ReAwakening the Spirit
of America

*Rebuilding Strong, Resilient Families
and an Informed, Healthier Nation*

Almerin Cartwright O'Hara, Jr.

REAWAKENING THE SPIRIT OF AMERICA

N.B. – Any Internet addresses, QR codes and telephone numbers in this book are offered as a resource. They are not intended in any way to be or to imply an endorsement, nor does the author vouch for the content of these sites, numbers or references.

Cover graphics design and artwork by the author, using *Canvas X 2018*, a product of ACD Systems, Miami, FL., with *Microsoft Paint* and *LibreOffice Draw*. Cover background illustration derived from "Sunrise", by Getty Images. Interior artwork and text by the author using also, *LibreOffice Writer* and *Microsoft Word*.

ISBN: 978-1-7915-0719-0
Createspace Independent Publishing Platform

**1Lt. Almerin C. O'Hara, Sr.
and the author
March, 1941
Anniston, Alabama**

Dedication

To Him who spoke the words of John 10:10-b
and
To my adorable wife, Sally who has made
my life abundant and this book possible.
and to
The memory and soul of my friend,
The recently departed
Rev. Msgr. Dr. John Oppong-Baah

Acknowledgements

As the poet proclaimed, "No man is an island unto himself." Indeed, no undertaking of this type could have ever been accomplished without those who raised, guided and taught me through the many past joys, trials and storms of life. Thanks and acknowledgements to all of them upon whose shoulders I stand today:

To my parents, who gave me life, and especially my mother who taught me how to sing; to my father who taught me respect for America and all people everywhere. to my Grandmother Cornelia, who made my life livable and my career possible; to Great-Uncle Charlie who taught me to love the outdoors and to work with tools; to Grandmother Anna who taught me to know and love America; to Donald Huddleston, teacher of history, who taught me it was OK to ask questions; to Harold Niver who patiently let me hang around his repair shop and ask innumerable technical questions; to Bob Smitherman who gave me my first full time job; to Jacky Knopp who taught me to question, to think and to love mathematics; to Mrs. Nichols who taught me to speed-read and understand and retain; to all the teachers and folks at Park School of Buffalo who helped me discover myself; to Herbert Monheimer, my chain-smoking Freudian psychoanalyst who taught me to think deeply and question everything; to Professor Edward Craig who mentored me and gave me my first big break; to Professor Alan Nelson who infused in me a living, deep love for American literature, history, culture, tradition and poetry; to Lou Hritz who noticed me and got me my first big job; to my many Jewish friends who taught this shaygetz the joy of being alive: L'chayim! to all the hundreds of others who gave me of themselves, in a thousand ways, as they taught me to inquire, to stretch and to search, especially all those people I interviewed and talked with who offered so much help and so many ideas in putting this book together. They are many; to Carl Mariconti and Bob George who pointed me to a new life; to Thomas Reynolds who provided the spark of the "aha! moment" that made this whole book come to life; to Franciscan University where I, a visitor, found the way, the truth and the life; to Jesus for loving me, teaching me and finally healing me; to Sally, my very dear wife, whose great patience and love has made this book possible; And to my four children who taught me that my parents were right all along.

And there were many more: teachers, preachers, extended family, friends, acquaintances and even a few past enemies who paved the road ahead of me over which I travel more easily today.

Special acknowledgment and thanks to those several reviewers who helped this amateur writer and by whose comments this book is better and more readable. Especial thanks to accomplished authors Cornelia and Brian Alley who made major suggestions early on and to reviewers George Burke, Irene and Larry Fischer, Bill Gage, John Jordan, Sally O'Hara, Tom Reynolds and Doug Sturomski.

If you find herein the true, the good and the beautiful it is because of all these good people. All else is from my own misperception, misjudgment and error.

Let me live in a house by the side of the road,
Where the race of men go by –
The men who are good and the men who are bad,
As good and as bad as I.
I would not sit in the scorner's seat,
Or hurl the cynic's ban –
Let me live in a house by the side of the road
And be a friend to man.

Sam Walter Foss

Contents

ReAwakening the Spirit
of America

Foreword

Our Republic is in Peril

Things are the way they are because they got that way

Our constitutional republic is under attack and in grave danger. If the republic goes, our whole way of life will go with it – our freedoms, our ability to speak freely, our prosperity – all will be in peril.

Things we take for granted – peace in our homeland, 24/7 electricity, clean running water, adequate food, freedom of speech and religion – these were not always ours and are just a broken thread away from being taken from us again.

Our families are falling apart – more than half of our nation's children are now born out of wedlock. Single mothers lead the country in poverty. Our young are leaving their faith behind for the trinkets of technology and social media and the consolation of free government stuff. The percentage of young adults with no religious affiliation has nearly quadrupled in the last 30 years. Our failing educational systems are being held hostage by labor unions and inept, corrupt politicians. Our economy cannot function without billions of dollars of borrowed money – some of it from our enemies.

Our Culture Began a Rapid Change

I watched it all begin to change.[1] After World War II the country had begun to stabilize and the economy boomed. Years later came the Vietnam War, made large under President Lyndon Johnson. Johnson feared that raising taxes to pay for the war would upset voters and he would lose the next election, so the Treasury *printed* the needed 80 billion dollars instead. This unearned currency injected into the economy started a massive monetary inflation which impacted every person in our country. We are still feeling the destructive ripple effects of that and the war on our culture.

When the Vietnam War ended, double digit inflation soon became rampant. Everyone's cost of living went sky high and many people could no longer afford their mortgages and basic necessities. Millions of married women with children had to go to work so a second salary would help their families survive. Women's Liberation was given real life and even when the economy began to stabilize, women stayed at work and child day care centers sprang up all over the country. The age of the respected stay-at-home mom who raised the children had come to an end and a new age of dysphoric, lost children had begun.

As the war in Vietnam was progressing a culture of tradition-estranged youth began to blossom. Hundreds of thousands of our young men were being drafted into the army to fight. The government claim we were winning the war was exposed as a series of lies and an anti-war rebellion grew among young men. Trust for authority evaporated.

The draft-vulnerable anti-war group fell into three categories. Some fled the country to Canada to avoid being drafted. Others were drafted and forced to fight. A large number dodged the draft using both legal and falsified options. Before the law was changed in 1971, large numbers escaped the draft by taking the Congress-approved deferment by entering college, graduate school or post-graduate studies. Many of those same anti-war, draft-avoiding, anti-culture rebels and their like-minded heirs now teach in and lead our universities and our news and entertainment media.

A totally new culture emerged among the young, epitomized by anti-cultural folk music, flowers, mind-altering drugs, communes and alternate life styles. At one time there were thousands of 'alternate lifestyle' communes in the hills east of Los Angeles. With this new generation, previously accepted

---

[1] I was almost five years old, living in California, when World War II started and still have vivid memories of the afternoon of December 7, 1941 and what followed. Since then I have watched with increasing interest as our history unfolded.

moral values and ethics were rejected and former taboos now accepted. Sexual "freedom" became rampant, aided by the newly invented birth control pill. The idea of marriage commitment became "old-fashioned" and divorce laws were changed to make it easier for families to dissolve. Most of the damage from these changes affected predominantly white families and their children.

The damage is still being felt to this day. "Deaths of despair," including from alcohol, drugs and suicide among white, non-Hispanic Americans have almost doubled in every state in America in less than two decades and continue to rise.[2] Studies by researchers Angus Deaton and Anne Case attribute this to "a failure of spiritual-social life…" and the breakdown of families[3].

But the Devil hadn't finished. He had further plans to damage our black families also.

Good Intentions Gone Awry

Meanwhile, progressive liberals initiated a nationwide "War on Poverty" out of real concern for the poor living in our city 'slums'. They were about to demonstrate anew the law of unintended consequences. Almost sixty years later there is more poverty, almost ten times more crime, more dependence on government, more suffering and an almost complete destruction of the families that held the black communities together and raised their children.

In Chapter 1 we discuss the nation-wide Urban Renewal Project of the 1960s Great Society program which destroyed the homes of hundreds of thousands of black Americans, and how it fractured and dispersed their families and crushed their children's and their grandchildren's hope for a decent future.

What Next? Who Will Lead?

There is a shrinking reserve of capable people who can be convinced to sacrifice their lives and families to serve in political and appointed office. Competent people often find too many disincentives to participate. Two examples come to mind: In August, 2008, within hours of Sarah Palin's selection as John McCain's Vice Presidential running mate, the Democrat Party hired an airplane and sent 27 lawyers to Alaska to dig for potential dirt on this former governor and her family to discredit her.[4] Separately, my own father who served in a non-controversial but very visible state-appointed job 45 years ago received frequent death threats.

Capable people can no longer afford to hold government office unless they are willing to endure less pay, more personal grief and threats of physical violence against them and their loved ones. They will almost certainly have irrelevant parts of their lives and distant pasts unearthed, disassembled and placed in the most embarassing public light by an irrepressible and irresponsible 'news' media.

Many of the people who do run are either the very brave and patriotic or they are the nebechs[5] who have no previous accomplishments or track records to attack and who are often regarded as losers. Being favored by the left-leaning mainstream news media can increase one's chances as well.

Career Politicians

Superannuated politicians on the left and the right have created an impotent national Congress as they seek increased power and personal gain above the needs of the people and the republic. Many of them have never held a productive job other than elective office, much less any military or similar public sacrifice.

---

[2] CDC statistics

[3] Deaton is a professor and Nobel Prize winning economist; Case is a professor of economics and public affairs at Princeton.

[4] Please! The proper name is the Democrat Party, not the Democratic Party. Many Republicans, Liberals and Socialists are democratic (adjective) but they are not Democrats (noun).

[5] An expressive Yiddish/American word, sometimes spelled *nebbish;* first cousin to a *schlemiel.*

The U.S. Democrat Party is being infiltrated by a radical Left Wing branch of Socialists. True Liberals still stand for improving America but the new Leftists stand for social disruption, division, destruction of the Constitution and gaining power.

The Republican Party has accomplished little of importance when it was in power due to its two or three opposing and uncompromising factions. Described by one astute observer as, "Two hundred Paul Reveres, all yelling and screaming and riding furiously in different directions."

Blind? Or Just not Watching?

We have become fat, dumb and happy – and seemingly blind to what is happening. Much of our country is run by young adults, intelligent and educated, yet mostly ignorant of our country's history and the values that have preserved it for almost two and a half centuries. They neither learned this at home nor in our broken educational system. Meanwhile as they complain about their latest *offense du jour*, many are ignorant how much worse off the rest of the world is.

Sweden, once a peaceful, well-ordered country, now has migrant enclaves in its cities where citizens cannot enter. Crime and violence is so high – including grenade attacks, gang-related crime, shootings, gang rapes –that citizens fear to venture in. For example, in Malmro, a suburb of Augustenborg, the country's postal system Postnord, will no longer deliver packages because the area is too dangerous.

Friends, just returning from Ireland, found that part of their ancestral small village in County Kerry had been walled off with signs forbidding entrance unless you are Muslim. This pattern is repeated all over Europe, but the news media gives it little coverage.

We have the beginnings of these "no-go zones" in parts of our own country as we bring in people whose culture and belief system discourages assimilation and which fosters a way of life totally opposite to American culture and at odds with many of our foundational values.

Where is Our Roadmap?

There has never been a better time to take stock of America and begin the long process of national revival. But first we need to examine what worked in the past and what might work in the future. If we don't know where we are or how we got here, no roadmap will suffice; if we don't know where we're going, it's just as easy to get lost on one path as any other.

And even with a clear goal, the signposts are constantly being moved and rearranged.

The Great Depression of the 1930s was the beginning of massive government control over our lives. The post-Vietnam era of the 1960s was the beginning of the voluntary surrender of our souls to big government.

The seeds of division had been planted. Now we are challenged to pull up the weeds, reawaken our national spirit and repair our brokenness.

The Spirit of America

If you are grateful for the gifts of freedom given us by our Creator, inscribed in America's founding document, *The Declaration of Independence*, and consummated in this great nation and if you are concerned with the direction we are headed, this book is written for you.

You struggling fathers and mothers and those others entrusted to raise and educate the next generation – this book is for your enlightenment, encouragement and support.

This book is focused on the needs and concerns of those among us who are alarmed by our country's present problems and would like to work together to begin a great national reconciliation and a revival of the American Spirit. It is directed especially to those practicing Christian men and women who are committed to dialogue, leadership and inspired rational action and who recognize that only Biblical truth, ethics and morals can overcome all the lies and deceptions that have gotten us to this present dystopia.

If there is to be a true reawakening, there needs to be several new conversations:

First, a dialogue among practicing Christians and those coming from a Judeo-Christian heritage to set aside our intellectual and theological differences and focus on our common interests and the chaos before us.

Second, there is an urgent need for dialogue with secular progressives with the goal of increased mutual respect and understanding. Make no mistake, this requires an ongoing awareness of the conflict between those who ascribe to our Judeo-Christian heritage values and those who do not. No easy matter, considering that we are beginning to think and speak separate, mutually unintelligible languages.

Dialogue will only be useful if directed toward understanding and respect for important common interests. We waste our time appealing to 'common sense'. It is no longer common and many of us, while we retain a common vocabulary, have diametrically opposite sense and understanding of important words.

What went wrong? What can we fix and what can we not fix? I don't know anyone who has all the answers – especially not this author – but I earnestly desire that we start a new conversation of discovery and common purpose.

What is the "Spirit of America?"

America is almost unique among nations, so much so that most Americans when asked the question, "Are people basically good?" will answer in the affirmative, because that has been their experience. But anyone with world travel experience will tell you the opposite. People are not inherently good. In fact people generally behave badly and selfishly almost everywhere. Corruption and bribery are taken for granted as a way of life in many countries.[6]

Try driving a car in some second- and third-world foreign countries where people seem to use their cars and motor scooters as weapons to challenge one another. At intersections, driving can become a matter of survival of the fittest. Driving is just part of the nightmare. In some cities when a person falls ill or dying in the street people often just walk around or step over them and unless a member of their family or tribe is near they are often ignored. When a person seeks something from a government bureaucrat, bribes are frequently expected.

Many other nations may boast constitutions and laws similar to ours but they are often ignored by corrupt officials and un-protective government agencies.

People are not born 'good' nor do we become better simply by aging. Jesus himself said, "No one is good but God." Little children may be 'cute' but, untrained, they are not naturally good or civil beings.

---

[6] "Corruption Perceptions Index 2016", *IEEE Spectrum*, Nov., 2017, p.22 (A ranking of 176 countries by perceived/measured corruption. Report by Transparency International, *www.transparency.org/cpi*)

Those of us who have raised children and witnessed an infant's rageful tantrum can be thankful its strength and destructive radius is constrained by its limited size and mobility.

Christianity acknowledges that we are all born flawed and ritualizes the washing away of this origin-sin by the rite of baptism.[7] Christian churches historically have taught rules of behavior that are contrary to our innate animal instincts. Witness the last seven of the Ten Commandments – rules for how we should treat one another. We are taught to internalize these rules and treat one another decently with love and respect even when no one is watching.

What we call "civilization" is not a genetic gift. It is a cultural gift of the values and morals taught and imposed by our parents, teachers, elders and peers.

Americans are generally naive about "goodness" because studies show we have one of the least corrupt countries in the world and – yes – people generally are fairly decent here.[8] We have a heritage spirit based on Biblical values and morals which until recently determined how we treated one another and how we educated our children. We seem to have internalized the parable of the Good Samaritan into our national psyche. Most of us unconsciously see others – all others – as potential neighbors like ourselves.

Our public educational institutions seldom teach the origins of this implicit code of behavior. That needs to change. Too many young adults are making risky political and personal life decisions that are beginning to negatively affect us all.

The founders of this country recognized that people, though imperfect, can work together and have a government that supports our freedoms while preventing one group from unfairly overwhelming another. Those protections are enshrined in our Constitution and our rule of law, but require a moral and religious people to keep them.[9]

The spirit of America is a civilization based on a voluntarily-accepted, God-given code of conduct that is passed from one generation to the next.

Trust and Wellbeing

It has been said that our whole American economy is built on trust. Many business deals are consummated with the promise of a handshake or a phone call. In places where people can trust one another – even strangers – society and commerce thrive and life is more peaceful.

But don't try 'the handshake' in some other countries. There you may even pay a person in advance and never again see him or your money.

Individuals and businesses prosper when trust rules commerce and where its participants respect one another and work together under the rule of law.

The current decline of our faith-based culture coincides with an increase in selfishness and greed. This seems to be one outcome of our greatly weakened family structures. As mutual trust declines, so also does our overall wellbeing. It is that trust which must continue to form an essential part of the traditional American spirit.

Both Hands on the Plow

Our nation differs from all others because it has been built on a trust in God.[10] The founders of this republic gifted us with the rule of law, freedom and a deep respect for human rights. Immigrants from every corner of the earth now work together in this land with its vast natural resources. The early

---

[7] One etymological source claims the word "sin" is derived from an ancient Hebrew verb meaning "to stumble."

[8] "Corruption Perceptions Index 2016", op. cit.

[9] Paraphrasing a famous quote by John Adams.

[10] United States of America national motto: "In God We Trust."

immigrant ethos of hard work that has been passed from generation to generation and the Judeo-Christian way of neighbor helping neighbor have made America strong and great.

We can increase our strengths, while vigilantly guarding against those ceaseless forces that, if left unchecked, can lead us to weakness, retreat and decay.

Our Creator and our nation's founders have blessed us with endless resources and a blueprint for a strong and good nation. But like good soil, if untilled, untended and left to itself it will only grow weeds.

Not a Recycled Past ...

We can never repeat our past – too much has changed – the good old days are gone but the good new days are ahead. A great deal has changed since we were a more civil society – the end of the Cold War and the Soviet Union, our technological revolution of computers and communications, significant advances in medicine and the discovery and mapping of the human genome, space exploration, discovery of distant new worlds, robots and artificial intelligence (AI) – and so much more.

We must take control and proactively mold and adapt these new tools and discoveries to our values, and on our terms or else they will control us – our resources, our time and our very lives.

... But a New Future

If we are to return our nation to stability and civil cooperation, we need to focus on the things that make a great and lasting nation. There are forces and people at work in America who don't want this to happen. We need to be vigilant. In every battle, every war, every heated political debate, each side thinks they are good and the other is evil. We must declare a truce between warring parties so we can begin to listen to one another. Not to agree, not to judge – just to listen and try to understand one another. Truce first, then perhaps tolerance and peace.

Imagine ... people once again treating one another with respect, able to disagree with peaceful and civil dialogue. Picture a nation of strong families that consistently love, discipline and nurture their children toward responsible adulthood and citizenship, where we are first responsible for ourselves, yet willing to help one another – especially the less fortunate among us. Living within our means – as individuals, families and as a nation. Being respectful of and careful to protect the great gifts we have been given by our Creator and the Founders of our Republic. No longer talking about "exporting democracy", but able to show the rest of the world a peaceful, moral and decent culture they can envy and desire to copy.

That's the America we were and the country we can be again – an amalgam of dozens of cultures, aware of our differences yet understanding and supportive of one another – not judging and condemning each other – but able to come together to face and solve our common problems.

We have so many broken American families and lost children. And we are a nation with half a million citizens who are homeless and thousands of suffering and recovering war veterans and all the others among and around us who are hungry, lonely, depressed, marginalized and forgotten. They are our brothers and sisters and their problems are *our* problems for our attention and help.

We must lift up one another if we are all to rise.

In the chapters that follow we will explore the origins of our unique republic and what made it so strong and different. We examine the rust and decay that have taken place in our *educational* systems, our *governance*, and our *national and personal economics*. To be renewed, all of these must stand on the firm foundation of *family* and *faith*. Extensive research confirms that no civilized culture on earth has ever begun *or endured* without strong families and the bond of religion and faith.

Better aware of how we got to where we are, we can then begin to set straight our goals and objectives and lay out the work before us.

It is not too late to respectfully turn to one another and unite the soul of this nation and re-awaken and invite that spirit which awaits our common call. *Smile at someone you don't know today.*

Introduction

Probing First Causes

This book is about problems and solutions. If we don't understand the problem and its causes, we are unlikely to stumble on the solution.

Foremost among our national problems are the major changes in our family structures due to the effects on our culture and our economy of past wars. Close behind is the impact of our technological revolution on the way we communicate, work and play. All these have combined to force major – and often unintended – changes in our family structures and our educational systems which in turn have had a profound effect on our children who must inherit this new, often dystopian future we have created.

Despite the wonders of our labor-saving technology, we work harder for less than ever before and our ceaseless struggles leave less time for family and community, and the religious faith that sustained us for so many prior generations.

Political emotion, government spending and mob mentality fed by old myths won't save us. Rediscovering and using the tools that worked before might give us a better chance.

Entanglements

In this book we deal with many intertwined facets of our American nation. Our families depend upon employment income and the support of one another and community. We all rely upon appropriate actions of our different branches of government. What we call civilization has been tied closely to strong families, bound by faith and religion. Our politics depends on selecting capable people to lead us. Understanding what does and what does not constitute significant local, national and world events requires trusted news sources. Carelessness, selfishness, and greed often derail well intended objectives and lead to more harm than good.

Having adequate resources – shelter, food, transportation, income, free time and all the other things we depend upon is a constant problem for many of us.

Among all these issues are complex interrelations and interactions where one affects another, which in turn eventually affects the first. There are many of these so-called 'feedback effects' that entangle them.

For example, increases in social programs and welfare costs results in higher taxes and thus, breadwinners and their spouses must work harder and longer hours and then they have less time for raising children who in turn then lose some of their family's moral heritage. They in turn create children out of wedlock – children who are doomed to greater risk of poverty and the need for more government intervention and social welfare programs. This is just one such cycle and there are others such as involve addictions, gang violence and crime and other forms of personal and social brokenness.

Politicians tend to promote simple answers that almost always involve passing new laws and spending more money. (Does anyone still recall the old aphorism, "If all you have is a hammer, every problem looks like a nail.")[11]

The time has come to take the problem from the professional politicians as we take stock, identify first causes, disentangle the mess we are in, propose reasonable fixes and begin to focus on truly attainable objectives.

---

[11] Why do we have so many new laws in our local, state and federal legislative bodies? While lawyers are only 0.14% of the total U.S. population they constitute 45 percent of members of the U.S. Congress (50% Senate, 42% House). 12% of all of the 450,000 U.S. lawyers work for our federal, state and local governments, (2015 statistics, per American Bar Association)

Our Present Challenges

Overwhelmed with life, too many Americans are too young to have experienced anything different – they think all this present turmoil and chaos is normal. They find little time to relax with family and friends and life is a constant rat race.

They work hard and have little to show for it. One quarter of our families have no savings for emergencies. Too many of our children are suffering from isolation and depression.

Mental illness and drug abuse and suicide rates are at all-time highs. Our mental hospitals are not much better than our prisons. As one patient recently told me, "If you're not crazy going in you'll be crazy when you get out." Much of the hospital "treatment" we provide is through drugs that put patients in a sleep-like stupor so they can be controlled more easily.[12] The discovery of these new drugs let us close many of our mental hospitals and supposedly allow many former patients to find a better chance at life on the streets.

Our educational systems have become political indoctrination centers which fail to prepare young citizens to make informed choices when and if they vote. Our republic, founded on Christian principles, is experiencing fewer and fewer faith practitioners and a growing and active number of atheist, pagan and secular groups, some of them quite militant.

The Law of Unintended Consequences

Starting in the 1960s a ruling class of progressive liberals, social engineers and do-gooders began the unintended destruction of the Black family structure in America and the result can be seen in our prisons. Our jails and prisons are bursting at the seams and we have lost most of a generation of black youth who, if they can graduate high school have little subsequent family or community support. Men released from prison often return to their earlier way of life and without any meaningful support to make the transition, they are soon re-incarcerated.

The Next Wave of Immigrants

We are a nation of immigrants. We can't live without them but the current uncontrolled flood of illegally entering foreigners is doing great damage to our nation and the ensuing partisan conflict is destroying anything remotely like decent political conversation.

In addition to overwhelming our social services – (For example, California has one eighth of the nation's population, yet consumes one third of our welfare resources) – immigrants are flooding into our country and rapidly diluting the culture, while bringing in many truly evil values, beliefs and practices, such as the widespread Santa Muerte with its worship of the skeletal "Saint Death." And we are importing hundreds of hardened gang criminals from Central America.

Islamic Sharia law with its diametrically different and radical social and political practices is creeping into our culture. It is a direct challenge and a growing threat to our republic and the rule of law. Neither our media nor our public educational monopoly exhibit any more depth of understanding of Islam's religious beliefs than they do those of Christianity or Judaism. Serious discussion of the differences is often halted as one side accuses the other of using "hate speech."

---

[12] Visit the day room at your local mental hospital if you doubt this. Psychotropic medicines do not cure mental illness, they only control it. The earliest such meds, e.g., Reserpine, Chlorpromazine and later, the whole family of Benzodiazapines all have side-effects of "drowsiness, dizziness or sedation," as do many of the more recent ones.

"We're Good and You're Evil"

The more we fight one another the sooner we will all lose. Make no mistake – our adversaries include progressive Socialists who sincerely believe that a properly educated, all-wise elite can rule us better than we ourselves.

There are powerful people among us who only want money and power and have little interest or use for our religious and moral or our community social traditions. They are happy to work with Progressives and Socialists until they have what they want.

Any nation whose citizens sit in their respective mud puddles casting muck at one another is ripe for takeover by political hacks. Their wealthy backers will do what it takes to manipulate our supposedly uneducated, uninformed minds, our thoughts and emotions and ultimately our votes until they have the control they seek.

It's not just the Russians and their computer hackers and false news interjectors who want to play the "Let's you and him fight" game. America is under attack from within.

If we don't stand together it is certain we will soon lose our republic and our way of life. Once the chains and ropes have been tied it is hard to remove them. Just ask the people of the once-wealthy, now-destitute country of Venezuela where 80 percent of the people don't have enough food and a privileged, well-fed dictator keeps them all in thrall.

What kind of society do we want our children to inherit? Are you and I going to be happy with that word of careless abandon, "whatever"?

Weeds in our Garden

A newly motivated citizenry can begin to repair our American Spirit but first we need to understand what went wrong.

There are several different 'weeds' growing in our American culture and each is sowing its seeds of chaos. They have been planted and nourished in different ways but (this book) examines how we can get them under control. Some can be plowed under now and others must await a later harvest. Most can be recognized by their poison fruits. Here are some of the weeds and their hard-at-work sowers, disruptors and devotees.

The Hysterical Mud-Slingers

Powered by emotion, uneducated in critical thinking – or incapable of it – and armed with social media, lefties and righties alike befriend and attract the like-minded into their respective mud puddles where they reinforce one another and hysterically demonize those in the other mud puddles each confidently shouting at the other, "We are good and you are evil!"

The Mobs Who Would Rule

Also polarized, but incapable of any dialogue beyond four-letter insults and armed with the tools of hatred, these Antifa,[13] White Nationalist and Anarchist groups march, disrupt public events, organize bullhorn rallies outside opponents residences and do things like publish the names and photographs and hometowns of 9,000 employees of the Immigration and Customs Enforcement (ICE) department. And sometimes they resort to actual physical violence.

---

[13] Antifa – A violent so-called "anti-fascist" group – but the recent actions of this group are the epitome of violent fascism and terrorism.

The Hapless Don Quixotes

Feckless and flailing against the wind, these ones can do nothing but resist and reject, such as refusing to serve a White House aide and her family and driving them out of a Virginia restaurant, "because she works for President Trump!"

The Government "Deep State"

The "deep state" has been described as "10,000 little left-wing Obamas, scattered throughout every federal agency" and making decisions biased by the politics of the previous administration. This is a serious state of affairs which never would have become evident had Hillary Clinton won the 2016 presidential election. The Department of Justice and the FBI, as of this writing have already demoted and/or fired six top level employees for extreme bias and potential law violations for trying to change the outcome of the 2016 Presidential election.

The Left-Leaning News Media

The mainstream news media with a majority 90-plus percent Democrat- or Liberal-voting membership[14], concentrates on negative, mostly leftist bias and opinion, while apparently unable to analyze and report positive accomplishments by the Republican/Conservative right. Struggling to compete for audience, they lead with opinion and sensational emotional content. Many false or just heavily biased stories, such as a recent full cover of *Time Magazine* which showed a crying child purportedly snatched by evil ICE agents from its mother.[15] This story was later shown to be false and the child was actually with her mother. Another report accused the Trump administration of keeping children in steel cages at the border. False again. It turned out those cages and the pictures were actually from the *previous* – Obama – administration. But not until thousands of (still) uninformed people became enraged at Immigration authorities because of these false reports. (Did you see any news media apologies or retractions? Possibly small type on page 547 ?)

The U.S. Congress's Games of Mutual Destruction

[*The following was written before the 2018 Congressional elections but is still relevant.*]
Supposedly there is a majority in the U.S. House of Representatives. Some say it is a majority of Republicans. Others believe it is a bunch of spoiled, bickering adolescents. But whatever it may be, they are so divided that they can't agree and pass any significant legislation. For example, 25 Republican members who represent corporate cheap-labor interests consistently block sensible immigration reform. Another Republican group, the "Freedom Caucus" has been unable to compromise ("We want it <u>all</u> or *nothing*, so *THERE*!!") and continues to block other important legislation or even any incremental change toward improvement.

Meanwhile the Democrat minority is much more united and uniformly able to resist and obstruct every important item of business as their leadership delays each Republican initiative, and all significant legislation. Individual Democrats who would prefer to see some progress are afraid to buck their powerful leaders (currently Rep. Nancy Pelosi and Sen. Charles Schumer) else they will be made to suffer by being kicked off committees and lose other power privileges.

---

[14] Goldberg, Bernard, *Bias, A CBS Insider Exposes How the Media Distort the News*, Regnery Publishing, Inc., Washington, DC, 2002
[15] ICE – Immigration and Customs Enforcement federal agency

Elite Oligarchs and Big Money

It's an old story; an entrepreneur gets lucky, formulates a great business decision, makes a bundle of money, and then apparently begins to think and act like an all-wise demi-god, destined to become a major political influence and power broker.[16] Many of these wealthy lefties and righties spend enormous sums on elections and wield disproportionally large influence on our elected leaders. For example, former Google executive chairman and CEO, Eric Schmidt, visited the Obama White House 260 (two hundred and sixty) times – more than anyone ever, before or since. Maybe he was there just for a few friendly tea and crumpet visits? Ya think?

Jeff Bezos, CEO of Amazon (and as of this writing the wealthiest person in the world) is another. He bought the *Washington Post* newspaper and later allegedly made them squash an article on allegations of worker abuse at his Amazon warehouses. The *Washington Post* has a reputation for its continual anti-President Trump rhetoric. (Google "American Oligarchs" for more detail.)

Foreign Invasive Species

Russia, China, Iran and others attack U.S. websites, steal information, spread false information and have armies of Internet and social media "trolls' whose job it is to incite and comment on current issues and conflicts and amplify them to create chaos. Thirteen Russians, including businessman and Kremlin advisor Yevgeny Prigozhin, have been indicted and charged with interfering in the 2016 presidential election. Alexander Malkevich, another Russian with ties to Vladimir Putin, runs the English language website *USA Really* whose sole purpose is to post false information on social media about U.S. issues, create chaos and destabilize us.[17]

Rounding Up the Weeds

These are the weeds and seeds of the Devil and the roots of the chaos we are up against as we move to reawaken and motivate America's Spirit again.

Why Bother to Vote?

Motivation is key. A poorly educated, often uninformed, emotionally susceptible – *and worn out* – people can be overwhelmed and frustrated by all this social and political chaos. They may take sides but shrug it all off and fail to act – or vote. It may be easier to turn on the sports channel where only *half* the people are losers at any one time.

Sadly, when it comes time to vote, too many stay home, as did 87 percent of the registered Democrat voters (187,006 out of 214,750 registered Democrats) in the recent primary election win of an avowed ardent Socialist in Queens, New York.[18] Chosen by only 13 percent of those eligible voters, she became a member of the U.S. House of Representatives in November, 2018 because Democrats always win in her district. They say she is so far left she makes Socialist Bernie Sanders of Vermont look like a Conservative. The result: 27,744 active voters were able to swing to the far left a community with a population of 700,000 people. That's only four percent of the total community that decided who will represent their interests in Congress. Failure to vote, especially in a one-party town, has its consequences.

---

[16] Being rich doesn't make one an oligarch. Being rich and commanding political influence makes one an oligarch.

[17] Johnson, Tim, "Russian website for U.S. readers tries to turn the nation upon itself", *McClatchy Washington Bureau,* *6/23/2018*

[18] Alexandra Ocasio-Cortez, 28 year old Socialist and community organizer, 2011 graduate of Boston University, with bachelor degrees in economics and international relations. Although she is relatively young, she is a very intelligent, hard-working person with experience in politics who should be taken seriously (worked as an intern for Senator Ted Kennedy).

The spirit of the Devil, the great divider, wants us to remain unmotivated and divided, and continue to waste our limited time and energy questioning the inane minutiae of each other's beliefs, so we will continue to remain a divided, impotent and neutered 'opposition'. In order for this evil to continue, decent but exhausted people will be encouraged to do nothing as they repeat the Devil's mantras, "*Live and let live*," and "*Whatever*."

Structure and Content of this Book

The above is the summary of the problems we face. But the purpose of this book is to help us find a way out of these problems. For that reason, the first six chapters conclude with a statement of "vision" and a list of suggested resources for getting started with the needed repairs.

Chapter 1 [*American Culture*] details the condition of our common culture and how it has changed to its present state. Without that understanding, any attempted change would be simply flailing against uncertainty. That has already been tried in several ways, notably by throwing money at its component problems. Congress is good at doing that and it is usually ineffective or even counter-productive.

Here we discuss the pros and cons of immigration. We discuss the current unrest in our culture and its major causes. The great mystery of why the black American family has suffered so very much since the 1960s is discussed and the blame squarely placed on our misguided government policies. Technology continues to affect our culture and we highlight some of the additional changes we can see on the horizon. Finally, the control of our culture by a few individuals of great wealth is laid bare and explained in political terms.

The chapter concludes with a focus on cultural renewal including information sources and groups with similar objectives and other resources for those who want to actually do something about the problem.

Chapter 2 [*The American Family*] deals with strengthening the American family and raising sturdy children.

Chapter 3 [*Our Tradition of Faith*] discusses our tradition of faith and religion and its essential part in the founding and continuance of our civilized culture. We highlight the importance and difficulties of dialogue in a changing culture where language and understanding are beginning to divide between the faith-oriented and the secular communities.

Chapter 4 [*Educating Future America*] discusses the need for more effective education to pass along essential knowledge of our system of government and laws in order that we raise generations of educated voters.

Chapter 5 [*Governance and Politics*] discusses why our government is becoming so ineffective and what we can do to fix it, including getting more capable people to commit to its service.

Chapter 6 [*Finance*] deals with the essential questions of improving financial control of the government and our own personal situations.

Chapter 7 [*Effective Dialogue*] discusses ways to improve our political and social dialogue in a culture that has devolved to mud-slinging and name calling among opposing groups that no longer talk with one another.

Chapter 8 [*America's ReAwakening*] this is a summary of much that is proposed in this book through the eyes of parents, children, adolescents and emerging adults. Summarizes some related needed changes in the way our government works.

Chapter 9 [*Stories from the Heart of America*] contains some uplifting and informative actual stories illustrating how we are a nation of people can care for and help one another, even strangers.

Chapter 10 [*Unanswered Questions*] is a list of some of the more difficult unanswered questions we will face in the future.

Chapter 11 [*An Open Letter to My Children*] is a personal letter that could serve as a model for anyone else who wants to convey the guidance of a Christian upbringing to their children and grandchildren.

Several appendices have been added to provide additional support for the main chapters.

Appendix A presents a chronology of the history of the struggle and suffering of Black America.

Appendix B discusses the cultural influence on America of Islam in greater detail.

Appendix C presents research and anecdotal information about the linguistic difficulties we face in attempting serious dialogue. This amplifies some of the discussion in **Chapter 3** where we talk about impediments to understanding one another's faith.

Appendix D is a prayer for the nation.

Appendix E is a sample civility pledge for political candidates.

Appendix F shows how all 50 states acknowledge God or a Creator in their constitutions.

Appendix G discusses help and recovery for substance abuse, a growing crisis in America.

Appendices H and I present additional challenges for families, children and our civilized society, augmenting some of the unanswered questions in **Chapter 10**.

There are and always have been powerful political forces which seek to irreversibly alter our great American culture and the rule of law. We must continue to be politically vigilant and exercise our right to vote but more importantly we need to focus our energy to fortify family, faith and community. That has always been the ultimate source of our national strength. Political reform can follow as we rebuild robust, cohesive communities based upon stronger families.

This book is the result of decades of research and consideration about America's persistent problems. It is the result of talking with hundreds of citizens and recent immigrants of all races and creeds, from all across this country and from all walks of life. I have been privileged to have been in the company and confidence of the very poor and powerless and the very wealthy and powerful.

This is the culmination of two years of intense work, reading dozens of books and hundreds of articles and listening to dozens of speeches from all sides of the political spectrum. And it is the result of many conversations with colleagues and friends and of much prayer. I offer this to you and hope it will shed some light in the darkness and show you why, although there are many challenges ahead, there is much hope for the future of America.

Almerin C. O'Hara, Jr.
January, 2019

1 – American Culture

Culture – The ideals, beliefs, preferences, pursuits and practices of the people who populate a particular region. American culture is determined by what we Americans think, what we want and what we do.[19]

Stable culture is the social oxygen one breathes in a well-functioning society. Two forces are working to change our culture: internal turmoil and massive immigration.

CHANGED BY IMMIGRATION

Not like the brazen giant of Greek fame,
With conquering limbs astride from land to land;
Here at our sea-washed, sunset gates shall stand
A mighty woman with a torch, whose flame
Is the imprisoned lightning, and her name
Mother of Exiles. From her beacon-hand
Glows world-wide welcome; her mild eyes command
The air-bridged harbor that twin cities frame.
"Keep ancient lands, your storied pomp!" cries she
With silent lips.

"Give me your tired, your poor,
Your huddled masses yearning to breathe free,
The wretched refuse of your teeming shore.
Send these, the homeless, tempest-tost to me,
I lift my lamp beside the golden door!" [20]

A Nation of Immigrants – a Working Amalgam

Like strong concrete, our culture is a distinct combination of many things. For example, where else in the world could you find a stadium filled with descendants of a hundred different foreign countries and ethnicities all cheering, in English, for their favorite baseball, football or basketball team? We are uniquely that amalgam and you will find it nowhere else in the world.

How America Became Exceptional – A Tale of Two Brothers

Two brothers lived in a distant land. They were poor and had little to eat. Their king was a tyrant and dictated the lives of his subjects. Obedience meant survival. There was only one official religion. Other faiths were forbidden on pain of death. The older brother was very strict and well behaved and ran his father's business prudently, so there was always a little something for the family to eat. The younger, like his older brother, was very disciplined, yet creative and often the first to solve a difficult problem.

One day a weasel tried to get into the chicken coop but the creative younger brother had foreseen the threat and made the chicken's home impregnable.

---

[19] Definition thanks to attorney and pastor Abraham Hamilton III
[20] Emma Lazarus (November 2, 1883), *The New Colossus*, Poem on the base of the Statue of Liberty in New York Harbor.

Five years earlier a weasel did get in and killed all 60 of their chickens. Because it had been late fall, the family almost starved to death that winter and had no meat or eggs, only some potatoes and vegetables in the cold storage and a little food saved for the chickens – old bits of garbage and some moldy corn.

They survived that winter and Eitan, the older brother, was able to reinforce the old coop and buy a few new hens and a rooster. But every morning they would see signs that the weasel had tried to chew his way into the coop. He clearly would not give up easily.

So one night, the younger brother, Caleb, took one of the new chickens and tied it outside of the coop. He built a small shelter of sticks around it with spaces small enough to keep out the weasel. And he tied a bell around the chicken's neck. The next night, when a furious bell commotion awakened him, he released his dogs and they caught and killed the weasel.

His brother Eitan was proud of what Caleb had done. And with better assured protection against these vermin, Eitan built a more secure coop and added 40 more chickens in the following spring. They flourished and the family was able to sell more eggs to the townsfolk. But he did not credit the improvement to Caleb's creativity, so much as to his own hard work. Eitan was happy with life as it was. Meanwhile Caleb wanted something more, but he couldn't quite put his finger on it yet.

Caleb was always thinking of new things and his brother called him a dreamer. They had very few disagreements. But Eitan had a low tolerance for impractical ideas. When family survival and preparation for hard times mattered most, he became impatient with too much of Caleb's dreaming.

Since their father had died six years earlier, Eitan had become head of the family. He was reluctant to let Caleb become betrothed, even though he was coming of age, and was afraid that the dreamer would not be able to run the family business should Eitan die.

Early one April, Eitan sent Caleb to buy some supplies in a nearby town. While there, Caleb met an older man in the local café. He had just returned from an ocean voyage of several months. The tales he told of faraway places and the freedom of the seas kindled a new fire in Caleb's imagination. But there was work to be done. So he bid adieu to the old man and returned the next day to the family business with the new supplies.

Many months passed. Winter came and went. And what a winter it had been! Colder than anyone could remember. Several townspeople had starved to death, not because they had no food – they had a very little – but because the King's Guard had come and demanded more food from everyone in the town. Winter's cold persisted beyond imagination, and most of the animals had been slaughtered for food. Planting season had to be delayed several weeks, and there was little food or hope for the poorest.

Caleb suggested they sell their business and move their family to a warmer place across the ocean as the old man in the café had described.

Eitan would not hear of it and told him he was crazy to think of such a thing. "Do you not realize that our father, his father and his father's father before him built this house and our business and we have the trust and good will of the entire town? And you would cast it all away for some dream? You are a fool! Now get to work for we have much to do if we are to survive another winter such as last!"

Caleb put all these thoughts aside for the time, but could not stop pondering what might another world be like? A place where he could build his own trade and be free to be successful on his own and raise a family, free from the constraints of his brother, the village elders and the king. He was about to find out.

Dreams turned to thoughts and thoughts became a plan.

========================

Eitan, normally a man of great reserve, exploded! "Caleb, you are a fool to leave your home! What will you find on the other side of the sea? You know the stories – there are savages and starvation! You will die out there no one will be there to bury you!" But Caleb was more than resolved. He was leaving.

The ship pulled away and Eitan, standing on the dock, grew smaller and smaller until there was nothing behind and the open sea ahead, with its many unknown terrors and wonders.

After what seemed an eternity of calm days interwoven with days of violent waves and rain, the fragile ship had survived and the long ocean crossing was over. Finally Caleb had arrived in the new land called America. His old home seemed so far away and its memories so long ago. His heart was suddenly filled with a jumble of excitement and apprehension, as the ship came within view of the harbor.

What work could he do? He knew only a little of English from the few years his brother had made him attend the church school. But where would he sleep? What would he eat? He soon discovered the little money he brought with him from his old country was worth little in the new land. He would need to make many compromises just to survive the next few days.

One brother stayed in the old country, the other departed and took the chance of a better life. Knowing he would struggle and having been hardened by past life, he vowed to try anew or die trying.

There were tens of thousands of young Calebs in America's past. They brought to America their faith, their skills, and their intelligence, but most importantly they brought a fierce resolve that life could be better. Many were guided by the Protestant Ethic that work is ennobling. Quite a few died on the ocean journey and others were later overcome by sickness or misfortune. But many more survived and succeeded and for many reasons these highly motivated immigrants kept coming, while the unmotivated and the unable stayed behind.

These immigrants often lived in squalid quarters and took menial jobs until they could learn the language and the new ways and save enough money to build careers and families.

Difficult work led to survival. They married and raised their children to respect hard work and pass on their own values. Those values included the belief that you could leave everything and everyone behind and cross a dangerous ocean to better your life. Leave your family and village and friends behind if necessary, but make your own decisions and put your shoulder to the task at hand. Work long hours. Help one another. Plant seeds. Harvest crops. Survive. Worship your God. Pray. Raise a strong family. Teach your children what is important and teach them to teach their children in turn.

If there is no tool to do the task, make one from what is at hand. If there are rocks in the field, clear them so the soil can be tilled. If there are trees, cut them down and burn the stumps and plant your crops. Innovate. Invent. Create. Fools will laugh at you and they may not prosper or survive but you will. Your children will take notice and your values and the story of your struggles will be reverently passed on from generation to generation.

So very many exceptional Calebs sent this determination and faith down through the generations to their children and through their children's children. We have inherited their hard won culture and their dreams. This is why America is special. This is why America is exceptional. They made America great and have inspired our hope for the future.

This was the beginning of the Spirit of America.

Why Immigrants Have Been Coming to America

Recently, immigration has become a two-edged sword and a divisive subject. We are learning we can't live with too much of it but we may not survive without it.

Peaceful Civil Interaction

Much recent talk and emotion about the value of immigration and immigrants has filled our news media and our conversation. But there are many different kinds of immigration. There are those who have come here of their own will and there are others who have been brought here, some against their will. Indentured servants. Slaves.

And then there are those who risked everything for a chance at a better life.

Immigrants have brought many cultures. Some have melted into the mix. Some have not. Most of the early American immigrants were either Christians or Jews. There is a definite bond between different Christian faiths, and an historical bond with the Jews. Some Christians and some Jews did not assimilate, but formed their own communities. Think, Hassidic Jews, Amish, Mennonites, River Baptists, Tibetan Buddhists.

But these earlier immigrants did not come here to take over the country, but rather to make a better life through their work and prayer and devotion to family. In the beginning of each large migration – Italian, Polish, Irish, etc., there was tension and strife. Now, most of these have attained peaceful, civil interaction, if not true assimilation.

Rapid, Forced Cultural Change

Immigrants are now coming in for a variety of new reasons. Our porous southern border has, over the past few decades, allowed many people, mostly of Hispanic origin, to enter without the usual immigration approval and process. There are currently in excess of 10,000,000 'undocumented' people in the country – illegally – now.

Republicans want them here because they are cheap labor for their farms and factories. Democrats want them so when they give them free stuff, they will enlarge the ranks of liberal voters who send even more Democrats to Congress.

Many Christians and observant Jews do not discourage immigrants because it is part of our culture to welcome strangers and take care of those in need. And while they may be adding much good to our culture, they are also transforming it so fast that most Americans cannot accommodate the rapid change.[21]

Gang members from El Salvador come here because there is more to steal and to escape their country's mandatory 12 year prison sentence just for belonging to a gang. In America it is not illegal to belong to a gang until they prey on our citizens and are caught. Salvadoran MS-13 and other lethal gangs are now all over America, in towns large and small, and flooding our prisons. To say they are disruptive to our way of life is like saying that being hit by a truck is disruptive to one's balance.

H-1B Visa holders – highly skilled in science and technology and in great demand by our laboratories, universities and technical industries – these visa holders come to fill needs that our inferior schools cannot fill, and many work in Silicon Valley and other advanced business areas. They make things like Google work – and a hundred other marvels we can no longer live without. In the past, I had the honor to work and consult with some of these skilled technical people and they were all brilliant, hardworking and very productive.

Tens of thousands of refugees from the wars in the Middle East are now pounding on our doors and climbing through the transoms. Many are desperate and starving and have lost family members. But some of them bring an Islamic belief system that is not just a 'faith', but a tripartite way of life that dictates political, economic and social behavior that is unable and unwilling to assimilate. It is entirely foreign to America's way of life. These are often older men and women. Their young have difficulty integrating and often become swayed and radicalized by Imams who teach that America's Christian and Jewish (and other) ways are heresy. The Islamic holy book, the Koran (also sometimes transliterated, Qur'an), teaches that we are all "infidels." Strict adherents of Islam who take the Koran literally know

---

[21] Our security systems – police and national security services – need speakers of foreign languages in order to monitor criminal activity. Just a few years ago, the New York Times reported that the NY City police had no one who could speak Albanian and there were many Albanians entering, some of whom were conducting criminal activities. Currently our Border Patrol has asked for expertise in some Central American and Mexican indigenous languages, such as Maya.

that they are allowed – indeed required – to kill all infidels. This is not a peaceful group when they practice their faith as it is written. America has some real soul searching to do as we try to assimilate this new wave of Muslims. Maybe we need to communicate our own values differently.

For more in-depth effects of Islam and its Sharia Law on our culture, see *Appendix B. Peaceful/Militant Islam* , beginning on page 133.

A Modest Proposal

Dr. Sebastian Gorka is a British citizen of Hungarian descent and a recent White House advisor. He has an unusual suggestion to deal with the politicized version of Islam. Tell the Muslim world about The Federalist Papers – those historic articles promoting the ratification of the US Constitution. "For the cost of one missile, we could probably translate (into Arabic) those papers, put them in a leather-bound book and give every Muslim in the world a copy."[22] Tongue-in cheek perhaps, but an interesting thought.

Pandering Politicians

In the past century and before, most immigrants eventually assimilated into the American culture and became part of everyday life. Many initially lived in ghettos with those of their own culture. Instructions and road signs were not printed in different languages. Only English. To survive outside of those ghettos, they had to learn to speak English. Intermarriage after several generations and a host of other factors, including two World Wars had a tremendous mixing effect.

Now, our political leaders have promoted a new communication standard with multi-lingual instructions, and separate telephone numbers to call if you need to understand and can only speak one of several dozen other languages.

Are we doing the right thing in our compassion? Is this really compassion, or, as some say, just a ploy by some politicians to encourage immigrants on a fast path to vote for them?

Common understanding begins with the first step of dialogue in a common language. This is becoming an urgent topic for calm, rational national discussion and understanding.

Why Immigrants Must Keep Coming

Aging and Shrinking America

Even though immigration is helping to stabilize the population, our educated and relatively well-off citizens are not replacing themselves. Our US birth rate is below the stable replacement rate and our 'native' population is getting smaller and older.

Euthanizing the Soul of our Nation

We continue to kill our babies – more than 3,000 *each day*. If that doesn't bother us, and it certainly should, then consider that our shrinking population means a smaller working force paying to support an ever increasing number who are not working and on Social Security and our many programs of welfare.

Fortunately, the Muslims and Latin Americans coming into this country do not abort their babies like we do and are reproducing at an excellent rate. Unfortunately, many of them are bringing culture changes that promise to permanently change America.

In Japan, since abortion became legalized, their social security system has begun approaching financial disaster because there aren't enough young workers to continue supporting it. Incidentally, the

---

[22] Ruth Sherlock, "The most powerful Briton in America on what it's really like in Donald Trump's White House.", *The Telegraph*, April 1, 2017.

Japanese have aborted over 90,000,000 of their children. (In America, we have aborted over 60,000,000 since it became legal.)

Even though so called 'pro-choice' advocates call abortion services 'health care,' most abortions have nothing to do with the mother's health. Rather it is more a matter of convenience. Parents who, for one reason or another, just would rather not have any (more) children, but can't stop creating them.

> *The definition of healthcare is to make a person well and to encourage health. The definition of a successful abortion is the complete death of the unborn child.*
> *Elizabeth Graham, Texas State Right to Life director*

In America our current replacement rate is 1.9 [23] Below 2.0, a population will shrink in size and grow older. Non-white America has a slightly higher rate, about 2.4 for Latinos and 2.0 for Blacks. People emigrating from predominantly Muslim countries have replacement rates between 2.5 and 5.0 – one of the highest in the world.[24] (Islamic culture forbids abortion.)

> *Today and every day in America over 3,200 babies are brutally killed by abortionists. As these babies die, the soul of our once great nation dies with them.*
> *Judie Brown, President of American Life League*

Who Will Pay our Bills?

But who cares if we don't sustain current population numbers?

Consider our national debt. $21,000,000,000,000.00 and rising. We have been on an easy spending spree for decades. We are borrowing money from foreign countries to pay Social Security checks to our retirees. The interest on twenty-one trillion dollars is a lot of money and we have to pay that every year as well, much of it to foreign countries. Money that might otherwise have gone to better use.

The more working immigrants we have paying taxes, the more this will help us economically.

Immigration Challenges

People are coming into America in droves for reasons very unlike previous great waves of immigration. This great volume is disrupting our culture and bringing in crime, cultural poisons and people who will not assimilate. Sadly, one of our greatest challenges is politicians – on the left and the right – using these poor people as pawns for their own political advantage.

Economic and Social Costs

U.S. taxpayers are spending vast sums helping these new waves of immigrants, paying for their food, housing, medical care and schooling for their children. Past experience shows that this creates a dependency class that struggles to get off the dole.

Well-intentioned government actions that have been placing large groups of immigrants in small towns has disrupted the social order all over America, and just like the forced affirmative action of past decades, it is causing unnecessary resentment and neighbor-to-neighbor hostility. Leave it to Washington bureaucrats to find clever new ways of creating chaos.

---

[23] The U.S. total fertility rate (TFR) dropped to 1.9 in 2010, per the National Center for Health Statistics.
[24] Source: *The World Fact Book*, U.S. Central Intelligence Agency, 2016

Uncontrolled Immigration

Existing immigration laws are inadequate to deal with both the volume and the needs of all the desperate people flooding our borders. We need either many more workers on the borders or somehow to set 'speed limits', probably with the help of Mexico.

Imported Poisons

One alien cultural change coming up out of Mexico and Central America is the growing folk-devotion to "Our Lady of the Holy Death." *Santa Muerte* has been called the poster girl of narco-satanic spirituality, admired by criminals, drug dealers and cultural Catholics[25] and is portrayed as a skeleton in a robe. The practice is widely condemned by Christian groups and the Catholic Church.[26]

Drug deaths are at an all-time high and most can be attributed to fentanyl/heroin mixtures and other addictive chemicals that are entering through our porous borders.

Child traffickers, bringing in children to be sold for sex is another horrific import. Adults pose as their 'parents' and require an overwhelmed Border Patrol to determine who is real and who is not.

Criminal gangs are rampant throughout Central America and many are sneaking into the U.S. through our borders to take advantage of our more tolerant laws. They are normally only arrested if they commit a crime, whereas in their original countries they can be arrested simply for gang membership.

Sanitary conditions vary and many diseases, once eliminated or suppressed, are now re-entering the U.S. such as Dengue Fever, Malaria, Chagas Disease, parasitic infections of the brain and other organs, to name a few. When immigrants sneak into the country there is no way to screen them for these diseases.

CULTURAL UNREST IN AMERICA

What Is Our Culture? Are We Unique?

Are we really so very different from other countries? Is our culture exceptional? Many elite globalists, trans-nationalists and world government aficionados would demur.

Independence

We declared ourselves to be a free and independent republic in 1776. Every other country I can think of declared their Day of Independence either at the end of a war, a colonial withdrawal, or a great uprising such as the attack on a prison (France, 1789.)

America is unique in that we declared our Independence at the start of our rebellion from our British overlord, six years before our war of independence ended, 12 years before we had a Constitution, 13 years before we elected our first president, and 39 years before the British finally gave up trying to re-colonize us (War of 1812 which ended in 1815.)

One Language

We have since become a great amalgam of the ideals, beliefs, preferences, pursuits and practices of many nations and cultures. We attempt to communicate using one language, from coast to coast. It has been estimated that American English contains about 800,000 words. Contrast that with, for example,

---

[25] 'Cultural Catholics', as differentiated from observant Catholics who follow the teachings of Scripture and Sacred Tradition.
[26] *en.wikipedia.org/wiki/Santa_Muerte*

Spanish with approximately 200,000.[27] Many English words were brought to America by our founders, but many more came to us from our immigrants. Lingustic history shows that American English has become a melting pot of all these many languages.

Christian Origin and Practice

We are still a traditional Christian nation and despite all the atheist hoopla to the contrary a majority of Americans still agree. In that tradition we treat one another generally better than many other places in the world and reflect this behavior in our laws. We accept more immigrants and refugees than any other country in the world. We are a nation of generous people. The US government sends about $42 billion in foreign aid around the world but individual Americans give *more than three and a half times as much* to developing countries, making us *the most generous country in the world!*

Led by Law, Not by the Whims of Men

We are blessed with a heritage of British Common Law,[28] Greek and Roman philosophy and a Constitution that has survived the test of balancing and checking human avarice and weakness for more than two centuries. We have amended that Constitution to attest to and demand human rights that other nations only dream of. We are a nation that rejects rule by king, dictator or tyrant – the rule of man – in favor of the rule of law.

Free Markets, Creativity and Free Choice

We are a wealthy nation, made wealthy by free choice of occupation and free market capitalism. By contrast, our poorest citizens seem wealthy to many of the truly poor in foreign lands.

We are a land of creators, inventors, medical researchers and builders. Most of the world's seminal technology of the 20th and 21st Century has originated with American inventors, engineers, scientists and builders. We are a nation built on the lives, fortunes and sacred honor of so many before us as we have been tested again and again by our enemies.

There is uniqueness in our music, our theatre and all of our arts which reveal the story of our history, our dreams and our present struggles – these arts reflect the very soul of our culture.

Blessed by Our Creator

Take all of this and place it in a country blessed by God with land so fertile and water increasingly more clean, where we produce more food than we can eat and send vast surpluses to other countries.

America's culture is unique, exceptional and unlike anything in history.

How Things Changed

When World War II ended, prosperity followed, which eventually led to over-consumption, disrupted families and culture. We got through the Korean War, but then came the Vietnam War and the invention of the birth control pill – two unrelated events that began the national breakdown in the 1960s.

Today we are surrounded by uncivilized children and adults who would rather clash than engage in productive dialogue – but why?

Following the Great Depression of the 1930s and widespread poverty, we endured the horror of World War II, after which businesses bloomed, prosperity followed and anyone who wanted work could

---

[27] Actual estimates vary but it is fairly well agreed that English contains from two to two and a half times as many words as Spanish and exceeds the word count of every other world language as well.

[28] This is true in 49 of our 50 states. The exception is the state of Louisiana. For historical reasons, the laws of Louisiana are based on the Napoleonic (French) Code.

find it. The middle class grew and many became wealthy. With full employment came great mobility and families left their hometowns to follow their breadwinners. But then our hometown-based extended family structures – grandmas, grandpas, aunts, uncles, cousins, brothers and sisters – the ones who used to help with the children and give us moral support in hard times – began to dissipate. Soon we became a nation of "nuclear families."

20 years later we tried to share our new national prosperity with those who lived in poverty, especially in our city 'slums'. Federally-funded Urban Renewal in 1,000 cities all across America, tore down old buildings – homes where generations of mostly black, mostly broken families, the legacy of slavery – had slowly begun to build extended family structures for raising their children. As the buildings came down those families were torn apart and many of the children had nowhere to go but the streets.[29]

We tore down their houses, broke up their extended families, put their kids on the street, told them they didn't have to work, gave them everything so they would continue to vote for the same inept politicians who ruined their families in the first place. That was part of President Lyndon Johnson's "Great Society" program.

The war in Vietnam was the final blow that set young against old, family against family and sacred institutions against one another. It was "patriots" and traditionalists on one side and "radical" students, "flower children," and pacifists on the other.

Young men feared being suddenly torn away, drafted into the armed forces and sent to die in Vietnam. Things turned very ugly when Daniel Ellsberg gave the New York Times hundreds of pages of top secret documents he had stolen from the Pentagon where he worked. These "Pentagon Papers" showed what the radical youth had been saying all along – the whole war and its progress was built on government lies. Many of our leaders knew we were at risk of losing the war, lied to the public about increases in troop levels and bombing in adjacent countries yet we kept sending more and more of our kids there to fight and be slaughtered.

Finally, with our tails between our legs, we abandoned Vietnam to the Communists – the only war the United States has ever lost. Returning veterans were scorned, shunned and abused, as if *they* were responsible for the war. We are still to this day paying the price for this horrible conflict and *it and its ripple effects remain the central first cause of the cultural divisiveness and decline we see today.*

As if things weren't bad enough during that war, Congress made the stupid – there is no better word – *stupid* decision to exempt from the draft our – mostly white – rebellious youth, if they would choose to enter college or graduate school.[30] College meant they didn't have to fight in the war and someone else, less gifted and financially able, could take their place. These were the kids who rebelled against the hypocrisy of the previous generation, its culture and everything it stood for.

Now these same social rebels have aged to become the new elite political Left which controls our news and entertainment media, teach and administer our universities and controls much of our government, as they change our culture and throw away whatever remains of the foundations of the longest enduring society ever created where free men govern themselves.

---

[29] And the former 'slum' buildings were almost always replaced with upscale condos, apartments and commercial units which the previous residents could not afford. Many of our state and city governments are still enabling this forced exodus and even homelessness of our most vulnerable citizens. For insight, read Kevin Bakers article, "The Death of a Once Great City, The fall of New York and the urban crisis of affluence", in *Harpers Magazine*, July 1, 2018 edition.

[30] Congress changed these rules as the war was closing down in 1971. See, Selective Service System website: *sss.gov/About/History-And-Records/How-The-Draft-Has-Changed-Since-Vietnam*

Killing the Golden Goose

These are troubling times for America. Our culture has become sick. While we slumbered, the ugly face of intolerance has appeared everywhere: in our families, in the media, in our entertainment and in our politics. Half the population is angry with the other half and fear and distrust are everywhere. Respect for human life is on the decline for the elderly, the sick and the unborn. Our educational systems are failing with a capital "F". Our families are crumbling and our children are wandering without purpose in minefields of our own making. Almost half of our people live from paycheck to paycheck and a quarter of us have no savings for an emergency. Their new motto might be, "In Big Brother we Trust."

Democracy is dead in most one-party cities whose perpetually re-elected representatives have continued to dominate and control their local and state legislatures for decades. Their seniority rank confers leadership and power and then these same legislative committee leaders often derail needed reform. Too many of these career politicians have never held any productive job other than political office. Aided by their poor management, many of their cities are either in or on the verge of bankruptcy.

Meanwhile, the atheistic political Left, hell-bent on destroying our culture, has perfected the art of stifling civil discourse and dissent. Anyone who doesn't agree is shamed into silence, usually by being called a racist, a hater, a sexist, a xenophobe or a homophobe. America has become a myriad of little dialogue-free war zones where people fight over words and feelings.

Rudeness and vulgarity prevail in public discourse. A quick look at so-called comedy on TV reveals what has decayed into a uniform cesspool of vulgarity, crudeness and personal disparagement.

Human life has become devalued as we perfect our growing *culture of death*. Every day in America we kill over 3,000 unborn babies because they are *inconvenient* – and few people even blink. If you are sick or just depressed with life your doctor is now allowed to kill you in some states. In past years a school child's greatest fear was being called upon to give an oral book report. Now the greater fear is being shot dead in the classroom by some deranged adolescent whose potential malevolence is obscured and protected by privacy laws.

We live in a world with an undercurrent of fear. Every new fear seems to provoke opposite and antagonistic viewpoints.

It's no surprise then that many children believe their world is falling apart with no purpose to their lives. They believe the adults running their world are totally clueless. Yet they depend on the government, their parents and their teachers to support and sustain them and protect them from 'micro-aggressions'. In fact, 40 percent of Millennials now believe Socialism would be a good form of government for America. These products of our failed educational system would throw away the goose they never knew who lays the golden eggs they take for granted. Too many of these kids, overwhelmed, purposeless, weak, anxious and depressed, escape to the brain-altering respite of drugs, fantasy and pornography.

Meanwhile, a few highly vocal minority groups poison the minds of confused adolescents who wonder about their own gender, and their very life's meaning and purpose. A recent study in the U.K. shows that only two thirds of young people aged between 16 and 22 are certain they are heterosexual.[31] One can expect similar figures in the U.S.

The spiritual and moral strength that sustained us for centuries is becoming unknown today. Too many young folks have little or no grounding in faith and many have never been tested through the kind of hardship which produces endurance and so they have little hope for their future. Interpersonal dialogue is an alien concept. Modern overprotective child raising 'theory' which restricts roughhouse and unsupervised play for young children prevents them from learning how to solve their own

---

[31] Rudgard, Olivia, "Only two thirds of Generation Z identify as 'exclusively heterosexual'", *The Daily Telegraph*, London, July 5, 2018

interpersonal problems and so their minor disagreements often escalate into major insults and problems. Studies show that these overprotected, bubble-wrapped kids have higher depression and anxiety levels – 21.6 percent of them, in one large study.[32]

Boys suffer the most in this culture that once looked up to strong masculine heroes and role models such as first responders, soldiers, astronauts and explorers. The media now give them imaginary, gender-neutral super-heroes, over-sexualized movie actors and vulgar rap musicians. Twisted, game-induced fantasy replaces reality. Unprepared adolescents and young adults now require trigger warnings and safe spaces to protect them from the 'horror' of differing opinions and ideas.

Our educational systems are failing to teach mutual respect, tolerance and critical thinking. One result – first-time voters have little to guide their electoral choices beyond their emotions. Public education has become a brain washing operation of the political Left. Teachers unions literally buy politician's votes with money allocated to them by those same politicians as they nourish each other. We spend tons of money on our public schools and produce some of the world's dumbest graduates. Teacher turnover is horrible – good teachers leave in droves soon after being hired, while tenured bad teachers remain forever.

Hope for the Future?

If we can ever get our borders secure and our immigration system working again, immigrants with starkly different viewpoints and experiences may yet shake us awake and save us from our foolish paths. Past immigration has made us different and stronger.

Today's immigrants are a different lot and many have troubled cultures and habits that some say could destroy our way of life. Many are coming to America for reasons we have never seen before and bringing challenges we have never in memory been required to face.

CHAOS IN BLACK AMERICA

Lost Children

All America but especially Black America is suffering from a rapid destruction of the family structure to the peril of current and future generations of children. Much of this is the result of our progressive social engineering and welfare laws.

A *Wall Street Journal* Op-Ed article summarizes the damage:

> *More than 50 years and trillions of dollars after Lyndon B. Johnson launched [the 'war on poverty'] with the best of intentions, all we have to show for it is the devastation of the black family and the dysfunctions of our inner cities.[33]*

I'm talking with John (name changed), a withdrawn and somewhat fidgety 23 year-old. We're sitting in a room in an upstate New York prison, where he is incarcerated. John looks uncomfortable as he shifts from side to side in his chair. I ask him if he's feeling OK. Then he tells me he's in constant pain from a bullet that's lodged in his right knee. He's been told it's inoperable. John is considerably overweight – apparently aided by depression and his physical inability to get much exercise.

---

[32] Peterson, Andrea, "The Overprotected American Child", *The Wall Street Journal*, June 1, 2018
[33] McGurn, William, "The Crisis of Good Intentions", *The Wall Street Journal*, December 9, 2018

As we talk he explains he was shot four years ago. Nineteen years old, out on the streets with the only real family he'd ever known – his gang – and no hope for the future. One of the guys in his posse did something really bad, they all got arrested, the public defender lawyer was less than helpful and now here he is, for quite a few more years. I'm the first person who's visited him since he went to prison.

John is just one of the hundreds of imprisoned young adults I've talked with since I started doing prison ministry 14 years ago. They're not there because they're black or poor – they're there because they were born, then ignored and abandoned to the streets – either by their families or their community or their government or – or by you and me. If we are to strengthen and re-awaken America we can no longer ignore those who are suffering, just because their situations may seem foreign and insurmountable to us. We are all in this together.

America's mostly urban Black Community is suffering from major family breakdown. It's not about economics or jobs – it's about drugs, prison and death and all those kids we're losing for lack of decent role models and fathers and strong families.

Helping the suffering youth of Black America isn't a Democrat or Republican, a Liberal or Conservative thing. It's a serious problem that affects us all and requires us all to work together.

Minority America, 1953

As a child, I lived all over the south and by my mid-teens became aware of tremendous oppression of black folks and their families. I had come from the North where black and white coexisted more or less peacefully. They lived peacefully in the South also, but only because, as I was reminded several times down there, they "knew their place."

Where I lived in the rural 'deep south' blacks couldn't own land, cars or in most cases, their own houses. Total segregation was an accepted way of life – accepted by the white folks.

I saw unbelievable brutality, discrimination and indifference to suffering. I was too young to understand or do much about it since I was a *damyankee* and had to keep in my place also. Small for my age, I was often bullied or beaten if I stepped out of line.

One large farm/ranch I visited had many black folks working the fields and they lived in run-down shacks on the land. When I asked how much they were paid I was assured that they were well fed and had all their needs taken care of. They were obviously not being paid for their work.

Several times my father and mother tried to help people and were reminded they were in a different place and they should also 'know *their* place' or suffer the consequences, including being ostracized and shunned.

It was in 1953 that my father tried to buy some land for a woman who worked for him. Mary's shack had burned down and Dad planned to pay to have one rebuilt for her but was told by the highly respected man who owned half the town including the land Dad wanted to buy, "Oh no, sir, we don't let them n*****s own no land. Can't sell you any." [34]

After many stories and adventures we moved back up north and some of these memories still haunt me. I became interested in why and what had happened to the black families in the south and the north and why it has taken so long for them to recover and rebuild their families from the hell of slavery.

How We Have Damaged the Black American Family

Before the founding of America, slavery was common throughout the world, in almost every country and culture. One of the worst decisions ever made was to bring a few African slaves to the pre-American colonies.

---

[34] This man happened to be the father-in-law of a well-known American President.

The invention of Eli Whitney's *Cotton Gin* began a large-scale demand for more slaves to farm the suddenly profitable cotton fields of the South.

Captured by other Africans and sold to ship-owning slave traders, these human beings were ripped from their families and communities and sold as property. Hundreds of years of stable family cultural structure and traditions were destroyed as fathers, mothers and children were torn from one another and sent to exist as slaves in an alien culture. (For a brief chronology see *Appendix A. Out of Slavery – The Struggle of Black America*.)

Damaged Again – Good Intentions Gone Terribly Wrong

100 years after the 14th Constitutional Amendment gave Black Americans equal rights and full protection under the law, and just when many of our black families were beginning to heal, we blundered again. Our Federal government decided to spend billions of dollars to eliminate 'slums' because they were regarded as a major cause of poverty.

But invisible to all but a few politicians who would actually go out and talk with these families, these 'slums' were the places where extended families had developed and grown over many decades since emancipation. Even where a father might be missing or absent, children often had other relatives nearby to help raise them. Many 'slum' residents were money-poor but family-rich.

This cultural reinvention of the extended family gave many urban black children a decent start in life.

Black Homes Destroyed, Families Wounded, in 1,000 US Cities

As part of the so-called 'War on Poverty', Congress approved and the President signed into law the Urban Renewal program. Enormous sums of money and other incentives were given to cities throughout the US to bring in the wrecking balls and the bulldozers and destroy the very homes where people – predominantly black Americans – were raising their families.

This massive Urban Renewal effort destroyed 'slums' in 1,000 mostly eastern US cities, resulting in widespread destruction of the extended family structure in black American families as hundreds of thousands of residents were forced from the only homes they had known.

Little was done to find new homes for the evicted residents, much less to preserve the contiguous extended-family structures. Opposition to these changes varied from city to city but the result was massive displacement and destruction of homes and the dissolution of families throughout the country.

In One City – 500 Homes Destroyed – Black Families Torn Apart

Kingston is an old Hudson River city in New York State. It proudly boasts of once being the capital of the State. In the 1960s the town fathers accepted 36 million federal Urban Renewal dollars and they used half of it to tear down 500 apartment and small business buildings.[35] Mr. Rufus C. lived in one of those buildings with his mother and his grandmother and had relatives in adjacent buildings. It was a community of extended families. I had briefly hired Rufus to do some part-time work for me so I was somewhat aware of what was happening. Too late, we all realized the terrible consequences.

When you drove through this old Rondout Creek section of town, you could see that some of the buildings needed repairs or paint. But they were old, sturdy, beautiful structures that had the imprint of careful architecture and had served their residents well for more than a century.

---

[35] *Lost Rondout, A Story of Urban Removal*, 2016, a video by Stephen Blauweiss and Lynn Woods. From the back cover: "In the 1960s, federally funded urban renewal projects destroyed hundreds of working-class urban communities across America. [This video] chronicles how one such project impacted the Hudson Valley city of Kingston, New York, demolishing 500 buildings and displacing thousands of people..."

Apparently well-meaning federal and local politicians and esthetic elites decided for this area's residents that these buildings would be condemned and government money would cure their poverty by tearing them down and replace them with nice buildings. Except there was no money or plan to build these nice buildings. It took decades to replace them and today's current residents are all middle and upper middle class and the businesses are mostly specialized boutiques. It would have all been forgotten except for a few unusual people.

One of them was a young delivery boy who worked for his father, a local florist. Every time he made one of his many deliveries he took pictures. Over time he amassed hundreds of them. He captured their architectural grandeur; and he captured the work of the wrecking ball. Now, because of him there is a video documentary using interviews to narrate this delivery boy's pictures, thanks to the hard work by two determined researchers, Stephen Blauweiss and Lynn Woods.

Trailer:
Lost Rondout

Blauweiss and Woods produced *Lost Rondout, A Story of Urban Removal*. This 2016 video chronicles how in "the Hudson Valley city of Kingston, New York, [the result was the] demolishing [of] 500 buildings and displacing thousands of people..." Trailers of this video[36] are online (click on QR code at right)[37] and the full 60 minute video is now available as a DVD or for online streaming (with subtitles) on Amazon.

Today, the Rondout section of Kingston, New York has become an area for tourists and artists. Some of the remnants of the original extended families occupy nearby public housing, built many years after the extended families had been fractured and scattered.

Urban Renewal – 99th Street in New York City

NY City:
99th Street

Urban renewal did untold societal damage all over America. A poignant six minute video details what happened in one New York City neighborhood. *The Tragedy of Urban Renewal: The destruction and survival of a New York City neighborhood* created by the staff of the Reason Foundation's *Reason.tv*, it is available for watching on YouTube[38] (or click your smartphone on the adjacent QR code.)

"Why Can't They Help Themselves (Like __(fill in name)__ Did?)"

So why didn't other ethnic groups who were displaced suffer the same as the black community. Some people still ask, "My grandparents (or parents or uncles … pick one) were dirt poor and they worked hard and lifted themselves up and today we are all contributing members of society."

In fact many non-blacks were displaced, especially in the smaller cities east of the Mississippi but the majority had a different cultural heritage to support them.

The Italians, the Irish, and the Polish and most of our other immigrants had a similarly common family ethic that helped them succeed. Central to that higher success rate was a more predominant two-parent family with its male role model for boys. That role model got its strength because earlier generations had intact families and had *not* been fractured through forced separation of father from mother and children.

---

[36] *www.youtube.com/watch?v=PPvK8MojSac*
[37] For help with QR codes, see *Appendix J. Using QR Codes in This Book*
[38] *The Tragedy of Urban Renewal: The destruction and survival of a New York City neighborhood*, This video is on the Internet at *www.youtube.com/watch?v=mWGwsA1V2r4*,

The Legacy of Slavery made it all Different

Slavery taught the American Negro that any family could be suddenly torn apart. A strong young man – a father – could be sold one afternoon at auction to a faraway owner while his children were of little monetary value and would stay with their mother or other women. They would almost certainly never see him again. This scenario was repeated thousands upon thousands of times and the lesson was clearly learned: Black mother will raise the children; black father is only useful for breeding and hard work. And so a large proportion of black America has developed into a matriarchal-dominant structure. A mother can do a lot for a boy but only exceedingly rarely can she can't make him become a man. But every healthy boy aspires to become one.

A hundred years later and before the start of the 1960s social engineering fiasco, black city dwellers, poor but thriving in their clustered ghettos had developed a sense of a neighborhood 'family' where people typically looked out for one another. Unlike other neighborhood ethnic groups the father was more often missing or absent – the cultural heritage of past slavery. Even so, there were male role models in the close neighborhood even though they often lived apart from the children. Uncles, older cousins, grandfathers – all of these gave young boys a chance to observe the difference and the pride and the unique sense of meaning that derives from being male.

Today too many young boys and adolescents find their role models in the streets and they in turn become role models for the next generation of lost boys.

Larry Elder is a radio show host, author and attorney who grew up in a poor neighborhood of Los Angeles. California. He makes a powerful case for the need for fathers in the black community in a short video.[39] Click on the QR code at the right to view it.

Larry Elder: Black Fathers Matter

'Street Families'

Extended families were destroyed and black families were disproportionately affected. Children were lost. Out in the streets, their need for missing family were met by gangs.

America's growing drug market helped support these gangs. Prisons began to overflow, so we built more prisons. Chaos had begun to overwhelm Black America.

From the 1950s through until about 1974 the national prison population – white, Hispanic and black – was about 200,000. After 1974, the rate started a rapid uphill climb to its present approximate 1,500,000 in 2015 – more than seven-fold increase.

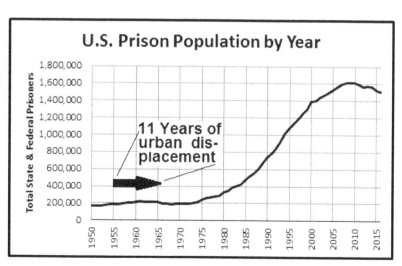

U.S. Prison Population by Year

11 Years of urban dis-placement

---

[39] *www.youtube.com/watch?v=FszQelEQ2KY*

The graph shows a more detailed picture and illustrates how within a decade after the great scattering and displacement of urban 'slum' residents, the U.S. prison population started its upward climb in 1975.[40]

Books could be written about what happened in that decade. A review of the aging statistics of prison populations during that period makes it clear that the displaced boys from these fractured families first were involved in minor infractions, then as they grew older, they moved from the streets, then to the courts and then to the jails and finally, within less than a decade they began flowing into the prisons.

The displaced children of the 1960s had found their substitute families in the streets and now they – and their children – are in prison. I know because I have talked with hundreds of them in many prisons over the past 14 years.

It all started in the 1960s with progressive social engineering

They didn't do it to themselves. Our liberal government ruling class did it to them.

According to a 2014 report from the National Research Council:

> Beginning in the 1960s, a complex combination of organized protests, urban riots, violent crime and drug use, the collapse of urban schools, and many other factors contributed to declining economic opportunities in many neighborhoods and too often to greater fear of crime.[41]

And the cycle repeats:

> Most studies find that incarceration is associated with weaker family bonds and lower levels of child well-being. Men with a history of incarceration are less likely to marry or cohabit and more likely to form unstable partnerships than those who have never been incarcerated, and children of incarcerated fathers tend to exhibit more problems in childhood and adolescence.[42]

When I hear naïve Americans complain about "why poor people can't lift themselves up by their own bootstraps", as they parrot phrases such as, [pick one:] "Like I did."; "Like my father did."; "Like my grandfather did."; "Like everyone else did."; …, my blood begins a slow boil.

If you still don't understand what happened to Black America over the past 60 years, please re-read this section again and then compare their tragedy charted in *Appendix A. Out of Slavery*, on page 132 with your own family's history and ancestry. See any differences? Look around and look behind you.

Try not to boast if you stand tall. You may have worked hard to get where you are but you are also standing on the shoulders of those who came before you.

---

[40] Graph is based on U.S. Department of Commerce and Department of Justice statistics from seven different sources (data can be provided on valid request to the author.)

[41] "The Growth of Incarceration in the United States – Exploring Causes and Consequences, *National Research Council*, Jeremy Travis, et. al, Editors, The National Academies Press, Washington, D.C., 2014, p.24

[42] Ibid., p.262

OVERWHELMED BY TECHNOLOGY

Internal Challenges

Did anybody see it coming, all this cultural chaos from our high tech inventions?

Technology is changing the way we interact with one another and is destroying the better fabric of our culture. It is literally reshaping the brains of our children. It has already made major changes to our way of life and is putting blue-collar workers and laborers out of work, many of them the very people who are immigrating to this country in vast numbers.

Meanwhile a few tech executives have become very rich and are using large sums of their money to 'dabble' in politics as they work to undermine the will of the common citizen in federal and state races. When a wealthy tech executive gives thousands of dollars to a political action committee, it seems less like a gift and more like a bribe. *Quid pro quo.*

Social Media, Hypervigilance and Hysteria

The Internet has given rise to social media which for many people has grown to become an electronic lynch mob. Unrestrained gossip now becomes 'news' at the speed of light and spreads like a deadly virus. Lives and reputations are ruined and the seeds of divisiveness are spread to grow in the minds of the foolish and the naïve.

Social media encourages formation and rapid growth of strange action groups. In earlier times a 'crazy' social action idea would often die from neglect. Now the most bizarre ideas can attract a large group of unhinged adherents from far flung places – in America and from around the world. These groups are more likely to coalesce when they feel threatened. This is the new 'globalization' of fear.

When all is calm, people go their various ways, each enjoying their comfortable differences in peace. But when things become tense, society's 'outliers' pull together like threatened sheep. Calm grazing sheep normally spread over a meadow. But when the wolf, or rumor of wolf appears they quickly congregate.

Agitated people do likewise, coming from far and wide, to group-up and march in protest. They sign petitions; they vote in larger numbers; they riot; they organize; they train for battle. And like hungry, wet infants, their shrillness over-proclaims their mass.

Social media has become a new kind of nucleating adhesive used to attract and encourage frightened, angry people to group action, often before they have had time to verify or comprehend.

Technology? – You Ain't Seen <u>Nothin'</u> Yet!

As if all the rest of the world's problems aren't enough for us to cope with, just wait a few historical moments. It used to take about 18 to 25 years from the time of a new invention until it became integrated into our lives. That was nice. It gave everyone a chance to find a place on the mantelpiece for the buggy whip and a new home for the horse.

What's This !?

But 18 years became ten and then four and now change is almost instant – or seemingly so. Remember how you used to order a taxi? Now there is Uber and Lyft. Pull out your smartphone, push a button and the GPS locator in the phone tells the nearest available car where you are and tells you it's on the way. And how long to wait.

And some of us older folks, born in the last century, remember when there were phone booths. Actual rectangular things with a door you could close while you made a personal call. You put in a few quarters (or used a plastic card) and made your call. Those booths were good to keep you dry when it rained.

And then, to the amazement of 20th Century old-timers, tiny pocket sized, 'analog' flip phones appeared.

Then came the smartphone. It's called 'smart' because now it can do everything a computer, camera, GPS locator, motion sensor, gyroscope, magnetic compass, wristwatch, alarm clock, thermometer and humidity detector can do. Among other things. Oh, did I also mention, it can also make and receive telephone calls. And send and receive text and voice messages. And act as a typewriter. And a weather barometer. And it can do voice recognition and real-time language translation. Oh, and these things come with internal radio transmitters and receivers to enable linking with other devices.

Apple Corporation's first iPhone was released in 2007. As of 2017, ten years later, there have been ten generations of improvements. This is unheard of progress compared to the average human ability to adapt.

Will artificial intelligence (AI) and robots and automation take over our jobs, our politics and our very lives? According to one study, "About half of today's jobs will likely be done by computers in a decade or two,"[43]

We were warned. Almost 50 years ago, Alvin Toffler told us all this was coming.[44] Almost 80 years ago the noted economist John Maynard Keynes blamed the Great Depression, in part, on "growing pains of over-rapid changes." Improvements in technology, he said were "taking place faster than we can deal with [them]." Did we pay attention? Have we prepared for this change? Could we have prepared? Or was it inevitable and is there much more to come?

What Next?

Brace yourself. Smartphones, computer tablets and the like are just the beginning.

Social media – the new way people are communicating and congregating is changing the world. Facebook, Instagram, Yelp, Google, LinkedIn, Twitter and a host of others are all fairly new.

Virtual reality – VR – lets us see things that are not really there, yet experience them as if we were totally together. Stuff comes to you, rather than you having to go to it. We can feel the thrill of riding on a roller coaster, the experience of flying over the Grand Canyon, or the intimacy of a loved one who is actually far away. Or even gone from this life. Deep immersion in VR can be intoxicating and lead to several forms of dysfunction. Similar to the LSD experiences of earlier times.[45]

Cloud computing and 'edge computing' are some of the new buzzwords. As I write this book, I keep several back versions on the 'cloud' – on remote computers 'out there somewhere' – as a backup against unexpected loss and so I can easily review and work with the text on other devices.

Blockchain – the technology behind the Bitcoin phenomenon – is a new and very real invention that is already transforming and improving transaction security in financial applications and other important areas of commerce. Professional publications are devoting entire issues to this subject.[46]

Artificial and Intelligent too?

Yes, *artificial intelligence* (AI) exists and is in your life now. AI is no joke. It is artificial and it can pass many tests of intelligence. These machines with artificial neural networks and other computer marvels can actually be trained and learn and they can improve their behavior over time. AI machines already have beaten world champions at the most complicated and difficult games, including Chess and

---

[43] Frey, Carl Benedikt and Michael A. Osborne, *The Future of Employment*, Oxford Martin School, University of Oxford, September 17, 2013

[44] Toffler, Alvin, *Future Shock*, Random House, New York, 1970

[45] This is reminiscent of the 1995 William Shatner movie and book, *TekWar* which is centered on a highly addictive computer-based virtual reality "drug" called "Tek."

[46] *IEEE Spectrum*, October, 2017 issue. *spectrum.ieee.org*

the Chinese favorite, 'Go'. But more general purpose AI is on the horizon – AI that can work in many and multiple domains and industries.

Today, AI is translating languages on Google and, as it learns, is getting better at it every day.[47] AI is now driving driverless cars and trucks. In 2015 there were approximately 36,000 traffic deaths in America. Driverless cars, with their collision avoidance systems and other safety devices are expected to lower that number significantly.

The popular media is almost completely clueless about AI and its promises and our need to direct its development. Their stories are full of misconceptions and are mostly dystopian. They are usually accompanied by an evil-looking robot carrying a weapon.

For a factual understanding of AI and its promises and problems, read the excellent book by Max Tegmark, *Life 3.0: Being Human in the Age of Artificial Intelligence*.[48] Tegmark is a very literate and articulate MIT professor and AI developer who has organized a top-flight group that seeks to direct AI's future development for the good of mankind.[49]

A "Right to Explanation"

One big problem with these AI computers that learn and ultimately perform according to their learning – there is not always a way to 'question' the machine to determine how it arrived at its decisions. This area of "explainable deep learning" is currently a hot research topic. The legal implications alone are significant. For example, why did a self-driving vehicle react in a certain way? Why did an airplane autopilot make a certain decision?

This is turning out to be a difficult technical research area that has important future implications for applications in medicine, law enforcement and financial operations. In April, 2016 the European Union issued a regulation that makes it a human right to request an explanation when a machine makes a decision that "significantly affects" an E.U. citizen. The law took effect in 2018.

Robot Servants

Human controlled and self-actuated robots are everywhere, from the farm to the production line to the hospital to the battlefield. They may not always have arms and legs but they perform our tasks and relieve us of much work. And more and better ones are coming. And worse ones are heading our way also.[50]

And then there is the 'Internet of Things,' or IoT, a somewhat geeky name for what happens when it becomes economically feasible to connect formerly separate devices in the home, office and factory. For example, sensors in your refrigerator may detect that the milk carton is only a quarter full. The refrigerator will communicate with the grocery store which will then send you a carton of fresh milk. This is but one trivial example, yet illustrative of what can be done when man's mind is free to imagine and implementation costs are reduced to near zero.

---

[47] Use your web browser and go to *translate.google.com* to see how it works. This AI website from Google's DeepMind project does immediate translations between any two of over 100 languages. Click on the loudspeaker symbol and it will speak the translation for most of the languages. User input and corrections are continuously being used to improve the neural network's learning.

[48] Tegmark, Max, *Life 3.0: Being Human in the Age of Artificial Intelligence*, Alfred A. Knopf, New York, 2017

[49] This group, the Future of Life Institute (FLI) has developed a set of 23 principles to guide future AI development. Those principles are broken down into, research issues, ethics and values, and longer-term issues. The complete list as well as the names of the experts comprising this vast group can be accessed at *futureoflife.org/ai-principles/*.

[50] On the battlefield and in the brothel. Amazingly horrid things are being planned and prototyped.

Wearable Electronic Devices

Many companies are actively working on devices that will become a part of our everyday clothing and what we carry with us. These so-called 'wearable electronics' will have the capacity to sense others in our environment, to locate, then record their pictures and voices and actions and read things such as their heart rate from a distance. Some of these devices have the ability to upload information to the Internet, all without our knowing about it.

Already there is concern in Europe where a committee of the European Commission is working on a proposed law to regulate these devices[51] and there is much research and concern on both sides of the ocean about the privacy and ethical implications.

Dangerous "Smart Toys" – A Cybersecurity Problem

A recent article in the technical press raises eyebrows about those cute, fuzzy new toys which can connect to a smartphone or the Internet. According to an article in *Computer* magazine they may be easily hacked. Some of these toys have hidden microphones and cameras which hackers can use to spy on families and children.

Some toys connect to the vendor's websites and upload information obtained from the children to support the fun applications. Hackers have been able to access some of this private information about families and children and in one case a hacker was able to communicate with a child through their toy.

Toymakers have limited technology budgets and many are naïve about the risks. The message to customers is, use caution in purchasing these toys. Some of these toys have become illegal in Germany because of their security dangers and the European Union is considering similar action. No such action yet in the U.S. *Caveat emptor.*[52]

Undetectable False Witness and Fake News

"Seeing isn't believing anymore. Deep-learning computer applications can now generate fake video and audio recordings that look strikingly real." That's the message of a recent article in the *Wall Street Journal.*[53]

Researchers from several universities, with apparently nothing better to do, are developing computer software that can make fake videos of famous people (or anyone else). They look and sound real and it is very difficult, without specialized analysis to determine they are fakes. As this software becomes more sophisticated is becomes harder to tell they are fake creations.

As one commentator recently suggested, imagine the consequences of and response to a fake video of the President announcing, "We have just launched atomic cruise missiles toward (name the country)."

One can question why are university researchers developing tools like this and why are they making them available to the general public? Are we better off knowing of the possibilities? What should we do to prepare ourselves for this kind of potentially deadly 'gossip'? In light of these developments, what is the role of responsible journalism? What safeguards can we recommend to other countries?

Robots, Intelligent Machines and the Meaning of Life

What will we become if all our work is done for us by robots, when the largest factory is staffed by fewer than four people and when the farm is planted and harvested by robots? Will we still be human? I

---

[51] The Article 29 Working Party (A29WP) legislation project requires that users and bystanders be granted freedom of 'notice and choice.'

[52] Kshetri, Nir, and Jeffrey Voss, "Cyberthreats Under the Bed", *Computer*, (IEEE Computer Society), May, 2018, pp.92-94.

[53] Schellmann, Hilke "Deepfake Videos Are Getting Real and That's a Problem", *The Wall Street Journal*, October 15, 2018, wsj.com/articles/deepfake-videos-are-ruining-lives-is-democracy-next-1539595787

contend that there are aspects of humanity and consequent work for each one that will remain as long as there are humans on the face of the earth (or beyond.)

So what will we do in our spare time? Will we sit in our recliners, fantasize with our VR devices, vegetate and ignore the rest of the world. Or will we find new meaning in our lives? People will always suffer. That is the nature of our existence. That also may change as medical advances eliminate causes of illness and prolong life. But life's end will always be nigh.

While we await this utopian fantasy, we might look for guidance in the words of Jesus near the end of Matthew Chapter 25 where he talked about our need to give drink to the thirsty, feed the hungry, shelter the homeless, clothe the naked, tend to the sick and visit the prisoner.

It is hard to imagine a time when all that will become unnecessary on this earth – no more hunger or thirst, no more sickness or loneliness. When hospitals and prisons become museums.

We may rely more and more on our machines to help one another but mankind has incredible creativity and surely we will be able to create more suffering than any machines can handle.

The mandate of Matthew, Chapter 25 will still prevail. Maybe therein lies our vision of the future and what we should hope for when all else is decided and taken care of for us by our new techno-servants and the elite few who would control them – and us.

And then there is the problem of compassionate love – try your best computer experts on that one. As one Saint proclaimed, "The power of love alone is able to lift up the soul from earth to heaven…" [54]

═══════════════════

(My advice to those who worry about the implications of our tech future: Don't believe half of what you hear – but pay close attention to the other half. Choose your information sources carefully. Most 'journalists' have zero technical knowledge or capability when the subject turns to science or engineering. Only a few of those written for the layman are trustworthy. One is the Tuesday *Science Times* section of the otherwise biased and politically left-leaning *New York Times*. Their Tuesday section has an excellent record for writers who truly understand and write well in most of its science reporting. Another is *Science News Magazine,* a biweekly publication of *Society for Science and the Public*.)

Culture and Ethical Considerations of Disruptive Technologies

In the interim as these changes take place a great number of people – particularly the elderly, the infirm and the poor – will be pushed to the margins or left behind.

Some of these changes will cause social upheaval resulting in stress, disagreement, fears and even open 'warfare'. (Remember the stories of the Luddites and the first saboteur, who threw his shoe (sabot) into the automated weaving machine?)

As a nation of many cultures, each of us may be affected differently. Consider the Amish way of life as one cultural example, and as a near opposite, the suburban or large city urban dweller who, at this very moment talks to his Alexa, Cortana, Google Assistant or Siri device[55] and orders groceries, or room temperature changes or music to be played or a host of other things, all of which are now a reality.

Still relatively undebated is the issue of *ethics*. No longer just an academic topic, this will affect every American. As artificial intelligence, robots and other new technology change life for some, and leave others further behind, how will we Americans respond and still retain our humanity and our caring for one another? How will we be able to have meaningful and peaceful dialogue and understanding, one with another?

These technical developments are inspiring a number of inquiries into legal, cultural and ethical requirements, studies of which are ongoing, especially, surprisingly, in the technical community.

---

[54] Saint Albert the Great, teacher of Saint Thomas Aquinas. St. Albert is regarded as the patron of scientists.

[55] Voice-recognition systems tied to intelligent computing and data facilities from Microsoft, Amazon, Google and Apple respectively.

McKinsey Global Institute has published a report on the potential economic and social impact of twelve of these emerging 'disruptive' technologies and it is available online.[56]

=====

I have a great deal of hope for the future and am not the least bit afraid of all these coming changes, since I have been working with and watching them for a lifetime. But many of us will be taken by surprise. We will need to help one another to learn, cope, and in some cases to defend.

But we need to become more aware – and prepare.

How Technology Has Been Killing Art, Music and Video

The arts are the soul of a culture and that soul is under attack and is being destroyed by our technology and its bottom-line focused elite leaders. Like the canary in the mine, when the arts begin to suffer, the mine is becoming too toxic for humans. The result is a rapid decline in creativity in all areas, especially in the performing arts, such as comedy, music, shows and movies (called "videos" by younger readers.) The literary arts and our local newspapers are also heavily under attack.

The Internet has Destroyed the Music Industry.

Internet sites like Google's YouTube have taken away almost all royalties from artists, song writers, composers and their associates. When 70-year-old Levon Helm was dying of cancer in 1990 he had to do a series of local concerts to pay his medical bills. His income – tens of thousands of dollars – from royalties had completely dried up. All his recordings had been illegally uploaded on the Internet to pirate sites and YouTube, and any royalty income he had hoped would support his wife and kids had vanished. When he died, friends had to put on a benefit concert so his wife could hold onto their Woodstock house.

A Supreme Court decision[57] and an act of Congress[58] had made all this unstoppable. Today only a very few artists receive decent royalties from their work. Where just a couple of decades ago 20 percent of performers received about 80 percent of royalties, today, *one percent* receive about 80 percent of all royalties.[59]

Unlike the past when an unknown performer had a chance to get a toehold on the industry, today the incentive has vanished. The result, we are in a musical Ice Age – there is practically no new music anymore, other than that from a very few wealthy artists, such as the likes of Mariah Carey, Taylor Swift, Beyonce and Jay Z.

Technology has enabled another strike against creativity in the music industry. Search engines push the more popular songs to the top of the list while lesser artists become even lesser known. As *Vanity Fair* writer Kurt Andersen pointed out, "… popular style has been stuck on repeat, consuming the past instead of creating the new." [60]

Hopeful Recent U.S. Legislation

In October, 2018, President Trump signed into law the Music Modernization Act (MMA), which updates copyright law to better protect song writers, performers and producers in the age of Internet and music streaming. Well known country music star and prolific song writer John Rich who attended the

---

[56] Manyika, James, et. al., *Disruptive Technologies: Advances that Will Transform Life, Business and the Global Economy*, McKinsey Global Institute, May 2013, *www.mckinsey.com/business-functions/digital-mckinsey/our-insights/disruptive-technologies* (Click on the 'full report' button to download the complete 156 page report.)

[57] *Quill Corp. vs. North Dakota*, 1992

[58] *Internet Tax Freedom Act* of 1998

[59] Taplin, Jonathan, *Move Fast and Break Things, How Facebook, Google and Amazon Cornered Culture and Undermined Democracy*, Little, Brown & Company, 2017

[60] Andersen, Kurt, "You Say You Want a Devolution?", *Vanity Fair*, January, 2012

White House signing ceremony stated, this is "the single most important legislation ever passed in the history of song writing in America." This law, which lingered seven years in the dark recesses of Congress, was finally passed unanimously by both the House and the Senate. The law sets up a 'Music Licensing Collective' to collect and pay out royalties from digital service providers, such as Spotify and iTunes. The result: artists, songwriters and producers will be able to make more money from streaming and other digital services.

European Union – Baby Out With the Bathwater?

A slight glimmer of light is coming from – of all places – The European Union Parliament Committee on Legal Affairs which has proposed updates to the E.U. copyright law, specifically intended to prevent online piracy of music and video and will also require websites that link to other news sources to pay original publishers. In September, 2018, the Parliament voted in favor, 438 to 226, of an update on the proposal, called the Copyright Directive. Full approval faces a final approval vote in January, 2019 but opponents say this is a draconian law that will likely change the way the entire Internet is used and will severely stifle further creative development.

The proposed changes have come under strong attack from multiple Internet companies and influential tech luminaries, such as Tim Berners-Lee, inventor of the World Wide Web and Jimmy Wales, the founder of *Wikipedia*. The proposal is unlikely to survive in its present form. But if its two controversial parts survive the January vote it will have a large and disruptive impact on the entire Internet, both in the European Union and the United States and in the rest of the world.

All the News You Need?

Most people now get their news through news feeds from Google and Facebook. They are targeted, by computer algorithms that examine their e-mail and other online posts, searches and preferences, and feed them news based on age, race, religion and nationality, all in the interest of maximum advertising effectiveness. These corporations are increasingly being accused of "doctoring" the news. This has had the effect of totally breaking the revenue model for newspapers and magazines, many of which are going bankrupt.

And newspapers throughout the U.S. are being bought up by hedge funds as these new owners lay off scores of staff and bleed them cash-dry until they can no longer function. The *Denver Post* is one such – Denver, Colorado, a city of 700,000 no longer has a single local daily newspaper. Without sufficient revenues, local papers can no longer cover local news, much to the delight of those political hacks who would prefer to work out of the spotlight and exploit our democracy for their own profit and power.

CONTROLLED BY THE WEALTHY

The Tyranny of Wealthy Tech Oligarchs

The World Wide Web has begotten a nightmare. Google, Facebook, Amazon and a few others have rapidly made their companies, founders and owners fabulously rich. Google, for example is making so much money that it has difficulty finding sufficient opportunities to invest its cash. The market value of these companies is unbelievable.

Controlling enormous wealth seems to give some people a feeling of minor deity. If you can make such impact in your own little corner, why not rule the world? Mark Zuckerberg, the CEO of Facebook was recently rumored to be planning a run for the U.S. presidency! He's been sidelined for a while by recent distractions and lawsuits regarding Russian false news and E.U. privacy challenges and deceptive security and privacy practices.

In their reach for political power, their enormous monetary power unbalances our political system and ordinary citizens are pushed aside. Google, Facebook and Amazon give enormous sums of money to *both* political parties and have tremendous clout with Congress and the Administration. We citizens are led, rather than us doing the leading. Many thoughtful citizens question whether the 2010 Supreme Court's *Citizens United* decision which opened these monetary floodgates was best for the country.

And don't rule out other wealthy minor deities who would try to rule us. I'm thinking of celebrities like Oprah Winfrey, made wealthy by her fabulous emotional appeal to women and her good business sense. Then there's George Soros who became wealthy by betting on foreign currency and has his fingers into social and political issues all over the world.[61] (He recently became *persona non grata* in his native Hungary because of his attempts to meddle in their politics.)

The World Is Hollywood's Cesspool

Hollywood dumps their filth in foreign lands, pollutes their cultures – and it's all about money and making wealthy people richer.

'Hollywood' has become a synonym for much of today's entertainment industry output although much of it is produced elsewhere than Hollywood, California. There are countless instances of foreign religious and political leaders admonishing America for our ostentatious, violent, lascivious and vulgar entertainment products which soulless big money and big business brings to their country. Millions of dollars are at stake in these foreign markets and the simple, naïve people who view them think, in their innocence, they then know who and what America is all about.

Make no mistake; Hollywood is the true representative of America to the rest of the world. Our foreign offices and ambassadors represent us to the culturally educated, the intellectuals, the cocktail party crowds and the politicians but not to the common people in these foreign lands. When an uprising occurs, as when the Ayatollah Ruhollah Khomeini overthrew the Iranian government in 1979, he had no difficulty getting the masses behind him to proclaim, "America is the Great Satan!"

Enemy of the People

Much of the video and evil gaming 'entertainment' our industries create is filth, trash, debauchery and gratuitous violence. But it is attractive – especially to the young and the emotionally marginalized – because it is titillating and reflects a degree of rebellion. And it entices us to be entertained by the evil of someone else's human brokenness.

Most of us have no idea how differently those less 'advanced' societies perceive what we have created. In many countries these perverse exports are causing cultural division and family decay.

Foreigners 'see' America for the first time. It should be no surprise that a majority of them reject us and the rest may want to come here to enjoy the fictional lifestyle. Neither reaction benefits us.

Six mega-corporations control almost all of our entertainment industry. We should not be surprised if they would move to block and lie about any popular effort to disrupt this, their foreign cash cow. Organizations like *Focus on the Family*,[62] the *Parents Television Council*[63] and the *American Family Association*[64] and others have been trying for years to change all this, to little avail.

We absolutely need to rein in 'Hollywood' – a generic term I use to characterize all this violence, smut, pornography and X-rated slime – that is destroying the minds of our children and creating a great deal of unnecessary hostility toward us in foreign places.

---

[61] Soros' activist organization – *The Open Society Foundation* – has offices in 50 countries around the world.
[62] *www.focusonthefamily.com*
[63] *www.parentstv.org*
[64] *www.afa.net*

Real America doesn't live this way and yet much of the world has come to believe that all Americans are greedy, rich, corrupt, violent and immoral; that we are warlike and only worship superheroes.

They think our wealth is as portrayed in the videos. They believe all our music is vulgar sexual-rhythmic hip-hop and rap.

As in Henrik Ibsen's play of the same name, Hollywood will undoubtedly portray our insistence on American decency as the real "enemy of the people" and that should only encourage us to push harder against this real satanic enemy of our culture.

Foreign Backlash against our Cultural Perversions

The Chinese government has recently begun seriously cracking down on online news and social media. From our First Amendment point of view that seems very draconian and unfair. But bringing ourselves to understand what they are trying to accomplish does not require that we agree.

There is something profound going on in terms of our social media and how it is rapidly changing the culture of every country it touches.[65]

China has blocked a number of our stars from performing in their country. Among them are Lady Gaga and Justin Bieber, two performers whom many parents will not allow their kids to see. According to a recent Reuters news feed, China has launched a campaign to cleanse the entertainment sector of content it deems inappropriate and unhealthy.[66]

China today is a vast land of 1.4 billion people, containing many different ethnic groups, languages and dialects. There are five different languages – the most well known outside of China are Mandarin and Cantonese, and there are about 200 different dialects – many of them mutually unintelligible.

There are 55 different ethnic minority groups recognized in China, in addition to the ethnic Han majority.

If it is difficult to manage one country with a single language and culture, imagine how difficult – nearly impossible China must seem to its leaders. Again, this is to explain, not to excuse.

The tiny Himalayan Mountain country of Nepal has just outlawed pornography websites in its nation. Their decree lists 25,000 such known obscene websites and a government team is monitoring their internet service providers. A similar ban was issued in 2011 but the current one has much more severe penalties for violators.[67]

China is no exception. If you want an eye-full, just Google "foreign perception of American cultural perversions." America is regarded, around the world, as decadent and perverted because of our 'Hollywood' exports. Read what the liberal *New York Times*, The *Atlantic Monthly* or the *Washington Post* have to say. When the liberal news media finally get concerned, we might all take notice.

We could get a lot more foreigners to respect us if we stopped exporting so much of this 'Hollywood' crap so they could begin to see who we actually are.

---

[65] For example, Boko Haram is a radical Islamist group in northern Nigeria. The name, "Boko Haram" means "Western Influence is a sin."

[66] "Grammys cleans up its act in bid to enter giant Chinese market", *Reuters*, 3, August, 2017, *news.trust.org/item/20170803114640-dbr95*

[67] Gurubacharya, Binaj, "'This is only the start': Nepal blocks 25,000 websites in porn ban, *The Washington Times*, October 14, 2018

Putting Our Best Foot Forward

Robert R. Reilly was Director of the Voice of America international broadcasting system from 2001 to 2002. In a recent article in the *Wall Street Journal* he quotes a video that VOAs Ukrainian service posted online last year before the November election in which Celebrity Robert DeNiro referred to candidate Donald Trump as "… so blatantly stupid; he's a punk; he's a dog; he's a pig; he's a con". The video was pulled after the service was criticized but nonetheless was broadcast for a turbulent part of the world to hear. [68]

VOA has been under an independent eight person Board of Governors and is now run by a CEO appointed by the President. For a number of years VOA has become politicized; having lost its original mandate and is no longer doing the job it was created for during the Cold War.

This is just part of what the political Left has been doing to undermine the values we export to other countries. No wonder we are not well thought of in foreign places.

The VOA should be helping America export our values and focus on decency rather than trying to build audience size.

Reilly suggests that President Trump should nominate someone to lead the Voice of America who understands that we are in an information war with Islamic State, Russia and China. [69]

Our Cultural Preoccupation with Death

It used to be sex. Now we have become a culture preoccupied with death. Our movies, our music videos, our TV programs and magazines are overflowing with zombies, skeletons, evil dolls and clowns, and teen suicide, not to mention the 'usual' WMDs, suicide bombers, ISIS and North Korean bombs and missiles.

Irresponsible people will say this is what the people want. Other irresponsible people give children addictive drugs, "Because it's what they want."

Most popular media reinforces the perversion that it is so much more exciting to destroy than to create. It costs more to make a non-boring movie about building something than it does to blow something else up. And thus we teach our youth to disvalue the good, the beautiful and the created.

A Martian watching our entertainment media might conclude that individuals want to live forever yet destroy everyone and everything else. Recently there have been a number of media reports about wealthy people trying to live forever by cryo-freezing their bodies after death in anticipation of eventual scientific resurrection. Other scientists are working on life-extending DNA replacements and other 'miracles'.

One can wonder if our diminished national faith – every year more adults profess to be atheists or non-believers[70] – may be causing ripples of uncertainty below the conscious surface.

The late renowned scientist Steven Hawking predicted the end of human existence and noted that we must soon leave this planet for somewhere else in the Universe. And of course, many of us who are older remember the dire predictions of *The Bulletin of the Atomic Scientists* whose doomsday clock shows its hands pointing just before midnight. (They recently advanced them to two and a half minutes before midnight.)

Zombies, clowns, bombs and death-fears are human creations designed to distract us from the path we were created to follow on earth. I may be incinerated or pulverized tomorrow but *today* I have work to do and that work will suffer if I let these fears overwhelm me. That doesn't mean I am unprepared to

---

[68] Reilly, Robert, "How to Make the Voice of America Come Through Loud and Clear", *The Wall Street Journal*, Feb. 18-19, 2017, p. A13

[69] Note: Radio Free Europe/Radio Liberty is a separate broadcasting organization funded by the U.S. Congress and was very active during the Cold War with the Soviet Union. RFE recently resumed broadcasting to "Romania and Bulgaria in a bid to debunk fake news and combat poor quality journalism," according to *Newsmax Magazine*, Sept., 2018, p.38

[70] Pew Research – *www.pewresearch.org/fact-tank/2016/06/01/10-facts-about-atheists/*

defend my family as appropriate. It simply means I refuse to be moved by the hysteria of the crowd and its Pied Pipers, the news and entertainment media. Keep the Faith.

A Different Perspective

What would practicing Christians do? Well, in some very significant areas there aren't many Christians (or observant Jews) involved.

For example about 96 percent of executives in Hollywood apparently are atheists according to one study and those executives may not have encountered many practicing Christians, observant Jews or anyone else who lives by their faith. Also, a current Wikipedia website entry names 272 living film, radio, TV and theatre personalities who have publicly self-identified as atheists[71]

> *Finally, brothers, whatever is true, whatever is noble, whatever is right, whatever is pure, whatever is lovely, whatever is admirable – if anything is excellent or praiseworthy – think about these things. Whatever you have learned or received or heard from me, or seen in me – put it into practice. And the God of peace will be with you.*
>
> *Saint Paul's letter to the Philippians, Chapter 4, verses 8 & 9.), (NIV)*

Do we want peace? Or money? Should we push for both? Think about these things.

> *For where your treasure is, there will your heart be also.*
> *Matthew 6:21, (NIV)*

CULTURAL RENEWAL

A Vision for Cultural Renewal

> *The value of culture is its effect on character. It avails nothing unless it ennobles and strengthens that. Its use is for life. Its aim is not beauty, but goodness ... The True, the Good, and the Beautiful are not the perquisites of those who have been to expensive schools, burrowed in libraries and frequented museums.*
>
> *W. Somerset Maugham*

Beauty can be perceived through our senses alone. But a deeper, spiritual awareness lies in the hidden glow of beauty beyond those senses. It is the sudden awareness of unspoken mystery in what our senses first announce. Our culture will be refreshed when we can seek and teach respect and understanding for all created things, including one another, especially the most annoying people and the very least among us.

---

[71] *en.wikipedia.org/wiki/List_of_atheists_in_film,_radio,_television_and_theater*

Cultural Repair

> *The way to reverse cultural decline is to connect with the hearts*
> *and minds of those who create culture.*
> *Abraham Hamilton III*

Our country has had several great cultural renewals when everyone acknowledged and faced a common enemy. But we should not need an enemy to bring us together. Young people, army draftees, factory workers – those who otherwise would not have had to work together – found a need to bond, with many contrasting ways of life joined in mutual cultural respect.

Mandatory Public Service?

Why can't we do this again? How about two years of mandatory public service after high school or college graduation? This would bring our youth together in a disciplined environment with job-related training where they would learn to get out of bed *every* morning and take orders and work under stress.

Whether it be the Peace Corps, mandatory Military Service, AmeriCorps (which includes a domestic Peace Corps,) or working for an NGO (Non-Governmental Organization) – there are many options, but *all* young people should serve in some capacity. Our country would be the better for it and our national culture could not get any worse when people start talking and working together on common issues.

I have never met a Peace Corps or other service volunteer who thought they wasted their time and who didn't grow in the job. Every one of the several volunteers I have met enjoyed their service and returned as a stronger, better adjusted person and a more dedicated citizen.

We have a giant cultural disconnect today where mainly the poor, the rural middle class and the minorities tend to fight our wars and serve in our military. Most members of Congress have never had any military or volunteer public service aside from politics. Mandatory public service would do wonders for improving our national culture and reducing the number of 'whiners' who complain about truly trivial problems once they have to deal with real life issues.

========================

Despite widespread censoring and distortion by mainstream news media, the Internet and alternative sources are beginning to awaken sensible people – and they are starting to rebel. The 2016 presidential election was one such result.

Half of our battle is to get to the truth of where we went wrong, avoid the past mistakes and strengthen and save what can be saved and not let ourselves get dragged down by the atheists, moral relativists and naysayers who helped us get here.

Can we improve our culture? Maybe. *Sociologists say that when about ten percent of a society begins to move in a new direction, that becomes a tipping point, a threshold, where the movement becomes self-sustaining and hard to stop.*

Now we need to begin the mighty job of repairing the crumbling infrastructure of our culture. The first ten percent will be tough. Let's start.

Help for Struggling Families

The foundation of all that is good in every culture is and has always been the family. Who would want their children to eat garbage, drink polluted water or breathe toxic air? Our culture is the air our children breathe and the bread their developing minds consume. We need to regain more of the spiritual and social part of family life as we focus less on the distractions of wealth, power, fame and material advances.

Culture Resources for Change

Help is available but knowing where to look is often the first problem. Here are some starting points that others have found useful

- ➢ Miss Manners, *Guide for the Turn of the Millennium*, An up-to-date book of etiquette and social conduct. (See Bibliography.) As dumb as this entry may seem, a great number of citizens have no idea and little training that "good manners" are the start of good dialogue and understanding. Good manners are simply a way to show respect for the other person's humanity.
- ➢ Mediation resources – There are many. One such is the *New York Peace Institute*. They are committed to "promoting peace in our communities. Whether a dispute involves two people, dozens of people, or several groups." – *nypeace.org*
- ➢ Another excellent mediation resource are the ideas in the book, *Getting to Yes, Negotiating Agreement Without Giving In* (See bibliography.) The focus is on finding *common interests* rather than *issue positions*.
- ➢ *Essential Partners –(See p. 115)* This non-profit organization works with individuals, groups and private or governmental organizations to encourage respectful dialogue – *whatisessential.org*

══════════════

N.B. – Any Internet addresses, QR codes and telephone numbers in this book are offered as a resource. They are not intended in any way to be or to imply an endorsement, nor does the author vouch for the content of these sites, numbers or references.

2 – The American Family

*Train up a child in the way he should go
and when he is old, he will not depart from it.*
Proverbs 22:6, (KJV)

CIVILIZATION'S ROOTS

If we are to keep our republic we have to save our families. That is not a call to big government, it is a call to each of us to help parents raise decent, informed, capable, responsible children and keep them from the cultural undertow that would destroy their souls.

America is rapidly becoming an uncivilized society. We have many of the trappings of a civilization without much left of the spirit. Most of those trappings resulted from earlier cooperation and progress when people could actively disagree and still discuss real solutions to our problems.

Researcher and sociologist Carle Zimmerman has conclusively shown that no civilization in history ever existed without fathers who lead and defend family and practice faith. Take away any one of these and you have a primitive society but no hope of a true civilization. [72]

Strong Families

Zimmerman has studied successful families extensively and found that strong families – what he describes as 'trustee families' – are bonded by strong religious faith and are led by strong fathers.

He points out that trustee families make the difference between ordinary human societies and those that became civilizations. Our children need to imbibe that faith, which will unite them to their families, their peers and their country if they are to survive the turmoil and the rocky roads that life will present. And they will need to be armed for the endless attacks that will surely confront them in our atheistic and secular humanist society.

Two Parents

The importance of having *both* parents present is essential to the proper growth and maturity of children, and the need for fathers has never been greater. Here's what one father had to add:

> Despite a society that tries to degrade fathers, study after study shows the important and irreplaceable role fathers play in the lives of their children... Children are less likely to take drugs, have teen pregnancies, and go to prison. Children raised in homes with fathers tend to stay in school, are less likely to suffer depression and attempt suicide. [73]

Many radical feminists and others on the political Left doubt – or deny entirely – that a father in every home is even necessary or possible.

The Marriage Covenant

In the Christian faith, a marriage is a 'covenant.' Unlike a civil marriage, as in one performed by a judge, a covenant is a three-way agreement among the couple and their God. When understood as such it becomes a binding permanent promise, not just to each other, but also to a higher power.

---

[72] Zimmerman, Carle, *Family and Civilization*, Intercollegiate Studies Institute, 1947
[73] Mahoney, Jeffrey, Letter to the Editor, *Poughkeepsie Journal* (New York), June 23, 2017, p. 13A

A stable family is the best breeding ground for a stable child who can make it to adulthood in one piece. Everyone has problems at some point in life but the child who has a strong family background has a much better chance.

Many young people get married before they realize the tremendous responsibilities involved. The romance doesn't last forever and without strong mutual commitment, couples break up when their 'honeymoon' is over and the day-to-day realities become overwhelming. Children of these unions frequently take second place to the parents' own self-interest.

Foundation of Trust and Confidence

Men and women are attracted for different reasons. A woman is more likely to be drawn to a man who can provide for a family and for its children. What a man may tell a woman in moments of starry-eyed romance can be partly 'sales talk'. But far more important is her feeling that he can make a deep and sustaining commitment to family and marriage. A man who has a strong faith foundation and has truly committed himself to his Lord is more likely to be such a person. Statistics show that marriages between religiously devoted couples are more stable and lasting.

Commitment

The best test of a couple's compatibility is not how romantic they may seem together, but how they will handle life's disappointments, problems and crises. Financial pressures and in-law problems are just a few examples.

When a couple can postpone marriage and children until they can better know each other's weaknesses and strengths and examine the long-term scene, that marriage has a better chance of lasting.

Some organizations offer pre-marital classes. The U.S. Roman Catholic Church provides a 'Pre-Cana' course and a mandatory six month waiting period before a marriage can be consecrated.

Study after study overwhelmingly demonstrates that children do best when raised by their own mother and father who have a lifelong loving marriage commitment to one another and who provide them with love and consistency.

STURDY CHILDREN

It is easier to build strong children
than to repair broken men.
Frederick Douglas

The First Three Years of Life

A child greatly needs his or her mother during the first three years of life as the child's brain is forming. Eye contact, touch and gentle talk from the mother is critical to forming the developing neurological system. During the first three years, as the mother holds and comforts the baby in moments of distress the child learns to regulate its own emotions. Recent brain development and hormonal research shows that a father cannot do the job as well as a mother.

This recent research is discussed in an easy-to-read book by psychologist Erica Komisar who spent several decades treating families as a therapist and later as a psychoanalyst. [74] As she began to see increasing diagnoses of aggression in boys, ADHD, autistic-like social problems and depression in little girls she began in earnest to analyze and study the problem.

---

[74] Komisar, Erica, *Being There: Why Prioritizing Motherhood in the First Three Years Matters*, Penguin Random House, New York, 2017

Komisar, an avowed liberal, has received a great deal of hostility – indeed, outright rejection – from some liberals and feminists, especially in the media, despite the scientific nature of her work, since it differs with much current politically correct dogmas about women's liberation and child-raising.

Understanding and acceptance of best practices for raising infant children will take a great deal of adaptation. Our culture and a mother's concern will surely conflict at some point. And many families will still need two incomes just to survive. This journey will not be easy.

Babies Are Healthier When Held by Their Mothers

An article in *Science News* discusses the terrible toll on unborn children of opioid use by their pregnant mothers. [75] The number of babies born addicted has increased 400 percent from 2000 to 2012 – a national crisis. Some states are reporting as many as 30 of every 1,000 births are addicted.

There is no clear consensus on how to treat these babies once born, to minimize the agony of withdrawal. For many years the approach in most hospitals has been to give the babies decreasing doses of opioids – morphine or methadone – to ease their withdrawal. This process is based on a scoring system developed more than 40 years ago by neonatologist Loretta Finnegan. Scoring – and treatment – is based on measures of baby agitation, crying, restlessness, breathing rate, etc.

Some doctors at Yale noticed that babies often cry, are restless and agitated for other reasons – such as hunger and wetness. They decided to see if 24-hour a day access to their mothers would help. It helped immensely and now in Yale's New Haven Children's Hospital the percentage of children previously treated with morphine has been reduced from 100 percent to about 15 percent from 2008 to 2016.

Mother love wins again. [76, 77]

Winning the Rat Race

One of the biggest impediments to family life, even when there are two loving parents, is our frenetic lifestyle. Everyone is so busy and there is very little time or energy left over for family or personal reflection – even for meditation, or for the religious among us – prayer. One man who has devoted his life to faith and families is Cardinal Robert Sarah of the African country of Guinea:

> In this busy world, in which there is no time for family or for oneself, much less for God, true re-form, consists in rediscovering the meaning of prayer, the meaning of silence, the meaning of eternity.

> Prayer is the greatest need of the contemporary world; it remains the tool with which to reform the world. In an age that no longer prays, time is, so to speak, abolished, and life turns into a rat race. That is why prayer gives man the measure of himself and of the invisible world. [78]

---

[75] Rosen, Meghan, "For babies exposed to opioids in the womb, parents may be the best medicine", *Science News*, June 10, 2017, pp.16-20

[76] Much early research suggests an infant's need for close proximity to its mother in the earliest stages of emotional development. Among the many studies, significant early work was done by Harry F. Harlow and Robert R. Zimmerman, "The Development of Affectional Responses in Infant Monkeys", *Proceedings of the American Philosophical Society*, Vol. 102, 1958, pp. 501-509

[77] Clare W. Graves was an inspired research psychologist and teacher and in the 1950s found that infant children who were held close to their mothers' skin during the first months of life developed more normally emotionally. He developed a kind of cloth sling which allowed a mother to carry her infant this way. (This was related to me personally by several of his early students.)

[78] Sarah, Robert Cardinal, *God or Nothing*, Ignatius Press, 2015, p. 150

Even in a two parent family, when both parents work, loving parents can soon lose control of their children. For the good of our future, we must hope to return to one-parent working and one parent looking after the kids.

Santa Claus, 'patron saint of merchants', will greatly object to one-income families and a moderate business recession might follow. But controlling our materialism will help bring us back to more social interaction and more stable families.

Self-discipline and Success

Childhood and adolescence often equate with impulsiveness. Sturdy children grow to become successful adults when they become able to defer present gratification to attain future benefit. This does not happen automatically – some people never grow up this way. Those who do tend to be more self-reliant and are more likely to rise from or avoid poverty, both spiritual and financial.

The Brookings Institute, a liberal think tank, recently published a long-term longitudinal survey of youth in which they discovered that a child born in poverty can advance to the middle or upper income bracket with an 80 percent probability by following one simple formula:
1. Finish high school
2. Get a job
3. Get married
4. Have children …
… *In that order*. This has been called, "The success sequence." [79]

Children who did not follow these steps were shown to have only a 44 percent chance of success. Those who procreate children before they obtain a job face continued poverty for themselves and the next generation.

EFFECTIVE PARENTS

Children Who Run Their Families

It is a dysfunctional reality that too many children are dictating to their parents. The following reflection from the evangelist Billy Graham captures the essence of the problem and the solution (Used by permission):

> *The spirit of lawlessness is in the home. There is very little discipline in many homes. Each child is a law unto himself. The modern rendering of Paul's familiar injunction might well be, "Parents, obey your children, for this is right." In many of our homes, if there is a voice of authority at all, it is the voice of the child. Parents have little or nothing to say about the life of the child. As a result of all this, there is a grand rush for amusement on the part of the children.*
>
> *If children do not hear in the home a voice that speaks with authority, how can we expect them to obey the voice of the national government? We are now reaping exactly what we have sown for many years. We have allowed our children to run wild without discipline.*

---

[79] "'The Sequence' is the Secret of Success", *The Wall Street Journal*, March 27, 2018.

Parents Taking Control

Before anything will change, parents need to understand their unique and vital role. And they need to be in agreement, especially in front of the children. One parent can absolutely destroy the other's authority by challenging it in front of the child and such discussions should always be done in private until the child has reached the beginning of mature understanding.

Effective parents don't ask their children to do something and then ask if their request is, "OK." Yet, how many times have we heard a mother of father say to a child, "I need you to _____ (fill in the blank) now, OK?" The "OK" is nearly unconscious but it can seem like the parent is asking the child's approval. Leaving off the "OK" is not pressuring or bullying. Rather it is teaching the child that something that must be done for his good or the family, needs his unconditional action. Requests and commands made with love and consideration are not unreasonable but the way responsible, respectful, kind and obedient children can be raised.

A child who lacks respect for authority is a future adult who will have difficulty working for a supervisor and holding a steady job. S/he is a child who will have difficulty working on tough family problems and holding a future marriage together.

Start the training early by giving children simple household responsibilities. Little jobs at first, bigger ones as they grow. Holding them to their responsibilities teaches character. When done with firmness, consistency and love they will learn respect for parental authority.

Dinner Time

Too many families seldom congregate, other than in passing. Without a plan, parents and children will find a hundred reasons to be in different places and eat at different times.

Dinner time can be an excellent time for the whole family to be together and share the day's experiences. Little else can bond a family better than a respectful, shared conversation time at dinner. Turn the TV off. Don't answer the telephone. Have everyone put their silenced cell phones in a basket outside the dining room. Then when dinner is over, everyone helps clean up and put things away.

Some people try to do this every night; some can do it only a few nights, but make it something the kids and parents always look forward to. A child's image of this family bonding creates an inner strength that will last for a lifetime.

Sensible Use of Cell Phones, Tablets, Games & Social Media

There are always wars going on somewhere on the face of the earth. It is almost certain there is a war going on in a home somewhere near you, between a child hooked on social media or games and his/her parents. These devices can become real addictions and the source of great stress between parent and child.

Psychiatrist Thomas Kersting, strongly recommends that children should not own their own screen devices (phones, tablets, computers) but that the parent should sign a written agreement with the child stating the conditions for use and the conditions that will not be tolerated and cause the child to lose the devices. Children should not own their own cell phones as long as they remain fully dependent upon their parents. [80]

On his website, *tomkersting.com*, Kersting offers a smartphone contract between parents and kids to establish agreement on sensible use of these devices.

---

[80] Kersting, Thomas, *Disconnected, How to Reconnect our Digitally Distracted Kids*, CreateSpace Independent Publishing Platform, 2016

FAMILY EROSION

As our family structures have changed and weakened in the past few decades our children have also suffered and weakened. The decline of the American family is illustrated in the accompanying diagram.

Loss of the Extended Family

An extended family can be a strong resource for raising a child. But parents move away from their hometown; grandmother or grandfather pass away; or the neighborhood and building where the extended family lives is condemned and the extended family becomes geographically scattered.

The Nuclear Family

If kids still have a mother and father – a nuclear family- – they can still be fairly OK. Most American families today fit this pattern.

One-Parent Families

But then if through separation, death or divorce one parent is left to support and raise the children, those children are more prone to suffer. Single parents comprise the majority of the poor in America.

So who will protect the children?

Who is Watching the Kids?

Today's school children spend a small part of their day in school. The rest of the time is either on a school bus or hanging around in the neighborhood. Kids need activity and guidance in their spare time until they become self-motivated. Unfortunately most public schools do little to help them transition to the world at 2:30 in the afternoon, or transition back again at 8:30 in the morning. The old saying that "The Devil makes work for idle hands" is as true now as it was a

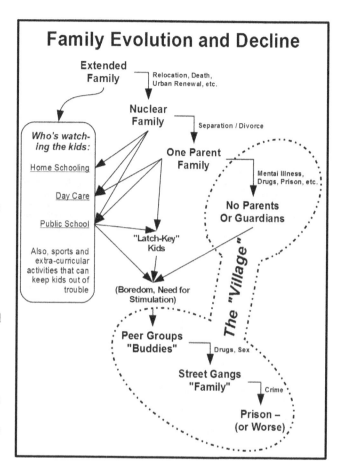

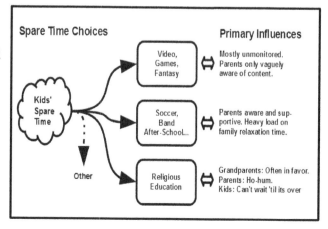

hundred years ago.

We can lose our children, little by little if we are too busy to pay attention. This is like the old, over-used aphorism of the frog that is slowly heated until it is boiled to death without its even knowing.

The figure "Spare Time Choices" illustrates that the top priority for many kids' use of spare time is fantasy, including video games and videos. This may not seem unusual to some parents, but is very foreign to many who did not grow up that way, including hard-working grandparents and newly arrived immigrants. Beyond the 'sports' and 'religion' options, beware of the 'other' choices.

Home schooled kids generally have better after-school structure set by parents and family. Public school kids are often on their own, particularly if they are the 'latch-key' kids whose parents aren't home after school.

Play, Fun and the Winning Team

Some kids can rely on after-school sports or other activities, if they are members of the select few who are chosen to be on teams or can find a place for their neighborhood game.

Twenty-five-plus years ago I took my older daughter to Paris for a weekend. She was on break from studies in London. We drove past a park and I was astonished that there were perhaps a hundred children of all ages running around and playing a variety of non-parent-structured games – just running around, having fun and being kids.

Returning back home, I started to look at our own neighborhoods and parks. What I saw was organized sports – soccer, baseball, and some football – that favored the physically and athletically capable kids (at the expense of those who were not.) But there were few kids just having fun in their outdoor neighborhoods after school or on weekends.

Some parents openly admit they are afraid of predators (there aren't very many, but those horrible few are constantly in the TV news.) Others over-protect and are afraid their kids might hurt themselves. A friend recently told me of a baseball game where a kid, running to third base, tripped and fell. His mother jumped from the stands, ran to his side and picked him up to see if he was OK.

A Loving Family, Not a 'Village'

> *With all due respect, I am here to tell you, it does not take*
> *a village to raise a child. It takes a family to raise a child.*
> *Bob Dole, Former Vice President of the U.S.*

All it takes to destroy a child is a village – the wrong village.

Few rational people doubt there is a crying need for solutions to the increasing brokenness in American families. So many children are being lost to crime and emotional problems and the failed educational system.

In 1996, First Lady Hillary Clinton gave us and heavily promoted a widely acclaimed book, *It Takes a Village: And Other Lessons Children Teach Us*. The book notes that many institutions are responsible in some way for raising children – including direct family, grandparents, neighbors, teachers, ministers, doctors, employers, politicians, nonprofits, faith communities, businesses, and international governmental groups.[81, 82]

Her book caused a great deal of controversy. However, fans of Mrs. Clinton made the book a best seller for several months. These were, for the most part, serious people who saw that we have a serious problem that somebody else – 'The Village' – should solve.

---

[81] Mrs. Clinton did not actually write the book. It was written under contract by ghostwriter, Barbara Feinman, a Georgetown University journalism professor. Mrs. Clinton never gave Feinman acknowledgment or credit, either publicly or in the book.

[82] *en.wikipedia.org/wiki/It_Takes_a_Village*

The Clinton doctrine would suggest the community can provide for the lack of a father and all the necessities of raising a healthy child. Clinton's audience was accustomed to having the government solve their problems and her 'village' idea fit neatly into that mold. But time has proven it hasn't worked and common sense and research show it makes us feel good but it does not and will not work.

Daycare

Children belong first to their parents and their families, not to their villages or their governments. Solid research continues to show that early and enduring, consistent *love* makes all the difference in the healthy growth of a child. Especially the love of a mother and a father. The nurturing love of a mother and the protective and guiding love of a strong father. No school or babysitter or daycare can give that.

> *Daycare is where a child can learn to*
> *be unloved all day long.*
> Dr. Laura Schlesinger

The Road to the Village of the Lost

Now we have a generation of latch-key kids – those who come home to an empty house – or kids who may have single mothers who are essentially absent from their kids' lives due to their own problems and addictions. These kids will seek and find their own 'homes'. That home is often on the streets, with a group of kids. Sometimes that group is a criminal gang. I have met and talked with hundreds of these young people – almost all of them in prisons, fatherless and often parent-less. They graduated from a home on the street to a new home behind walls and barbed wire.

What I don't understand is the great resistance to proven family values among some of our country's political Left and media elite. Those proponents tend to magnify the few exceptions – the successful survivors – mothers who can hold down important jobs and careers while still raising normal kids.

These anti-family advocates should go out on the streets and talk to the thousands of other mothers – the majority – who are poor and desperate and who struggle daily with issues as far reaching as mental illness, drug abuse and just plain hunger. Few of them can afford day care and those who can may fear for the safety of their children.

Fatherless Children

This year approximately one million American children will experience the divorce of their parents. Many others never had a live-in, biological father to begin with.

Every school age child today knows someone whose apparently happy family has suddenly disintegrated. Parents disagree, parents argue, children observe in fear and wait for the other shoe to drop. That's the 'fortunate' 59 percent who currently live in two-parent homes. And then there are the other 41 percent who are being raised by unmarried mothers.

Starting in the 1970s states changed their laws to permit easy "no-fault divorce" and families began to dissolve everywhere. Pop psychology and neo-feminism made it clear that fathers were not important. Out-of-wedlock births skyrocketed. Where there had once been many reasons to marry and for couples to bind and for fathers to stay, our secular society eliminated all of them and decided that *fathers should be optional*.

In the '70s, as divorce became more common, societal 'experts' opined that if the separated parents were happier, the children were almost certainly going to be happier also. Actual studies later proved this to be dead wrong. Divorce can do severe, lifelong damage to children.[83]

The Terrible Toll of the Fatherless Home

Today, the only thing left to bind most parent relationships is the fragile, volatile bond of mutual affection. Fathers were once called providers. Now, absent the father, government agencies step in to fill any void. The typical secular home provides little other reason for the father to remain.

Fast-forward to the present. Endless studies have removed all doubt that single parent, female-led homes have become a major cause of poverty and instability. Unstable homes have produced many unstable individuals. The result has been devastating:

- About 40 percent of children in father-absent homes have not seen their father at all in the past year[84]
- 71 % of all high school dropouts come from fatherless homes[85]
- One study shows that 85 % of all youths in prison come from fatherless homes[86]
- 90 % of all homeless and runaway children are from fatherless homes[87]
- Fatherless children are at a dramatically greater risk of drug and alcohol abuse[88]
- Of the seven deadliest mass shootings between 2005 and 2015, six were by young men from fatherless homes. (The one exception who was raised with a biological father had been mentally unstable since childhood.) [89]

Children are the future of America. We need healthy, stable and sturdy children guided and raised by devoted, at-home fathers.

Wake up, America!

GOVERNMENT MEDDLING

> *The scariest words you will ever hear is, "Hi, I'm from the*
> *Government and I'm here to help."*
> *Ronald Reagan*

Monetary Policies

With the societal upheaval that followed the Vietnam War and the 1960s, our whole way of life changed. President Johnson and the U.S. Congress relied heavily on the Federal Reserve to print war

---

[83] Popenoe, David, *Families Without Fathers: Fathers, Marriage and Children in American Society*, Routledge, 2017
[84] Some other statistics on the effects of fatherlessness can be found at
   https://thefatherlessgeneration.wordpress.com/statistics
[85] Ibid.
[86] Ibid.
[87] U.S. Dept. of Health and Human Services (U.S. DHHS) and Bureau of the Census statistics
[88] U.S. DHHS report
[89] Hasson, Peter, "Guess Which Mass Murderers Came From a Fatherless Home", *The Federalist*, July 14, 2015,
   thefederalist.com/2015/07/14/guess-which-mass-murderers-came-from-a-fatherless-home/

money and lend it to the government.[90] The vast new Great Society social programs were also funded with borrowed and printed money.

Out of control price inflation soon followed which made it difficult or impossible to raise a family on one income. The result: Hundreds of thousands of mothers had to leave their children in someone else's care and go off to a second job just to keep the family from sinking in a sea of taxes and debt. And the children's 'bonus' was increasingly less parental guidance.

Family Financial Struggles

Family economics are at a low point. Americans pay more in taxes than for food and clothing combined. We have just come through a major national economic downturn from the Obama era. Things are still not rosy and many families must still rely on two incomes. Half of American families are living from paycheck to paycheck. One quarter of Americans have zero money saved for emergencies.

Working Mothers

Parents saving for college wonder why the costs keep rising faster than inflation. Look no further than the federal government that has been setting the tuition rates (for Pell grants, etc.) which rise each year. Colleges take advantage of this and raise their rates accordingly. Surprisingly, only a trivial amount of these increases have gone to pay teachers and professors, but most have been used to expand bloated school bureaucracies and administrative staff.[91]

A similar pattern exists for rapidly rising medical expenses. Government-set reimbursement rates for Medicare and Medicaid give providers and Big Pharma's drugs a rising target to play with. Governmental over-regulation and taxation are seen as the root cause and help to explain why, for instance, U.S. hospital prices are 60 percent higher than Europe's.[92, 93]

Meanwhile almost 70 percent of mothers need to trudge off to work so their families can pay the bills and survive.

Bureaucrats to Raise Our Children?

Enemies of Parental Control

Parents who want to raise their children by their own values have little choice in some areas of the country. State education departments, school boards and many teachers often have more control and power than parents. Parents are astounded to find that sex education is taught and condoms are being handed out to *grade school* children.

In some districts, a child cannot bring a headache remedy to school but the school can refer the child to an abortion clinic or for birth control pills, all without parental consent.

Many public schools politically and socially indoctrinate children without parental knowledge or consent.

And when school is over, there are the endless TV programs, social media and gaming websites and the big one – pornography. Studies show that a large percentage of grade school children age 12 and over have already viewed pornography. These studies also show that these kids are forever warped in their understanding of the sacred marital bond between husband and wife.

---

[90] In like manner we have been borrowing to pay for the recent Iraq and Afghanistan wars.
[91] Campos, Paul F., "The Real Reason College Tuition Costs So Much", *The New York Times (Sunday Edition)*, April 4, 2015
[92] Patton, Mike, "U.S. Health Care Costs Rise Faster Than Inflation", *Forbes Magazine*, June 28, 2015
[93] Amadeo, Kimberly, "The Rising Cost of Health Care by Year and its Causes", *thebalance.com*, May 5, 2018

Most parents have little clue as to most of this, especially if they are frenetically busy trying to make a living, pay taxes and keep their heads above water.

School Choice

Parents who can afford it often send their children to private school to shelter their kids from these hazards.

Charter schools, which have much more freedom to hire and fire teachers and set curriculum are a good choice for many families but Liberal/Progressive politicians and teachers' unions are uniformly against them because they detract from their own power.

One good sign of future change is the recent Supreme Court *Janus* (union dues) decision that prevents teachers' unions from demanding dues from non-members. This is expected to reduce but not eliminate the corrupt relationships between politicians and teachers' unions.

Legislative Options

Paid Family Leave

Government should not meddle in family business. But government can help establish policy which creates a level playing field for corporations and organizations that seek to simplify family life and retain experienced workers. One such policy would incentivize companies to provide paid family leave.

In a recent lengthy letter to the *Wall Street Journal*, Ivanka Trump proposed a national paid family leave policy.[94] Among the most important benefits, would be healthier children and parents in more tightly-bonded families, with greater financial stability and stronger attachment to the labor force.

A paid leave policy will encourage both parents to share parenting responsibilities. Trump states that in 63 percent of American homes with children, both parents are working.

Today, women without a college degree are far more likely to lose or quit their jobs after childbirth. Meanwhile the poorest and most vulnerable workers in our society get left behind.

Trump cites a recent study that women who took advantage of available paid leave were more likely to return to their careers and were 39 percent less likely to receive public assistance.

She concludes that 82 percent of voters think Congress should consider a paid-leave program.

FAMILY RENEWAL

A Constitutional Amendment to Protect the Rights of Parents?

In recent years there have been numerous cases where government tries to take on the role of parents – from deciding what foods can and cannot be served in school cafeterias, to which schools a child must attend. Forced sex education and psychological testing continue to elicit parental anger.

And then there are controversial health treatment issues such as forced vaccinations and end of life medical decisions. Officials and professional elitists intervene where parents once had full authority. We have arrived at the point where bureaucrats and third parties often have authority over parents.

Proponents say a parental rights Constitutional Amendment would set a wide-ranging legal precedent leading to stronger families.

---

[94] Ivanka Trump, "Paid Family Leave is a Good National Policy", *The Wall Street Journal*, July 7, 2017, p.A16

Here is one version of this proposal, variations of which have been introduced in more than half of our state legislatures:

> *The right of parents to direct the upbringing and education of their children shall not be infringed. The legislature shall have the power to enforce, by appropriate legislation, the provisions of this article.*

Other proposed additions to this amendment would force the government to demonstrate, by appropriate evidence, that it has a compelling interest where it may attempt to intervene in family matters. Most variations also protect against ending life and the interference in our courts from effects of international treaties, such as the United Nations Convention on the Rights of Children.

Many issues remain to be debated and resolved, including how to maintain protection against child abuse, to support officials in prosecuting parents who abuse their children, and to discourage excessive lawsuits against schools and other agencies.

Progress Toward a Constitutional Convention

By law, making such a change to the Constitution requires one of two starting initiatives – either by a two thirds vote in both houses of Congress or by two thirds of the states (34 states).[95] Final approval of any new amendments or changes requires affirmative votes by three quarters of the states (38 states).

Critics rightly point out that, if a Constitutional Convention should result, it might open a whole new can of worms, encouraging more new controversial amendments and a new flurry of more left-right political bickering.

Some opponents question whether an amendment for parental rights is even reasonable or necessary, given the existence of the Ninth Amendment. That amendment protects other rights already presumed to be "retained by the people." However, given the legislative and judicial creep away from that presumption over the past fifty years, a specific protection for parents has now become essential in my opinion.

Newsweek recently reported that there is a Conservative push called *Convention of States Project* which is proposing that state legislatures call for a convention, as is permitted in Article 5b of the Constitution. This would be the first time in our history that a constitutional amendment effort had been initiated by the states and not by Congress. But it is permitted in the Constitution and Congress is regarded as so dysfunctional that there is no chance of it acting.[96, 97] A six minute video describes the proposal. (Click your smartphone on the QR code ➔)

Newsweek reports that 12 states have already passed this legislation and it is being considered in 18 other states.

Convention of States

Well-funded leftist organizations such as the inappropriately named People for the American Way, backed by teachers' unions and others, have been fighting this proposal for more than twenty years.

You can read more about parental rights – support and opposition – at one of several websites, including *ParentalRights.org* and a detailed discussion of pros and cons on the *Wikipedia* website.[98]

---

[95] See Article Five of the U.S. Constitution

[96] Hutzler, Alexandra, "Conservatives Aim to Bypass Congress to Amend the Constitution Next", *Newsweek*, *www.newsweek.com/conservatives-aim-bypass-congress-amend-constitution-1200369*

[97] Convention of States Project (website), *conventionofstates.com/*

[98] *en.wikipedia.org/wiki/Parental_Rights_Amendment_to_the_United_States_Constitution*

A Vision for a Strong, Effective and Peaceful Family

A strong family with a committed Christian marriage at its center can weather the storms of life. The purpose of marriage is to raise and treat children as a supreme gift of that marriage and to raise them and prepare them for life according to their unique individual skills and gifts.

Christians who understand that the purpose of life is to know God, to love him and to serve him above selfish desires will pass that on to their children. Knowing God involves family prayer and studying and reading the Word of God – the Scriptures. It also is in seeing and exploring the wonders of his creation and learning respect for the environment and all his people and his creatures. Children should learn to serve and respect one another, especially those who are in trouble, sorrow, adversity or need.

Purpose of the Family

For the first few years of life a mother who holds and comforts a baby during moments of distress will help the child learn to regulate its own emotions. This maternal nurturance produces emotionally more stable children and is something fathers cannot do as well.

Children are not automatically born with good character but must be raised and trained to become civilized good citizens. Fathers and mothers who show good examples to their children will teach them to forgive one another for offenses, quarrels, injustices and neglect as they acquire the spirit of justice and mercy.

Kids learn moral values best at home, starting at an early age. Fathers who practice their faith and teach their children with gentleness and respect will find their children following their faith later in life. School choice should be completely up to the parents to make sure these lessons are not diluted by those of the secular world.

The Christian family forms the foundation for freedom, security, charity and fraternity within a Christian society. A solid Christian family can provide an evangelical role model for the suffering, wandering and lost souls of the world.

Strengthening Bonds

Strong families find time for one another – in fact they actually *make* time for one another. Time for prayer and scripture reading, time for meals together when possible, play time, and just horsing around with the kids. These are all good bonding for growing children.

Family dinner is a time to give thanks and teach children that food doesn't just magically fall from the sky but is a gift from God.

One of the Ten Commandments says we should "keep holy the Sabbath." That can mean different things to different people, but strong families, in addition to communal worship, try to avoid unnecessary work one day a week, to be refreshed and to share time with family and fellow man. This is also a time to bond with church and community.

A Prayer for Parents

Most loving Father, the example of parenthood, teach us what to give and what to withhold. Show us when to reprove and when to praise. Make us gentle and considerate yet firm and watchful. Keep us from weak indulgence or from great severity.

Give us the courage to be disliked sometimes by our children when we must do necessary things which are displeasing in their eyes. Give us the imagination to enter into their world in order to understand and guide them.

Give us all the virtues we need to lead them by word and example in the path of righteousness. Amen

Action Items for Family Renewal

- Restore our two-parent families – Raise infants at home with their mothers. We need to restore and reaffirm the essential cultural perception of a mother's role. Let mothers understand that it's acceptable and necessary to stay home with their children for the first few very formative years of the child's life. Mothering can produce more "return on investment" than paid work. "Quality time" is no substitute for "quantity time" in the words of researcher Erica Komisar.[99]

  Re-prioritizing family life can often require some serious temporary economic bullet-biting but when the kids are older, parents will not regret it.

- Support real faith-bound manhood in fathers who love and stay with their wives and children. This is a kind of manhood that helps fathers keep the family together in stormy weather times.

  Fathers: Teach your children the faith of *your* fathers – the faith that will someday bond and bind *their* families. Don't leave this job just to the mothers. One study shows a child is more than *twenty* times more likely to practice his faith in his adult years if his father practices his.

- And while we're at it, let's begin the process to *legally recognize a father as a mother's equal.* For in-depth examination, see Chapter 3, "Reclaiming Fatherhood" in the excellent book by Armstrong Williams, *Reawakenig Virtues.*[100]

- If there is no active men's support/prayer group in your church, ask your parish priest or pastor why not – and keep on asking. Studies and common sense show the importance of fathers to the continuance of faith and family bonding. (Churches that don't understand this can be quickly identified by the lack of young attendees on a Sunday morning.)

- Families should strive to eat dinner together. This needs to be a sacred and productive time together where children can find good conversation and bonding. Don't allow any TV or electronics and silence your own phones and your children's phones. Parents can set an example for their kids by limiting their own screen time and TV time.

- Our local religious institutions should be encouraged to sponsor programs for children and young adults that teach the faith rather than try to mindlessly indoctrinate. Use programs that are *proven* to motivate with *tested* material that is relevant to their lives, not boring to them until they drift away. These new kids are the video generation and good wholesome, interesting and effective teaching videos are everywhere. Let's use them effectively.

- Priorities: Husbands and wives – for a successful marriage and a happy family, make sure your spouse comes first, then the children. Parents should decide how the family is run, not the children. Too many couples let their children subtly or overtly dictate. When we allow this we undermine the whole family and the children ultimately suffer the most.

- Just as we regulate other things that can harm our children, smartphones, social media and computer games need to be regulated. First in the home by parents, then by the community. Our legislatures should be involved. But failing a loud and unavoidable chorus from families and community organizations, nothing is likely to change while politicians have their hands out to the big businesses whose profits depend on corrupting our youth.

- As a nation, we must encourage, support and rebuild *extended* families, especially in our minority communities and never again permit public policies that put these family structures

---

[99] Komisar, Erica, op.cit.

[100] Williams, Armstrong, *Reawakening Virtues: Restoring What Makes America Great* (See Bibliography)

at risk.

- Petition your state legislators to back legislation to call a national Constitutional Convention to pass a Parental Rights Amendment to limit government interference in our families. (See section on this topic on page 41.)

- Provide your kids with interesting, clean entertainment, including family activities and videos and wholesome TV programs – there are many. Get kids interested early before they start to stray. (Check with websites or other publications of family organizations mentioned in the resources list below.)

- As our children grow to adulthood they need to be encouraged to pursue education first, then work, marriage and parenthood – in that order.

- Each community needs to develop a 'rescue plan' for troubled kids and a transition plan for them and those who are discharged from prisons. These ones must never be forgotten.

Family Resources for Change

Here is a partial list of resources that have been found useful for families that want to strengthen. Help is available but knowing where to look is often the first problem.

- Your local (and regional or national) church or synagogue
- *Focus on the Family* – Prayer and marriage assistance – *www.focusonthefamily.com*
- *Marriage Encounter* – The world's largest pro-marriage organization holds weekend courses to help couples communicate better and bond more closely in their differences. *www.wwme.org*
- *American Family Association* – www.afa.net
- NFP – *Natural Family Planning* – A good place to begin learning is online at: *www.beginningcatholic.com/catholic-natural-family-planning*
- NAMI – *National Alliance on Mental Illness* – the nation's largest grassroots mental health organization – *www.nami.org*
- *Suicide prevention hotlines* – the National Suicide Prevention Lifeline: **800-273-8255** or TEXT: **HOME** to **741741** (In Canada, text 686868). For trans or gender non-conforming persons: LGBTQ youth 24 and younger can call the Trevor Project Lifeline at **866-488-7386**. The Trans Lifeline can be reached at **877-565-8860**.
- Drug and Alcohol addiction recovery – See the section in this book on available help, *Support and Treatment* – on page 158.
- On his website, *tomkersting.com/resources-for-parents*, Author and psychiatrist Tom Kersting offers a smartphone contract between parents and kids to establish agreement on sensible use of these devices. (See discussion and footnote on page 34)
- *Teen Challenge* – A faith-based drug and addiction recovery program. Very tough and controversial. See *Wikipedia* summary for more details: *en.wikipedia.org/wiki/Teen_Challenge*
- Medical insurance – *Liberty Health Share* is one of several ACA-exempt Christian health expense-sharing organizations: – *www.libertyhealthshare.org*
- An excellent book for marriages facing mid-life problems by Kathryn Cramer, *Roads Home: Seven Pathways to Midlife Wisdom*, (See Bibliography).

N.B. – Any Internet addresses, QR codes and telephone numbers in this book are offered as a resource. They are not intended in any way to be or to imply an endorsement, nor does the author vouch for the content of these sites, numbers or references.

3 – Our Tradition of Faith

FOUNDATION OF THE REPUBLIC

A Christian Nation

Up until now our free expression of faith has been protected by our Constitution, our laws, its juridical precedents and tradition. Whether you are a Christian, Jew, Muslim, Hindu, Buddhist – whatever your faith – you are here free to worship and practice your religion without interference from the government. Even if you are an atheist, your choice is likewise protected. This freedom did not materialize by accident.

It is no accident that our Republic has endured for almost two and a half centuries. It has lasted and thrived because it was built on the solid foundation of the precepts of the Christian faith. John Adams, a devout Christian, a founding father of the Republic and our second president declared:

> Our Constitution was made only for a moral and religious people. It is wholly inadequate to the government of any other.

Adams believed the study of politics and government was a "divine science" essential to freedom and the prevention of anarchy and tyranny:

> I must study politics and war, that my sons may have liberty to study mathematics and philosophy, geography, natural history and naval architecture, navigation, commerce, and agriculture, in order to give their children a right to study painting, poetry, music, architecture, statuary, tapestry, and porcelain.

Serious study affirms there is no question that America was founded as a religious, moral Christian nation. In the early years, 98.5 percent of the new residents of this land were Protestant Christians. The remaining 1.5 percent were Jews, Catholic Christians and some few others. In later years, in the 19th and 20th centuries, immigration changed the mix as many Catholics and Jews immigrated until today 22 percent of Americans profess the Catholic faith and approximately two percent profess Judaism. Fewer than one percent are Muslim.

Despite the current atheist and pagan hoopla, we remain a Christian nation. Two presidents, Wilson and Truman, affirmed this and two Supreme Court rulings have so attested. [101] A balanced discussion of our Christian heritage can be found in a recent book, *Christian America? – Perspectives on our Religious Heritage.* [102]

Christian principles are reflected in the U.S. Constitution and in the constitution of every one of the 50 states of the union. *Appendix F* on page 153 lists the preambles and witnesses of these states, each of which gives thanks to God or the Divine Creator.

---

[101] We are a Christian nation according to two Supreme Court rulings: 1892 (*Church of the Holy Trinity vs. United States*) and 1931 (*U.S. vs. Macintosh*).Many state court rulings over the years have likewise affirmed.
[102] Cornet, Daryl C., Editor, B&H Publishing Group, Nashville, TN, 2011

DIVISION AND BREAKAGE

New Gods, Mammon and the Devil

We may be nearing the end of the greatest experiment in government in the history of mankind. Founded on Christian principles, our constitutional republic has lasted more than 240 years. Yet there are many atheists and pagans hard at work to destroy and redirect our society to the worship of powerful new pagan gods. Make no mistake – atheism is a religion. It just worships different gods.

Old classical gods like Zeus, Isis and Thor are seriously passé and have been consigned to the dustbin of history. But we have powerful new gods, the likes of Google, Facebook, Twitter, personal computing and communication tools, modern medicine, CRISPR/Cas9, artificial intelligence, cruise missiles, laser guns, nuclear and nerve-agent bombs and missiles, etc., etc. They can create and they can destroy. Whatever we ask of them they give us!

Worshippers of these gods no longer see any human problem that science and world government cannot tackle. They recognize no miracles. The Internet is their temple and they congregate on social media. Morals and ethics have become a matter of personal choice. Believers offer praises to one another and denounce, punish and excommunicate 'heretics'. Their human sacrifices, 3,000 each day, are offered at the *Temple of the Abortion Clinic dedicated to the god of Inconvenience.*

The clever workmen who fashioned these new gods from bestowed talent have become fabulously wealthy and wield enormous political influence and power. Their awesome power brings the un-united common man close to modern serfdom. Divisive political activists continue to be funded by wealth-backed organizations such as the Open Society organization of billionaire George Soros.

Our Creator made us capable of working together for the common good. But there are those among us who would rather see our nation devolve to the chaos of class conflict so they can pick up the pieces after their induced 'revolution' and rebuild a society after their own vision.[103] This evil Marxist[104] concept has not succeeded but there are those pagan and atheistic optimists among us who keep on trying.

The Atheist Proclaims:

There is no original higher power – a God – who created the universe. I and everything around me developed by random natural selection from an original primordial swamp of dust and chaos. Yes, there was a 'big bang' because science has proved it, but no big guy in the sky did it.

When I die, it's all over – there is no continuance after death, no after-life. None of that 'pie in the sky bye and bye.' There is no such place as heaven and there definitely is no devil and no hell. People get their reward for good deeds right here on earth.

Man's purpose in life is to get everything – as much as he can – for himself. (He who dies with the most toys, wins.) The Golden Rule is nice, and it means that if I don't mess with other people, they won't mess with me. Live and let live.

If I have any 'faith' it is faith in science. There are no absolutes, no absolute truths, outside of science. Only the fundamental axioms of math and science are 'true'. (One plus zero always equals one.) If science doesn't have an answer, you and I are free to believe whatever we want.

It is wrong to teach children about God and religion. They should be able to form their own opinions when they grow up. And don't get me started about public prayer!

It upsets me to see people suffer but there is little I can do about it. In a well-run country the government will handle it. There is no such thing as 'sin'. I believe I'm a nice person and I hope I live to be old, healthy and happy and die a quick and painless death.

---

[103] Worthy of note, the late historian Arnold Toynbee once stated that "stratification of class" occurs during the decline of a civilization. Although he was more focused on economic stratification, in a sense we seem to be experiencing this in the domains of social and political tribalism and the rise of 'identity politics'.

[104] Marx, Karl, and Friedrich Engels, *The Communist Manifesto*, 1848

Atheism – Enemy of Civilization

Atheism is a cancer to our nation, sowing division and discord. This belief system leads to social division and promotes and encourages the self above others while it destroys civilized communities. The 'common good' is reduced to a meaningless aphorism of relativism.

Today, we are facing challenges from a vocal but very loud and well-funded few who profess and promote atheism, such as the *Freedom From Religion Foundation* which has brought many law suits to eliminate Christian symbols and practices. They and their ilk have many followers of this evil in their cheering sections.

When I speak of workers of 'evil', I refer to those who would break what they cannot fix, destroy what they cannot build, and condemn the beliefs and needs of others whom they refuse to understand.

For example, I recall one politician who recently judged a quarter of American voters to be 'deplorable' and another who disparagingly described people in a rural area as those who "cling to their guns and their Bibles." (For what it's worth, both of these politicians conveniently profess to be Christians.)

DELIVERY FROM EVIL

The Need for Revival

Without faith, very few civilizations would ever have existed.[105] It is faith that binds families together in civilized community. It is the lack of a common faith that causes people to become divisive and corrupt and to transgress greatly against each other, themselves and their Creator and ultimately causes the civilization to dissolve.

If we want our great nation to survive, we need first to understand the very roots of this nation – including the faith and religion of its founders, beyond the usual stories and myths of a British tyrant King and a Parliament and tea parties and Paul Revere and all the other usual banalities shoveled into the brains of our public school students.

We need to understand why we have endured so very long, while every other nation's similar attempt to form a constitutional republic has failed in just a few years. Our endurance derives not only from the important right to own property but especially from the rule of law, derived, partly from British Common Law, but backed by a Constitution and a set of sovereign laws solidly based on the teachings of Moses and Jesus.

We need to examine honestly why this has recently begun to falter. Clear understanding leads to the inevitable conclusion that Christian spiritual revival is our only viable option.

Our founding fathers would not recognize the divisive, dystopian battleground we have become. Nothing but a complete turnaround and revival of the Christian spirit can save this republic.

> *Those people who will not be governed by God*
> *will be ruled by tyrants*
>
> *William Penn*

---

[105] Zimmerman, Carle, *Family and Civilization*, Intercollegiate Studies Institute, 1947

IMPEDIMENTS TO UNDERSTANDING AND DIALOGUE

We of opposing viewpoints need desperately to understand one another; but dialogue is only a beginning when the biggest impediment to peace is the confusion of basic ideas once commonly understood.

Twisted, Deceptive Language

If I were the Devil and wanted to divide the faithful and destroy the Church, I would do three things:

1. I would convince people they didn't need to talk and pray with one another to understand God or his will. "Don't go to common worship services – stay home and avoid all those hypocrites."

2. I would give them a new language that made it more difficult for them to conceive of anything spiritual or eternal. A language that would convince them that everything they needed to understand was here in the material physical world. And I would place new meanings on old words to make them feel comfortable with their sins and disordered lives.

3. Finally, I would convince them I didn't exist.

According to the Old Testament story, in the beginning there was only one language. (Cf. *Genesis 11:1-9*). In this story the people of Babel, an ancient urban city, became so proud they ignored God who then confused their language so they no longer understood one another. The people were then scattered over all the earth.

A divided world now experiences endless battles over language and religious concepts. Today there are more than 30,000 Christian religious denominations on the face of the earth, many of them the result of disputes over the meaning of words of Scripture.[106]

In *John 17:21* Jesus was talking about his followers when he prayed, "… that all of them [believers] may be one, Father, just as you are in me and I am in you." But what did he mean? What could possibly divide them?

Language is primarily a tool for thought, and secondly a tool for communication. But it can also be an impediment to clear thinking, used to manipulate, divide and control people and ultimately to manipulate their thoughts.

Omit Words ➔ Suppress Thought ➔ Censor Behaviors?

What happens when certain words and notations are forbidden or changed in meaning? Is it possible to control people by controlling their language and then their thoughts?

Could an unfriendly opposition be eliminated simply by controlling their language?

> *The purpose of Newspeak was not only to provide a medium of*
> *expression for the world-view and mental habits proper to the devotees*
> *of Ingsoc, but to make all other modes of thought impossible.*
> George Orwell [107]

---

[106] As 'denomination' is defined by The World Christian Encyclopedia: "An organized aggregate of worship centers or congregations of similar ecclesiastical tradition within a specific country."

[107] Orwell, George, *Nineteen Eighty-Four*, The New American Library, 1949

Language, Culture and Meaning

Communicating with a common language is only a beginning to understanding. Words often mean different things to different people. People who have not learned to think clearly and critically at an early age are often at a disadvantage in matters of complex dialogue. And modern human life *is very complex*. Language and its correct use are learned early in life or not at all.

Scientists who have studied feral children, raised wild by animals – and there are about 100 cases on record – have found that it is impossible to teach language or civilization to those rescued after about the age of six. It has nothing to do with simply being human or our inherited DNA. It's a matter of culture, passed through parents and family, starting with the child's earliest years.

We disagree over our differing tiny buckets of ignorance – we argue over the meaning of words and forget that sometimes we seek understanding of that which mere human words cannot easily express. Our spoken and written languages are inadequate in many ways…

Are There Weaker Languages? Stronger, More Eternal Languages?

The way that can be spoken is not the Eternal Way;
The name that can be named is not the Eternal Name.
Lao Tzu, Chinese philosopher, 5th Century BC

If individual languages have their own unique strengths and weaknesses, which natural language is it that best helps us conceptualize God and the Eternal? And conversely, are there languages – natural or artificial – that absolutely confuse people and push them farther from understanding God and each other?

This may seem like a philosophical diversion, but I contend it is at the heart of much of our current inter-group identity politics 'warfare'.

I would propose that the lexicon of materialism and of the pagan gods mentioned above is a significant part of such a degenerate language and is more than sufficient to inhibit further awareness of spiritual things.

If the nation needs a spiritual revival and half the country can no longer conceive of spiritual concepts, we are in deep trouble and all the dialogue and yelling and frustrated name-calling will just drive us farther apart.

Since we are each created so very different with dissimilar interior thought languages, is it any surprise that we might have diverse conceptions of God, his creation and things eternal? Or no concept at all? As we become aware of each other's differing understandings, perhaps we could adopt more of a sense of patience and humility in our dealings with one another.

(More anecdotal and scientific information on our mutual misunderstandings with language and thought can be found in *Appendix C. Mental Differences, Language and Understanding* on page 140.)

We mere mortals cannot possibly comprehend the whole truth of God's being. His words are eternal and his being is infinite and almighty and our tiny, finite human brains cannot be expected to see things from God's perspective, except our egos deceive us into believing we see the whole picture – or enough of it to be 'sufficient'. As in the parable of the seven blind men and the elephant, our senses and cognitive limits can falsely convince us we don't need to know any more.

He who claims to have knowledge of the complete truth of God blasphemes. The Apostle Paul understood these earthly limits to our understanding:

Now we see but a poor reflection as in a mirror; then we shall see face to face. Now I know in part; then I shall know fully… 1 Corinthians 13.12a, (NIV)

God's plan for us is to give us a new language – one that will bring us back together in common service to Him. Some say we have to wait for Heaven (Paul's "then") – I propose we not wait but seek as much of it as possible while we are here on earth if that is our Creator's will. (Consider this: "... Thy will be done on *Earth* as ... in *Heaven* ...")

A More Robust Language?

Several passages of Scripture suggest a new language will be revealed:

> For at that time I will change the speech of the peoples to a pure speech, that all of them may call upon the name of the LORD and serve him with one accord. *Zephaniah 3:9, (ESV)*

> I have told you this in figures of speech. The hour is coming when I will no longer speak to you in figures but I will tell you clearly about the Father. *John 16:25, (NAB)*

> I heard a sound from heaven like the roar of rushing waters and like a loud peal of thunder. The sound I heard was like that of harpists playing their harps. And they sang a new song before the throne ... No one could learn the song except the 144,000 who had been redeemed from the earth. *Revelation 14:2-3, (NIV)*

Music has been called a very special language and certain forms have always been part of worship in almost every culture. (But many parents will agree that some secular music presents an impediment to communicating with their children, and perhaps with God himself.) The psalmists enjoin us to, "Sing a new song unto the Lord" *Psalm 98:1, (Cf. also, Psalms 33:3, 96:1, 144:9, 149:1, NIV).*

Out of the Darkness

We need to pray for the wisdom to find that clear language of mutual understanding that will bring us, once again, in unity to the defense of this God-given republic. Pray that the looming spiritual darkness will instead become light by the power of God's Word to his people.

LIVING A CHRISTIAN LIFE IN A CHRISTIAN REPUBLIC

> *Christianity has not been tried and found wanting;*
> *it has been found difficult and not tried.*
>
> G.K.Chesterton

Josh McDowell in his book, *More Than a Carpenter*, offers this:

> *Wherever Jesus has been proclaimed, lives have been changed for the good, nations have changed for the better, thieves are made honest, alcoholics are cured, hateful individuals become channels of love, unjust persons become just.*[108]

The Rise of Christianity

Why did Christianity arise through all the scorn and persecution of the early church, from a rag-tag band of followers of an itinerant Jesus, to become the largest religion on the face of the earth? A belief system that has caused immense positive change in the entire world!

---

[108] McDowell, Josh, *More Than a Carpenter*, Tyndale House Publishers, Wheaton, IL, 1977, p.28

When everyone else was getting closer to their own kind and ignoring the poor and the outcast, along came radical Jesus who proposed that we actually get to know strangers, lepers and outcasts and feed and clothe and welcome and care for them. He said everyone is our neighbor and we are encouraged to love everyone. No exceptions. And forgotten people are to be noticed.

It has been carefully and statistically estimated that seven years after Jesus' crucifixion there were approximately 1,000 converts to the new way. Less than three hundred years later, when Emperor Constantine declared support of the Roman Empire for Christianity, more than half the population of Rome had already become followers. Constantine had no choice. Just a few decades later, Christians comprised half the entire Roman Empire – approximately 30 million people.[109]

The message of the early Christians encouraged many to convert as they observed followers of Jesus feeding hungry pagans and strangers, providing them water, taking care of their infirm and their sick, practicing marital chastity and respecting their women – all things that pagans avoided or fled from. And Christians were joyful and mutually supportive with social networks centered on congregations. Pagans did not have congregations. All the pagan gods were invisible and generally merciless and to be feared, but the people could relate to Jesus who had taken visible human form to spread a gospel of forgiveness, love, community and mercy.

Guidance for Our Times

Practicing Christians have a number of guidelines from Scripture and tradition to direct their actions, prayers and daily lives. Among these, are the Ten Commandments,[110] The Corporal works of Mercy,[111] the Beatitudes and all of the Sermon on the Mount[112], and Jesus' instructions on how to handle offenses.[113] When Jesus was asked by his followers how to pray, he gave then a format – a guideline – called the Lord's Prayer which has been called the summary of the entire Christian Gospel.

Communities Joined Through Christian Love

The Christian faith is inclusive and peaceful. It works from inside us, rather than by force from outside. What other religion is there that tells us to *govern ourselves* – each and every one – rather than *behave out of fear* of a whip or a sword? If threat of punishment is all that holds a society together, history shows that when it is removed, subjects soon revert to their old, often degenerate ways.

In communities where Christianity is observed and *practiced* and people genuinely care for one another, there is little need for police forces, government handouts, or lawyers.

C.S. Lewis describes agape love as the highest form of love known to humanity.[114] Agape (from the Ancient Greek, ἀγάπη, pronounced: *agápē*) love is beautifully described in the Bible in St. Paul's first letter to the Corinthians (1 Cor. 13:1-13). 'Agape', roughly translates to mean good will and caring.

Contrast 'agape love' with the popular use of 'love' in the English language. In secular media 'love' has many meanings and often commonly refers to sexual love. The New Testament was originally written in Greek and the Greek word for this kind of love, 'eros', *does not appear anywhere, not even*

[109] Stark, Rodney, *The Triumph of Christianity, How the Jesus Movement Became the World's Largest Religion*, HarperCollins, 2011, Chapter Nine

[110] Different faiths – Jews, Protestants and Catholics – number these slightly differently. The source scriptures are the same however: *Exodus 20:1-17* and *Deuteronomy 5:4-21*. For more detailed analysis, refer to the *Wikipedia* website: *en.wikipedia.org/wiki/Ten_Commandments*

[111] *Matthew 25:35-36*

[112] *Matthew chapters 5-7*

[113] *Matthew 18:15-17*

[114] Lewis, C.S., *The Four Loves*, Harcourt Brace Jovanovich, 1960

once, in the New Testament. So much for feeling all fuzzy at the next wedding when the lector reads First Corinthians chapter thirteen.

Who is Welcomed?

One mark of Christianity is a welcoming hospitality. Jesus taught us, in essence, to draw a circle around ourselves and make that circle larger and larger until it surrounds every created human being. None should be excluded and no one should be rejected.

> *And if you greet only your own people, what are you doing more than others? Do not even pagans do that?*   *Matthew 5:47, (NIV)*

And he also said,

> *If you love [only] those who love you, what reward will you get? Are not even the tax collectors doing that?* [115]   *Matthew 5:46, (NIV)*

My wife and I have visited many Protestant and Catholic churches and only occasionally been welcomed or greeted by parishioners. Left to stand alone, even at their so-called 'fellowship' times, I felt sad for them that they could not break away from their old friends and greet this stranger.

When we seek out new people in our congregations (and our communities) and welcome them, our churches will grow, while other congregations shrink as their confident, regular members burnish one another and hardly notice that the socially un-included quietly disappear.

And it's not just about feeling welcomed. Statistics show that many are leaving their churches because they are hungry for the Word that Jesus offers – but they are lonely and not being fed.

Go ahead — s t r e t c h — yourself. Next time you are in church, go talk to someone you don't know and welcome them. You may see them again.

> ### The Broken Lamp
>
> Many have wondered, why did Jesus offer himself to die on a cross for us? Let me tell you an illustrative story.
>
> Little Susie's father had told her not to run in the living room but one day she ran anyway and slipped and broke a very expensive lamp. Susie was very sorry and asked her daddy for forgiveness which he gently and immediately gave her.
>
> That's like us asking Jesus to forgive us for breaking a commandment, which he will lovingly do for us when we confess and ask forgiveness.
>
> But it didn't end there. Even though she was forgiven, Susie's dad still had to pay for a new lamp; she broke it but he paid for it. And like Jesus, we broke it but he paid for it for us – with his life.

Caring for One Another

During the 1960s Civil Rights movement, Christian activist and lawyer Thurgood Marshall[116] once challenged us, "The question," he said, "is not, 'Am I my brother's keeper', but rather, am I my brother's brother?"

The U.S. Government through FEMA (Federal Emergency Management Agency) has done a fairly good relief job in recent hurricanes and natural disasters to help suffering people. But most of the relief has come from Christian groups and faith-based organizations who have taken the major lead. Groups from the Seventh Day Adventists, the United Methodist Committee on Relief, The Convoy of Hope, Samaritan's Purse and others have brought everything from food to chainsaws, according to one

---

[115] Has anyone noticed? These poor tax collectors have never in history had a good reputation!
[116] In 1967, Thurgood Marshall became Associate Justice of the Supreme Court. See: *en.wikipedia.org/wiki/Thurgood_Marshall*

report.[117] The fact is that Christian organizations *gave much more support and resources than the government*, but the news media mostly ignored this.

Christianity is not alone in helping the needy. Many expressions and good works of faith, such as almsgiving, are to be found in other religions as well. For example, one of the five pillars of Islam (*Zakat*) requires Muslims to give a portion of their wealth as alms to the poor. Observant Jews practice charity (*Tzedakah*) and as with observant *tithing* Christians, typically give 10 percent of their income. The difference, however, when one looks at the statistics – non-Christian religions typically give most of their alms first to their own groups.

I know of one young man in our community who practices his faith and sets an example for each of us. A few years ago he borrowed a truck from his father's business and filled it with hundreds of blankets. On a cold pre-Christmas December night, he and some friends went out and gave them to all the homeless they could find. He is a credit to the honor of his father and his synagogue.

Sharing Our Faith, Healing Our Nation

There are many ways to share our faith. For example, legend has it that Saint Francis of Assisi insisted, "Preach the Gospel wherever you go, and if necessary, use words." Or we might recall the voice of our grandmothers reminding us, "Actions speak louder than words!"

Meanwhile a large and growing minority of timid churchgoers conceal their faith. They often have been poorly taught or are misinformed about their own professed religion. They too easily submit to the silence which the loud, clanging atheistic disruptors demand. These folks may have inherited their religion from their parents but cannot explain it and have little idea of its graces or gifts and are dumbstruck in the 'village square' when they have an opportunity to share that heritage. They mumble if asked, "Why are you a Christian?" They may be aware of the treasure they have inherited but for fear of being mocked or persecuted they remain silent. It may be time for some serious adult education.

Saint Peter enjoins us to:

> *Always be prepared to give an answer to everyone who asks you to give the reason for the hope that you have. But do so with gentleness and respect. 1 Peter 3:15*

Vaclav Havel, former president of the Czech Republic had this to say about hope:

> *Hope is a feeling that life and work have meaning. You either have it or you don't, regardless of the state of the world around you. Life without hope is an empty, boring and useless life.*

Several studies show that fathers who are active in their faith are more likely to have children who follow the faith themselves – into old age. A Swiss study found that among Christian families, between 2/3 and 3/4 of children whose fathers regularly practice their faith, practice theirs for the rest of their lives. These fathers and the families they lead, support and bond, are essential to the healing and continuance of our great nation. Their kids are the next generation who will re-invigorate and renew America. And children who have the gift of faith are better able to avoid and survive the potholes of adult life.

Faith is staking your life on the promises of God. Before the Freedom From Religion Foundation makes its next attempt to take away our national motto, do we truly believe, **"In God We Trust"**?

---

[117] Chumley, Cheryl K., "Christians beat FEMA, and in so doing, tame Big Government", *The Washington Times*, Sept. 12, 2017.

RENEWING THE FAITH OF THE NATION

Time for Action

If men – husbands, fathers and mentors – can be so influential in spreading the faith, what are we doing to encourage them – in our neo-feminist dominated society that regularly demeans and emasculates men and mocks them as bumbling idiots and 'unnecessary extras'?

What does your house of worship do to help men to better lead their families? *If you don't have a men's ministry, prayer or mission group, ask your pastor or priest, "Why not?"* These groups provide mutual encouragement and faith strengthening for men who are struggling with their families through the briars of today's culture.

Keep asking your pastor– and press for an answer. This may well be the single most effective thing you can do to help America, your community, your congregation and your family.

What this nation needs is a good old fashioned Christian revival. Many people need to hear the message but all they get from the media – and sadly from too many local pulpits – is sugary, substance-free Kool-Aide®.

Christian Visibility in Our Present Age

Our present government has taken from us many of the acts of kindness and mercy that the early Christians performed as they socialized and evangelized. We have a socialist government that now feeds the hungry, shelters the homeless and clothes the naked, gives them money and encourages them to vote for more of the same. That's just the way it is.

But the government cannot love. It cannot welcome the stranger, cannot show hospitality, cannot uplift the lonely, the grieving or the saddened ones and cannot spread the Good News to the people or the prisoner. Those many things are left for us to do.

We need to come out of our shells and speak out and take a bold stand for Biblical Christian values. Be more active in government – run for the school board, the local city, town and county councils, our planning boards and other offices – and above all *be more faithful in voting*. It is time for the voice of Christians and of the Church to be heard – with gentleness and respect – but loudly and clearly.

How are we to live a Christian life in a world opposed to our faith? Consider the early Christians – they stretched themselves, exposed themselves to ridicule and persecution. That's why the world changed.

Act II is now up to us. You and I will be ridiculed and persecuted. That's just the way it is.

A Vision for National Renewal

If we want our great Republic to survive, spiritual revival is our only option. I have found no better vision for renewal of faith than the timeless words of the renowned Christian evangelist Dr. Billy Graham. (Excerpted and used by permission):[118]

"*... Lawlessness and revolutions have now become the spirit of the age. And it has penetrated into every realm of human thinking. ... Mental revolution is in the air. ...*

"*There is a revolt against authority of all kinds. Lawlessness is the spirit of the times. Analyze every expression of it, and you will find in it an unwillingness to be controlled. Tradition, substance and precedent*

---

[118] "Overcoming the Spirit of the Age", by Billy Graham, © 2017 Billy Graham, used by permission, all rights reserved. (The full text can be found online at: *billygraham.org/decision-magazine/october-2017/billy-graham-overcoming-the-spirit-of-the-age*)

are all discarded. Governmental authority is questioned, moral standards are laughed at and the church is considered a useless institution. In the United States, even the Constitution is considered out of date.

"Jesus Christ can give mental rest to those who are confused and bewildered. He can quiet your heart and give you inner serenity and joy if you will let Him have control of your mind and heart. ...

"The spirit of lawlessness is in the home. There is very little discipline in many homes. Each child is a law unto himself. The modern rendering of Paul's familiar injunction might well be, "Parents, obey your children, for this is right." In many of our homes, if there is a voice of authority at all, it is the voice of the child. Parents have little or nothing to say about the life of the child. As a result of all this, there is a grand rush for amusement on the part of the children.

"If children do not hear in the home a voice that speaks with authority, how can we expect them to obey the voice of the national government? We are now reaping exactly what we have sown for many years. We have allowed our children to run wild without discipline. ...

"Never in the history of the world have we seen such a casting aside of moral restraint. ...

"The moral restraint placed by God upon men and women is now laughed at and ridiculed. Every person wants to do what is right in his or her own eyes. ...

"There has never been a nation in the history of the world that has ever improved morally apart from a revival. Nearly all great nations of the past have been destroyed by disintegration of moral character. That is now happening in the United States. History gives us only one remedy, and that is a spiritual revival. ... turning to Christ can save us now.

"... the issue in the United States at this moment is not political. It is spiritual. ... The modern expressions of revolutions are the natural results of a lawlessness in the hearts of men. We are rebels against God. ...

"There are times when revolts and revolutions are right and just. ...

"We have come to a place where we must have another revolution if we are to be saved. The church must lead this revolution. We must have a revolution against corruption in high places, against immorality, licentiousness and sensuality, which are pervading every realm of our society. We must have a revolt against alcoholism and drug trafficking. We must have a revolt against lying, cheating and cutting corners in business. We must have a revolt against discrimination because of race, color or creed. We need a revolt against hypocrisy, spiritual indifference and slothfulness on the part of church members.

"I call upon the church today to fall on its knees before God and ask the God and Captain of our salvation to lead on in a spiritual revolution that will shake the very foundations of the social structure.

"Christianity is not a religion for weaklings. The challenge of the hour in which we live is so tremendous that it calls for the very best in us. We must be strong, virile and dynamic if we are to stand. The only thing that can give us this moral spiritual strength is a return to Christ. Unless we turn to Christ, I despair for our future. I am convinced that unless we have a great spiritual revival, we cannot endure much longer. We are at enmity against God. We have disobeyed His laws. ...

"... The Bible teaches that there is no way back to God except through Jesus Christ. And if God says that to the individual, God also says it to the nation."

Faith Resources for Change

> *To one who has faith, no explanation is necessary;*
> *To one without faith, no explanation is possible.*

> *St. Thomas Aquinas*

Here is a sampling of the many resources available to those of us who wish to start this journey. There are many more. "Seek and you will find."

- ➢ Your local (and regional or national) church or synagogue
- ➢ *Start a men's prayer and fellowship group* – One of the better plans is from *Man in the Mirror* author Patrick Morley on his website: *maninthemirror.org/2013/09/17/220-how-to-lead-a-weekly-mens-small-group/* Also, there is a short but useful "Discussion Leader's Guide" in his book *Man in the Mirror* on page 371 (See Bibliography)
- ➢ *Cursillo* and *Tres Dias* – These are short weekend courses that will increase your understanding of Christianity and deepen your faith. *Cursillo* (pronounced ker-see-yo) is Catholic, *Tres Dias* is Protestant. *www.tresdias.org* and *www.natl-cursillo.org*
- ➢ *Alpha* – An excellent, highly successful ten-week evangelistic course that introduces the basics of the Christian faith on which all denominations are in general agreement. *alpha.org*
- ➢ *Reawakening Virtues* – An excellent book by Armstrong Williams. Everyone who is serious about revitalizing American society, politics and culture and strengthening the faith upon which our nation was built should read this book. (See Bibliography)
- ➢ *Teaching children* – There are a number of good (and mediocre) videos on the Internet. Google: "teaching the faith to children through videos" but make your selections carefully and prayerfully.
- ➢ *Faith and Family Entertainment* – PureFlix is a movie studio that produces, distributes and acquires Christ centered movies. Watch movies online on your mobile phone, tablet or TV. *Pureflix.com*
- ➢ *Teaching older children* – *Billy Graham Evangelistic Association.* Good, clean family movies: *billygraham.org/videos/cat/movies*
- ➢ *Catechism of the Catholic Church* – Available as a hardcopy book, or online at *ccc.usccb.org/flipbooks/catechism* (and click on the 3-line icon in the upper left). (See Bibliography)
- ➢ *Understanding true evil* – Book by Francis MacNutt, *Deliverance from Evil Spirits – A Practical Manual* (See Bibliography)
- ➢ *Prayers Against the Powers of Darkness* – A book of meditative, patient, trusting quiet prayer, available from US Conference of Catholic Bishops (See Bibliography).

=========

N.B. – Any Internet addresses, QR codes and telephone numbers in this book are offered as a resource. They are not intended in any way to be or to imply an endorsement, nor does the author vouch for the content of these sites, numbers or references.

4 – Educating Future America

*We... are not really free if we can't control our own government
and its policies. And we will never do that if we remain ignorant.*
Charley Reese, Conservative columnist

WHY BE CONCERNED?

If you are one of the fortunate few who live in an excellent or very good school district with excellent or very good teachers then you are surely blessed. And unless you are concerned about the low quality of the average U.S. public school education and how its failure to perform is damaging America, you probably don't need to read this chapter.

But if you are one of the unfortunate many who do not have adequate public schools, or you wonder why each year it gets more expensive and less effective, this chapter is for you.

A Costly System Gets an "F"

Our American educational system is broken at all levels, from pre-kindergarten through college and graduate school. By every measure we are at or near the bottom among developed nations in educational success and near the top in what we spend to educate a child. The cost of a good college education has risen beyond the reach of the average American. Much of our public system indoctrinates rather than educates; much less does it teach students how to think and reason beyond emotion and group identity prejudice.

We are raising a generation of adolescents who will be unprepared to take over this democratic republic. At the rate we are going they are on course to bring us to a state of ruin as 40 percent of the new millennial generation, according to one survey, considers turning our working free market system into a socialist nightmare.

Take This Quiz

We need to have a thoughtful national discussion about educational goals – not about standardized tests and ill-conceived, time-wasting evaluation schemes like 'Common Core' – but about answers to some serious questions:

What is a proper education for an informed citizen? What is the proper role of the family, the church and the school in matters such as morals, ethics and religion? How do we re-establish the authority of the teacher in out-of-control classrooms? Do students work harder and more effectively when learning becomes interesting?

When and how do we fill little minds with facts and information and when and how do we encourage and direct their natural curiosity? At what age do we begin to guide them to find their own unique talents and skills? What subjects beyond the current faddish STEM should we be teaching? [119]

What are we, as parents, as citizens and as a nation, trying to accomplish at each stage of our children's education? Do we know; do we have a plan; do we care? How best can we invest our resources for maximum return on investment? How should public education be funded? What choice options should parents have?

Are we happy and content to continue to allow unelected bureaucrats to decide the educational path and thus the future for our children?

---

[119] STEM – Science, Technology, Engineering and Mathematics.

Some of us remember when teachers were more highly respected and called "teachers." Now they are called by the fancier name, "educators." Is there a difference? Why did this change, who decided on the change and who else call themselves "educators?"

So-called 'educators' have had their turn at trying to successfully teach our children and they have failed again and again. Now it is time for the rest of America's stakeholders to dial in, fix the system and *let good teachers teach and manage their classrooms*, once again.

We Can Do Better

It's time to take an honest look at our schools, fix what can be fixed, throw out what is beyond saving and replace it with educational systems that have been shown to work. There is no lack of experience and supporting data to that end; we need only the will to oppose the entrenched politicians and labor unions that have been slowly degrading what once was an excellent, affordable system.

Every stage of education has value but the largest impact can be had by working with the youngest students. Their minds are flexible, their curiosity has not yet been stifled and they are always the hope of the next generation.

If there is a single message I would impart it is this: **Let good teachers teach** *and remove the others*, that 95 percent of the non-teaching, rule-making bureaucrats who never interact with real students and who are now referred to as "educators." They need to find different work.

An 'Educational' System that Fails to Educate

*"The goal of education is to enable individuals
to continue their education."*
John Dewey

Immigrants Do Better

Every three years an international test, Programme for International Student Assessment (PISA) is given to 15-year olds around the world to assess their scholastic performance in math, science and reading. The United States consistently scores near the middle when compared to all countries and near the bottom when compared with advanced industrial nations. The U.S. scores have always been worst in math and are continuing to decline.[120]

According to the National Assessment of Educational Progress (NAEP), high school math scores have remained stagnant since the 1970s, with only about 25 percent of 12th-graders scoring at or above a level of proficiency.[121]

But math is only a part of the problem. Students continue to demonstrate their lack of understanding of the origins of our country, the intentions of our founding fathers and the bases of western civilization. A current study found that only one third of Americans can pass the required test given to new citizens.

The Problem – Screwed-Up Priorities

The problem hinges on who runs the public schools and whom do they serve? With our current system, government bureaucrats run them and these schools serve, first and foremost, the teachers' unions and the teachers. The children are last. Businesses and stores that no longer properly serve their customers close. When was the last time we heard of a failing public school that closed?

But in a free market system – where parents can choose – only those schools that serve the needs of the family and the children will survive. So why don't we all just get in line and make this happen?

---

[120] Ryan, Julia, op.cit
[121] *www.nationsreportcard.gov/*

The line forms on the left. At the head of the line, first come the politicians, then the elite educator-bureaucrats – what I call the 'educrats' – then the state and district money counters, then the teachers' unions and finally the teachers themselves and last of all, if anybody has time to notice, the students and their parents.

America's schools are at their lowest ebb. The more money we throw at them the worse it gets. Studies are conducted,[122] books are being written[123] about the problem, laws are changed, committees are formed, conferences are held, learned papers are written and published in obscure journals that no one reads and yet there is no one to stand up and solve the problem. Teachers' unions make a big fuss and demand more money for public schools and their salaries and benefits grow and now exceed those of the average non-government employee. *But more money won't fix this disaster.*[124]

Meanwhile, those very teachers' unions give millions of dollars to help elect people to the legislatures who will in turn support their demands for more of everything except what is good for the students. It is no secret that teachers' unions were not created to look out for students or their parents and families. They were created to look out for the teachers.

Indoctrination Centers

The result – we have a failing school system. Failing our students. Failing their parents and communities. Failing our nation. Judeo-Christian values are no longer part of public education. The only religion allowed in our schools today is atheistic secular humanism under the guise of science and identity politics. What can we do?

Many of our government-run primary and secondary public schools have become 'indoctrination centers' or worse. Students learn little except boredom. Too many of them get little or no support from their families and homes for a variety of reasons. Subjects taught are not assimilated and students are graduated to a world in which they are unprepared to work and interact effectively. Those parents who are aware and who care and have the opportunity and means send their children to private, church-run or charter schools or else they home-school them.

The self-interested unions and the widely used school property tax system have combined to destroy much of our public educational system.[125] It doesn't take an Einstein to recognize that doing the same thing over and over again and failing each time is pure insanity. Our public primary and secondary schools are failing and we need to phase them out as soon as possible to restore some measure of sanity to the educational process.

Unprepared for Life

A generation or two from now, assuming our republic lasts that long, most of our tenured, second-rate, liberal public school teachers will be retired or dead. That might provide an opening for change. But can we, our children and our nation afford to wait that long?

---

[122] Still relevant today is a 1966 report, "Equality of Educational Opportunity", better known as the *Coleman Report*. This was a large national survey of U.S. schools, commissioned by Congress, and has been called the most influential piece of educational research ever published. The study concluded that school funding has little to do with student achievement, yet we still hear voices, mainly on the political left, that disadvantaged and minority students do poorly in underperforming schools because of inadequate funding. The *Coleman Report* conclusively put this idea to rest. More money does not fix these schools, rather, what happens in the home and the classroom was found to be most important.

[123] One good book, 30 years old, but still very relevant: Allan Bloom, *The Closing of the American Mind – How Higher Education has Failed Democracy and Impoverished the Souls of Today's Students*, Simon and Schuster, New York, 1987

[124] See note on *Coleman Report* in previous footnote.

[125] In most places, of all the dozens of different taxes we pay, the school property tax is the *only* one that taxpayers can vote on. When a school budget, put to the voters, is defeated, educational priorities often take a back seat.

College is too late to repair the damage done to our kids. Without proper preparation, by the time they get there, they have little idea why they think, behave and feel as they do. They will have become half-educated and indoctrinated and parts of our economy will continue to depend on better-educated foreigners. (And colleges and universities are creating their own kind of intellectual damage. See *Fixing Our Broken Colleges and Universities*, further along in this chapter on page 67.)

Why Do We Teach What We Teach?

The STEM Curriculum – Half a Loaf

STEM – Science, Technology, Engineering and Mathematics.[126] This is the new buzz-word in teaching. Few people are aware of or remember the great hullabaloo that occurred among 'educators' after the Soviet Union astonished America by launching their Sputnik, the world's first artificial satellite, into earth orbit in 1957.

Sputnik took the general public by total surprise and led to a great uproar and broad condemnation of our educational system. We Americans had become so proud of our technology and skills. (After all we had won WW II and invented the hydrogen bomb!) People wondered aloud, "How could those 'primitive' Soviets be so technically capable and do something this amazing?"

The answer in retrospect is very simple. The Soviet Union's communist regime put great emphasis and much money and resources into science and mathematics – and ICBM rocket technology. They developed and rewarded many brilliant mathematicians and physicists (and they borrowed and stole the best ideas from the West that they could get their hands on.) Science became the religion of their atheistic state, to the detriment of their national soul. (Some say that America is on course to repeat this soul-deadening, technocratic path.)

After the Sputnik launch dozens of panicked experts, committees and self-flagellating books suddenly appeared, explaining how our educational system had failed and how we needed to re-tread our whole approach to education. We spent billions of dollars on school laboratory equipment and other sudden new curriculum 'necessities' and realized we then had to consolidate our local schools into mega-districts for 'efficiency'.

All this enthusiasm lasted for a while. A couple of decades later, we turned the art of teaching over to the educator-bureaucrats – the 'educrats' – and then we drifted back to sleep.[127]

Today we have corporations begging for capable job applicants who can read, write, and think and speak coherently. Our schools have become so dysfunctional they can't handle all the demands. Corporate America is pushing STEM because they say they need capable workers who won't require remedial training.[128] STEM training[129] is useful for half an education but does little to produce well-

---

[126] STEM subjects are needed to prepare students for work in technical industries. Corporations and educrat elites push hard for these subjects. Even today, many corporations have to conduct remedial courses for new hires who are weak in these subjects.

[127] The companies that made school busses did not sleep. They started working overtime to produce, what is now approximately half a million U.S. school busses, so that the half of our nation's children who ride them could spend an average of two hours every day learning to 'commute'. This is part of the 'school bus culture' education provided for our children so the young riders can learn all the (in)appropriate things the older kids can teach them. A friend of mine who drove a school bus was constantly bombarded by pennies thrown at him. At the end of the year he had accumulated over $100.00 from his daily sweepings. (Home schooling, anyone?)

[128] There is little question that the average student is STEM-illiterate. But a recent article in a publication of the Institute of Electrical and Electronic Engineers, *IEEE Spectrum*, makes a strong case that there is no shortage of STEM experts if industry wants to pay them enough. See, Charette, Robert N., "The STEM Crisis is a Myth", *spectrum.ieee.org*, August 30, 2017.

[129] Most STEM math instruction is out of date. In addition to classical math, the kind that leads to calculus, it needs to also focus on combinatorial mathematics because of its importance to computing and programming.

rounded citizens, capable of expressing themselves, voting intelligently and raising the next generation. Our schools must support and emphasize those other subjects that make a well-educated, whole and decent citizen.

Interrelationships – Tasty Mixed Salad, Not More Boiled Cabbage

Governments allocate increasing funds for education and then hire more bureaucrats for implementation and oversight. Since these educator-bureaucrats – educrats – often aren't skilled at teaching, they manage by setting *measures of success*. The first, easy measure is a test – test the student; test the teacher. Other measures look at graduation failure rates, and of course it is too late to do anything useful with that measure. And so we have tests and tests and more mandatory tests which drive teachers and students crazy. Teachers often spend an inordinate amount of time preparing students for these tests at the expense of achieving effective teaching. At one point, Common Core testing as adopted by New York State consumed six whole school days of student time – just to take the tests!

Since it is easier to create tests that focus on single subjects, educrat-ordained testing, as one dismayed teacher recently told me, discourages the teaching of *how these subjects interrelate*. She describes how a top-ranked public school in New York State's Westchester County dropped to mediocre after standard subject-oriented testing became mandatory. Teachers could no longer teach how topics were interrelated. For example, how math and biology or art, literature and religion are intertwined in the real world. Several of their best teachers then resigned. Standard tests are graded by single subject but real life success is graded by relationships – between multiple interacting ideas and between people.

Elite Educrats Control our Children's Minds

Once upon a time local schools set their own goals and hired teachers who taught what kids needed to learn. There have always been standards, such as the time-honored *McGuffy's Reader*, a group of primers for the first six grades, first published in 1836 and which were used in some schools up until as late as 1960.

Today, every state now has a bureaucracy that sets standards, curricula and rules. In my own state of New York there are several thousand such bureaucrats whose job is to design and promote rules, curriculums, syllabuses and approved text books. Few of these bureaucrats have current, if any, teaching experience. Many of them rely on outside groups of experts to design parts of their required curricula, teaching materials, tests and text books. The College Board is one such subcontractor that sets standards for AP (Advanced Placement) high achieving students.

In the past, the *AP World History* exam covered everything from the dawn of civilization to the present. But now, according to a recent article in *Time Magazine* The College Board is proposing to eliminate teaching *everything* before the year 1450. [130] So why is that of concern?

Using multiple authentic sources, *Time* compiled a list of 200 of the "most influential individuals in documented history." They found that 40 percent of these most influential people in history were born *before* the new College Board AP cutoff.

If this proposed change is accepted we could begin to educate our best and brightest youth with little or no understanding or knowledge of history, including the Greek philosophers, the origins of the major world religions and how early human societies organized, transformed and interacted. The result would teach students that every important world event began in Europe, while ignoring major contributions from the rest of the ancient world.

---

[130] Wilson, Chris, "Jesus, Genghis Khan and Joan of Arc are Just Some of the Major Figures That Could Be Cut From AP World History Classes", *Time Magazine*, June 25, 2018

Whether or not this goes forward – and there is significant opposition – this is just one example of how ivory tower educrats set standards which give capable teachers little maneuvering room to do what they are trained to do best: to educate, inform and inspire.

UNIONS, TENURE AND TEACHER QUALITY

Guaranteed Employment for Life

Tenure – guaranteed permanent employment – was created in the public universities a long time ago for a good reason – to protect professors and researchers from administrators and oversight boards with opposing philosophies. But why in Heaven's name does a first grade teacher need or deserve tenure? Private school teachers don't get tenure. Nurses, doctors and medical researchers don't get tenure. Unionized mechanics and machine operators aren't given tenure. Astronauts and airline pilots don't get tenure. Why are public school teachers treated so differently?

The practice of public school tenure was originally established as an anti-nepotism, civil service solution to prevent politicians from appointing favored friends and relatives. But there are better ways and we will examine one later in this chapter.

In one state, tenure is now awarded after *one year* on the job! Three other states award tenure after two years! 31 states grant it after three years and eleven other states after four or five years.

One year! Two years! Three years! Imagine that! How often have we known or heard of people who have toiled and sweat for 25 or more years in a factory or laboratory only to find out on a Monday morning that they will no longer have a job the following week. Not for poor performance, but because of poor management planning or lack of company business.

Teachers' unions, aided by lap-dog politicians, have forced teacher tenure upon us, falsely claiming there is no alternative.

Bad Teachers Stay Forever

Too many of our public school teachers are poorly prepared academically or personally for their assigned subjects. Consequently their classes are uninspiring and potentially-good students are never adequately challenged.

In New York City it is virtually impossible to fire a non-performing teacher. To get rid of one bad teacher costs an average of $200,000 and several years of investigation and litigation. Incompetent teachers? Crooked teachers? Perverted teachers? It doesn't matter, these union contract-protected teachers are almost never fired.[131]

Instead, they are sent to the Absent Teacher Reserve (ATR) or what is jokingly called the "Rubber Room," a building where these un-fireable teachers have no contact with students for the rest of their careers. They sit at desks with nothing to do, where they spend each day – at full salary and benefits and eventual retirement at full pension. They have paid summers and vacations and holidays off, as per union contract.

This is less expensive than firing them and it prevents teacher union backlash.

---

[131] News update: The New York City Department of Education has begun forcing schools to fill hundreds of vacancies from its Rubber Room (ATR), putting failed instructors back in the classroom full-time according to a Nov. 8, 2017 *Wall Street Journal* article, "New York's Not So Finest" New York Mayor Bill DeBlasio supports this action, which is pleasing to the teachers union which financially supports his reelection campaign.

Good Teachers Leave in Droves

Teachers' unions have a stranglehold on public schools everywhere. They guarantee that bad teachers stay and demoralized good teachers leave. But there are no similarly powerful groups to represent the educational interest of parents and children.

Even with the possibility of life-long guaranteed employment – tenure – studies show teachers don't stay in the classroom. 40 to 50 percent of teachers leave *within the first five years!* And that includes the almost ten percent who leave *before the end of their first year!* [132]

At this writing, New York State alone is reported to have a revolving door deficit of over 6,000 teachers for the coming school year! Enthusiastic young graduates look forward to teaching until they find out how bad the environment is. One example of how unions interfere with the student-teacher relationship – in some school districts union contracts forbid teachers from voluntarily staying after normal school hours to help students! The teachers want to help, the students need the help and the union contract forbids it.

Surveys show those new hires leave for lack of support from administration and the mind-boggling amount of non-teaching work they are required to do, including dealing with unruly, out of control students with little support from administrations. And there is the constant threat of disciplinary actions if they dare punish misbehavior. Students who abuse and assault teachers are often left unpunished.

I have a relative – unnamed for obvious reasons – a highly skilled certified teacher who teaches in a youth prison. When asked why she didn't teach in a public school instead, she replied, "Because it's safer in the prison."

Unions vs. Right-to-Work Laws

For many years, public labor unions have been allowed to force non-union workers to pay partial dues on the premise that these workers will benefit from union negotiations and other activity. But in June, 2018, the U.S. Supreme Court ruled that forcing public sector non-union members to pay was illegal.[133] Now, many unions, including teachers' unions, and the left-oriented political causes they support have begun to lose significant revenue. The old rule stated that fees collected from non-union members could not be used for political activities, but the truth is this additional money made union coffers healthier for all their activities, including support of – mostly – left-wing politicians.[134] This new court ruling will begin to weaken the political clout of teachers' unions.

Unions are already mobilizing and fighting back with everything they can muster and can be expected to push even harder for new legislation when the political Left again regains control of Congress.

---

[132] "Why do Teachers Quit?", Liz Riggs, *The Atlantic Monthly*, October 18, 2013

[133] *Janus vs. AFSCME*, June 27, 2018, The Supreme Court ruled that public unions could no longer collect a portion of regular dues from non-members because the funds were being used in 22 states to advocate for positions against the will of the payers, thereby violating their First Amendment rights. This is of great concern to a number of organizations on the political left.

[134] For more in-depth, see: "Turns Out, Those Forced Union Dues Did Go To Liberal Advocacy Groups", Editorial, *Investor's Business Daily*, July 3, 2018

CORRECTING PAST MISTAKES

Fixing Our Public School Systems

> *'tis education forms the common mind;*
> *As the twig is bent, so the tree's inclined.*
> *Alexander Pope*

If we want the best return on our education investment we will need to invest heavily in the early years of childhood. This is where we should be using and rewarding our best teachers, the best curricula, the best evidence-based teaching methods and the best administrators we can find – and then *give them the support and authority they need* to perform.

The Rights of Parents to School Choice

Throwing more money at public schools will simply make them more expensive failures.[135] But we never close failing public schools. We just keep them half alive, promise parents better results and make superficial changes until they fail again.

In America we pride ourselves on being able to make free market choices in just about everything we need – except education. It is patently unfair that taxpayers who opt for private education are required to pay twice. Paying once through their school taxes and again for tuition when they choose the non-public school option.

Despite special interest propaganda to the contrary, the relatively new concept of publicly funded charter schools are succeeding everywhere they are being tried.[136] In 2018, New Orleans, Louisiana became 100 percent charter schools. In 2005, the state of Louisiana took over New Orleans' failing schools, abolished the old bureaucracy and closed nearly every school. The state hired independent contractors to operate the public schools. These schools are union-free and run by principals who are given the necessary authority to hire and fire as needed. Autonomy and accountability make the difference. Thirteen years later in July, 2018, the state turned over these schools to a locally elected school board. Time will tell how this works, but the results so far have been outstanding.[137]

It is no accident that charter schools' educational improvement is the fastest-growing in the nation. African-American and low-income students are doing equally well or better in charters, even though the per-pupil cost is often less. Interestingly, when some of New Orleans' earliest charters failed to perform, they were permanently closed while the remaining successful ones took in their students.

Despite these proven successes, teacher unions continue to strongly oppose charters or any other system that will diminish their power.

---

[135] See footnote on earlier page regarding findings of the *Coleman Report*.
[136] Osborne, David, "Charter Schools are Flourishing on Their Silver Anniversary", *The Wall Street Journal*, Sept. 7, 2017
[137] Leonhardt, David, "How New Orleans is Helping its Students Succeed", *The New York Times*, July 15, 2018.

The Importance of Family Support

When curiosity is set afire, kids' imaginations set their own goals. Motivated students, guided by competent adults, can trek through mountains of details to find the gems they seek. In a home where there is a disciplined family that cares, with open and available resources – books, magazines and newspapers – and peace, love and caring, developing minds can be set ablaze.

But for most kids, school is total boredom and parents who are themselves products of the same broken system, often don't know how to help. Add to this the distractions of childhood – and the later major hormonal distractions of puberty – and all is lost if there are no early interventions.

It is tragic that many very talented kids never attain the full use of their talents. There are many reasons, including poverty, misfortune, family dysfunction and sadly, some families that just don't care.

Unsupportive families, especially those in poverty, are often so dysfunctional that their kids can't succeed – a major problem in America. Family is and always has been a great strength in our nation but unfortunately the supportive family structure is weaker now than at any time in memory.

Currently 27 percent of all American children are in single parent homes, according to one report,[138] but these kids account for a whopping 62 percent of all children living in poverty. And more than half of all children are now born out of wedlock. All these facts are enmeshed in poor education and child poverty.

Knowing the truth may "set us free," but there are no easy paths to emancipation.

Hope for Kids in Poverty

Research shows that the constant stress of poverty changes the brain. The limbic system – the part of our brain that handles emotion and stress actually interferes with the development of the prefrontal cortex – the part that solves problems, sets goals and tasks. Studies show that children of poverty have very limited ability to handle 'process'. That includes the ability to take a job and break it down into attainable, sequential parts.

Success through Science and Natural Brain Plasticity

A Boston non-profit organization, Economic Mobility Pathways, or EMPath, has developed a new and reputedly highly successful approach to helping kids, adults and families get out of the vicious and destructive spiral of failure, defeat and more failure. The EMPath program is built around proven brain science, and has been shown to be 86 percent successful with kids and families. *www.empathways.org*

People in the program are making it out of poverty into family-sustaining wage occupations.

Alternatives to Tenure – Protecting Good Teachers

Teachers unions protect all teachers, the good ones and the bad ones. But administrators should be able to reassign or fire bad teachers without jumping through so many union and political hoops. In the few schools without tenure protection, or where 'sweetheart deals' exist between administration and unions and those unions fail to protect the teachers, bad things can indeed happen to good teachers.

I was recently told of a private school teacher who had a twenty-five year career without a single blot on his record. When a new administrator took over his school he was summarily fired without being given any reason. This man was devastated and hired one of the best education-law attorneys available.

---

[138] "Why Children Need Married Parents", *U.S Conference of Catholic Bishops, www.usccb.org/issues-and-action/marriage-and-family/children/children.cfm*

The lawyer concluded the teacher had no case and there was nothing he could do. *There had been no formal hiring agreement with forethought to protections.*[139] His school failed him and a written agreement could have saved him.

Fear of loss can bind teachers to their unions. For example, unions step in when there is fear of too much government interference. Witness the recent teacher union backlash against government-mandated Common Core testing. Other teachers fear losing salary, benefits and control of their venue or even their jobs. Unions retain their power when they are able to successfully keep the fear alive and portray themselves as guardians against change or unreasonable and overreaching administrations.

But many of these concerns – job security, pay and benefit changes – could be handled without a union by *a properly constructed standard contractual agreement* between each teacher and the school administration at the time of hiring. Such a contract would discourage arbitrary dismissal or punishment without a formal hearing and include a mandatory arbitration clause and remuneration terms. To keep these agreements from becoming too lopsided in favor of the school district, a teacher's advocate should be available. A public ombudsman might be made available to assist new hires with contracts and help teachers with grievances.

Such standards exist in other domains and private businesses. They could do a great deal to return the job of teaching back to the many good teachers and improve the quality of our schools, both public and private. We need to refocus our efforts on protecting good teachers and allowing them to teach without all the current bureaucratic red tape and union-induced fear of benefit erosion.

Curriculum beyond STEM

Emphasis is needed for non-STEM subjects such as Art, History, Language skills, Poetry, Law, Debate, Ethics, Religion, Classical Literature, Geography and Political Science, to name a few. All of these are useful in preparing well-rounded future citizens for civic responsibility and for civilized life.

Most public primary and secondary schools all teach a smattering of these but a majority of their graduates are notoriously ignorant in these subjects. Few public school teachers know how to teach these in such a way as to kindle passion for further learning. Most students who are excellent in these subjects have historically been educated in private, religious or charter schools or they were home-schooled.

===========================

Government publications are too often regarded as instruments of bureaucratic horn tooting. One notable exception that is as relevant today as it was when first published in 1986: *What Works: Research About Teaching and Learning.*[140] This extensively researched 65 page booklet by the U.S. Department of Education presents a series of proven ideas, each about one page long with footnotes for further information and study. It was written for parents and teachers. The presentation is clear, terse and easily understandable. An extensive introduction explains these subjects and recommendations and how they were evaluated and chosen.

The booklet has been updated with most of the original information unchanged.[141] What has been added in 30 additional pages in two new sections on "Teaching and Learning Language Skills" and "Teaching and Learning Mathematics Skills." Additional entries have been added relevant to today's technology, including computers and calculators. Unfortunately, none of the original research reference footnotes have been included in the updated edition. Also, the interesting introduction by the person who led the original research has been omitted in the update.

---

[139] Personal communication.

[140] *What Works: Research About Teaching and Learning*, U.S. Department of Education, 1986; (Developed under Secretary William J. Bennett)

[141] *What Works: William J. Bennett's Research About Teaching and Learning"*, Edited and Updated by Dana B. Ciccone, PhD, Published by The Wooster Book Co., Wooster, OH, 1996

There are three sections to the original booklet: Home, Classroom and School. These findings are focused on the needs of parents and elementary school teachers and not so much for the educrats who make policy. The original table of contents provides a good overview of the scope of the publication:

Home: Curriculum of the Home; Reading to Children; Independent Reading; Counting; Early Writing; Speaking and Listening; Developing Talent; and Ideals.

Classroom: Getting Parents Involved; Phonics; Reading Comprehension; Science Experiments; Storytelling; Teaching Writing; Learning Mathematics; Estimating; Teacher Expectations; Student Ability and Effort; Managing Classroom Time; Direct Instruction; Tutoring; Memorization; Questioning; Study Skills; Homework Quantity; Homework Quality; and Assessment.

School: Effective Schools; School Climate; Discipline; Unexcused Absences; Effective Principals; Collegiality; Teacher Supervision; Cultural Literacy; History; Foreign Language; Rigorous Courses; Acceleration; Extracurricular Activities; and Preparation for Work.

Fixing Our Broken Colleges and Universities

In his new, very readable book, *The University We Need: Reforming American Higher Education*, professor Warren Treadgold states, "The main identity that the university should encourage among its students and faculty is that of a thoughtful and educated person, not of an ideologue or a member of a race, class, sex or other group." [142] Many stories in the news are about college students who cannot discuss uncomfortable ideas and who require 'safe spaces' and 'trigger warnings'. These same students are often pandered by college administrators who allow or sometimes encourage them to protest against faculty and visiting lecturers who cross boundaries of the politically correct, left-wing, identity-political, socialist ideas that are common on almost all campuses. [143]

Treadgold goes to the heart of the problem of declining universities – the error-prone manner in which PhD candidate professors are selected and hired. He suggests an approach to greatly increase the quality of the professorial staff. Treadgold, who has taught at five different universities and served on faculty search committees, examines several reasons that things got to the present crisis and he thoughtfully dismisses many unworkable current proposals.

He makes the case that schools often hire PhD professors at the same level of mediocrity as those who do the interviewing, for a variety of reasons. The result is that most universities today perpetuate the cultural failings of their existing faculty and continue to be hostile to free speech and free market capitalism and "discriminate systematically against moderates, conservatives, religious believers and people interested in traditional education."

His proposal would provide a more rational examination of a candidate's PhD thesis before he or she is interviewed and ultimately observed in person for ability to present and teach.

Dissertation Review Board Proposal

Treadgold proposes the establishment of an independent, government sponsored review board that would evaluate and score PhD theses on five equally weighted measures – *originality, importance, accuracy, rigor* and *clarity* – which would give hiring search committees better understanding of

---

[142] Treadgold, Warren, *The University We Need: Reforming American Higher Education*, Encounter Press ,2018

[143] Langbert, Mitchell, "Homogeneous: The Political Affiliations of Elite Liberal Arts College Faculty", *National Association of Scholars* publication, nas.org/articles, April 24, 2018 (Brooklyn College professor, Mitchell Langbert, has checked the political party registration of every PhD professor at American "top-tier liberal arts colleges" and concluded they are almost entirely staffed by registered Democrats. 31 percent of these colleges are "Republican-free.")

candidates. This new scoring method would also provide university administrators better understanding of a search committee's recommendation. Today, few people actually read a candidate's PhD thesis and administrators simply 'rubber stamp' search committee recommendations.

To critics of government involvement, Treadgold answers, "If the United States government can inspect and grade food and drugs and examine the competence of elementary and secondary teachers and students, why should it not examine and evaluate doctoral dissertations and academic publications?"

Academic Honesty Board Proposal

As part of his reform idea he proposes a board charged with examining the honesty of academic publications. This board would analyze publications and theses for plagiarism and where possible, validity of underlying research. Plagiarism and falsification of research unfortunately have become all too common.

Both boards would use the services of retired professors as referees, aided by undergraduate assistants. Each thesis would be scored by three referees. Undergraduate assistants would prepare the theses and redact all references to the author's race, sex and ethnicity as well as his/her name and institution.

In addition to his near-term practical suggestions for changing hiring practices, Treadgold devotes an extensive portion of his book to a comprehensive vision for planning, designing, funding, administering and staffing a new university that would compete with the best of the world's existing universities.

SUCCESS STORIES

Outstanding Teen Scientists and Their Education

Every year students from around the country enter a pre-college science competition to compete for up to 3.1 million dollars in prizes. The top prize is $250,000. On March 14, 2017 the top winners were announced. The competition is sponsored jointly by The Society for Science & the Public and The Regeneron Corporation.

This is the nation's oldest and most prestigious science and math competition for US high school seniors. Finalists are selected based on the scientific rigor and world-changing potential of their research projects. The majority of the 2017 contestants were 17 years old.

Who Are These Students?

It is interesting to see the ethnicity and national origin of these students' names and the schools from which they come. A quick review of their website suggests that the vast majority of the 300 contestants have Asian-origin names,[144] – predominantly Chinese, Korean and Indian.

If you eliminate these, and the rest with Russian, German, or Jewish-sounding names, you can count on two hands those remaining. The list looks nothing like the telephone book. Why aren't there more of the other American names? What is going on in America's educational system?

It is hard to believe that being of Asian origin somehow makes one more intelligent than a person of non-Asian descent.

---

[144] *student.societyforscience.org/regeneronsts-scholars-2017*

Where Were They Educated?

Also interesting in this list is what one can infer from their high schools, most of which have names indicating either non-public or special public or charter. These are not foreign schools, but US schools. Most of these kids were educated in the USA, just not in our government-run public schools.

I have to believe, with all the other things I have encountered, that family influence matters a great deal to these children. Their families chose their schools. Their families set standards for education. And their families cared for their children. And maybe they were more motivated to make the financial sacrifice to send their children to good schools?

What About the Rest of America's Students?

But what about the rest of America's children? Asian-Americans are a small minority of our citizens – less than six percent. Why can't other children attain what these do? Is it because they have less guidance from home? Is it because the public schools which they attend have lower standards?

Almost every foreign country does a better job of educating their children than America – a national embarrassment. Immigrants coming into this country (legally) are often better educated and sought after by corporations for their drive and their skills.

Algebraic Boredom – A Personal Account

My family moved quite a bit and I went to five different high schools (well, actually one of them twice.) I had two semesters of algebra at two different schools. I learned that two different teachers were totally unprepared to teach a subject they barely knew themselves.

Then there was that geometry class where the kid in front surprised me and pulled from his mouth a total set of false teeth and clacked them up and down in time with the teacher as she rattled on and on. She never noticed it and several of us laughed so hard we almost fell on the floor. We learned very little from that teacher.

Then at my last high school – a private day school in Buffalo, New York – I encountered the best teacher I had ever had. Dr. Jacky Knopp made math come absolutely alive. Strict on discipline, he knew the subject inside out, and he knew how to make it fun and fascinating. At the end of the first year I wound up winning the Mathematical Association of America award for our school. A total shock to me because previous schools had made me believe that I was just another dumb student. This was the beginning of a very new and successful path that led to many fascinating destinations, including earning a degree in Electrical Engineering and designing some of the equipment that got the first American astronauts into space and working briefly with one of them.

One teacher made the difference: I began to set goals that interested me and to educate myself. It has never stopped.

By the way, Dr. Knopp began teaching at a private school since he wasn't yet certified to teach in New York State public schools. The reason? His credentials were unacceptable – they were from a university in Cairo, Egypt. One more fruit of the endless and frustrating impediments of our educational bureaucracy.

EDUCATIONAL RENEWAL

Fixing This Broken System

To begin to recover and repair our educational system we desperately need a kind of resolve that this country has not seen before. There has to be a national uproar and demand for solution or else nothing will change. We need to understand and focus squarely on the major problems. We need a plan. We need leadership and we need motivated citizens who can get off their TV chairs and vote in a way that our republic's founders gave us. Or else we will no longer have a republic and the loud clanging voices of the opposing minority will rule and their anarchy and hapless historical ignorance will soon give way to an irreversible tyranny we could only imagine.

Our families, our common traditions, our government and our very way of life are all intricately interdependent and intertwined with our educational system which complements the culture and faith that starts in each home. Fixing a system so historically complex will be a difficult undertaking, but we must begin. Our future is at stake.

Several Things Need Fixing

First, school can be *absolutely boring*. Ask any middle school student. Most will agree. They can't wait to get out of school so they can stop the drudgery of learning. But soon they grow older, then they vote – and are more inclined to vote their emotions rather than with facts and reason, because they have never learned *how* to reason. We have many excellent teachers in our public schools but we make them work with their hands tied behind their backs. When they try to teach, if they are not buried in paperwork, they spend much time dealing with disruptive students whom they are not allowed to effectively discipline.

▶ **FIX IT** – *Support and enable our good teachers.* ***Let good teachers teach!*** – Look at schools that have solved this problem – most of them are private, but there are abundant solutions everywhere and we should start with what has been proven to work. Students are not automatons. They are by nature curious creatures who can be challenged, given the opportunity to pursue course work that teaches required material. When allowed to do so and not burdened by requirements from bureaucrats in faraway marble buildings, most teachers can make school work interesting. I know – I attended such a school and haven't stopped studying and learning yet because it's *fun and fascinating.*

Second, teachers' unions – predominantly the AFT and the NEA – have a strangle hold on the entire system. They essentially bankroll and choose the same politicians who raise their pay and their pensions. Their message is, "You vote for our increased benefits and paychecks and then our millions of dollars and our 'volunteers' will see that you get re-elected."

▶ **FIX IT** – *Change the law to prevent unions from funding political parties and candidates.* – The laws need to be changed to prevent what amounts to a bribery situation at taxpayers' expense. This may ultimately require action by the Supreme Court.[145]

Third, national tests, such as the six days of testing for Common Core and its state-wide descendants do nothing other than give schools reason to cheat and manipulate the students to pass the tests so the school looks good. Since the 1950s most students no longer study the Constitution and a host of other critical subjects to prepare them for good citizenship.

▶ **FIX IT** – ***Let good teachers teach!*** – It is no matter whether the tests are 'good' or 'bad'. The *teachers* should decide on a local basis how, when and what to test. That was done in decades past while our schools were turning out capable citizens.

---

[145] Note: This section was written before the June, 2018 Supreme Court *Janus v. AFSCME* decision. But be aware – unions are not taking that decision lying down and are actively looking for political and legislative work-arounds. And the *Janus* decision does not prevent unions from funding and supporting political campaigns. It only makes it a little more difficult.

Fourth, new teachers, full of enthusiasm go to work in our public schools and burn out – largely because of lack of administrative support – within five and a half years. They quit. Turnover is very high. The ones who stay are not always the best.

▶ **FIX IT** – *Let good principals administer. **Let good teachers teach**!* – Let local school administrators run their schools like any other business. Establish separate public charter school boards to oversee charter schools. Prevent the politicians from meddling, and let capable people be hired to run the schools. Most principals have little real power over who works in their school. With better administrators – managers with full authority – better teachers will stay longer and schools and students will thrive.

Fifth, In most states, schools are funded by a tax on real estate property.[146] That is the *only* tax – with few exceptions – in the whole United States of America on which taxpayers can vote 'yes' or 'no'. And when taxpayers get angry they flood their local school boards with tax-reducing members who often have less regard for good education. And schools suffer. This is serious. Having lived in several school districts, I have seen more than one good school bite the dust when a sudden influx of new residents caused school taxes to rise. The resulting changes in their boards of education demoralized and eventually destroyed what was good and very good. They became just one more mediocre district as the good teachers and administrators threw up their hands in defeat and left.

▶ **FIX IT** – *Eliminate the property school tax and fund schools from other stable tax sources.* – Schools need to be able to plan for growth (or shrinkage) and – just like any other business – need budgetary predictability. Highly paid bureaucrats in faraway places might best use their expertise to help advise schools to predict growth, based on industry changes and other factors. But they need to stay out of the way and let the locals run their own schools. (And while we're at it, let's encourage career changes for most of the states' educrats.)

Sixth, In America, we supposedly believe in free markets and free choice. In everything but education. Why? Why can't parents choose which school their children attend? Why are they presented with their only choice of a specific tax-funded government-controlled school, or having to pay to send their kids to their choice of private school? A very expensive option which makes parents pay twice. Once with their taxes and again with their limited disposable income. But the powerful unions – AFT and NEA are violently against private and charter schools where they have no control over hiring or firing. And even home schooling has been attacked or forbidden in some districts. Unions and their political lap dogs refuse to help private schools – the term is often unjustly equated with church or parochial schools – and they rationalize this as "separation of church and state." We are supposed to forget that everyone's taxes would rise astronomically in many districts if church and other private schools could no longer function.

▶ **FIX IT** – *Permit more Charter schools. Support some private school infrastructure funding, but not operational costs.* (Operational cost assistance would be an invitation to lose control to the politicians.) We need to 'inspire' the political will to find a way to keep the state separate from the non-public schools and accept the benefit of private schools to the entire country. And by the way, it has been

---

[146] The history behind the school property tax is complex and varies from state to state. There have been many legislative attempts to fix it and numerous court cases as precedents. The fact is, property is politically easier to tax than income or other assets and smooth revenue is more predictable from year to year. But with modern computer technology we may be at the point where we have the ability to create a more equitable way to pay for our schools. One impediment is in states whose legislatures are dominated by city dwellers who do not own land and prefer not to have other of their assets or income taxed.

widely reported that many politicians in Washington, DC, both on the political left and the right send their kids to private and charter schools – while they continue to vote against them for the rest of the people.

========

Seventh, We have allowed our system to become totally out of balance, filled with anti-American, anti-free trade, anti-cultural, biased teachers whose personal philosophies are anathema to our republic and to most of our citizens. Biased students become biased adults who have no knowledge of how our democratic republic works – and who are rapidly changing it in ways they would reconsider, had they been effectively taught.

▶ **FIX IT** – *Eliminate tenure in grades one through twelve (and possibly in taxpayer-funded community colleges as well)* – Too many poorly prepared teachers at the lower levels – elementary, middle and high school – are unprepared to teach their subjects. Basics of American culture should be taught at lower grades before student hormones begin to cloud any possible new learning. If teachers cannot teach their subjects they should be terminated, retrained or properly reassigned and replaced with teachers who can.

In Summary

Here is the take-away from what we have discussed in the pages above. Now, we need to begin the hard part – to begin the rallies, the angry parents meetings, the lawsuits, the re-election challenges to long-term lapdog politicians – to begin the tedious legal process of changing the balance of power back, from the unions and the lazy, self-serving politicians to the parents and ultimately to their children.

1. Good teachers must be allowed to teach according to their professional skills to encourage, excite and make relevant every hour of every day for every student.
2. Teachers' unions must no longer be permitted to fund, or pressure their members to support campaigns of politicians who then guarantee their tenure and raise their salaries, benefits and pensions.[147]
3. Teachers alone must decide how and when to test their students, not state and federal bureaucrats.
4. Knowledge of our Constitution and the foundation of our rights and responsibilities must be re-established by state and local education boards as a requirement for high school graduation.
5. School governance – principals – must be given the power and authority to hire and fire and to run their own schools, without interference from state and federal politicians and bureaucrats. Independent public charter schools should eventually replace all other public schools.
6. Property tax funding of schools is archaic and counterproductive and must be eliminated to prevent irate taxpayers from disrupting and ruining well-functioning schools.
7. Parents must have the final decision on where their children are educated without financial penalty.
8. Teacher tenure – which guarantees employment for bad teachers – must be eliminated in grades one through twelve. New standards and agreements are necessary to protect good teachers while giving principals needed administrative flexibility.
9. Citizens should be encouraged to run for local school boards, attend school meetings, make themselves heard and be informed voters.

---

[147] See previous footnotes on this subject.

A Vision for Educational Renewal

We need to focus our best efforts on our youngest citizens. Teach the sciences, math and technology but not at the expense of the true the good and the beautiful. Show how different subjects and disciplines are interrelated. And remember that the arts are the soul of a culture; teach respect, understanding and love of all the arts, literature and history.

Until charter schools replace them, we are stuck with our public schools and will need to work with them.

Primary-Secondary Education

* Focus dollars on early years. Best teachers. Highest pay
* Take cues from Finland, e.g., hire only best graduates for teaching positions
* Work to increase respect for teaching as a profession
* Eliminate public schools and transition all to charter schools
* Provide vouchers for families that prefer the private school option
* Develop special incentives for parental involvement in children's education; analyze and remove any disincentives
* Tamp down over-control by teachers' unions
* Eliminate tenure.

College

* Improve quality of new hires (professors)
* Encourage diversity in matters of thought, opposing ideas and political viewpoints
* Establish federal incentives and rescind unnecessary federal and state regulations to encourage (and require) reduction of administrative staff and their spending so as to address the major cause of rising college tuition.

Education Resources for Change

Many resources exist to enable understanding and promote action in important areas needing change. Following are a few that have proven useful:

> * Home schooling resources – *Parents Magazine* has published a list of more than 30 websites that cover the philosophy of home schooling, legal matters, online curriculums, online learning resources, and information sharing sites, including blogs and Twitter and Facebook communities[148]
> * Home schooling resources – Another resource which includes art, music, language arts, math, science, geography, history and other resources is at *www.christianbook.com/page/homeschool*
> * Also relevant to homeschoolers is the publication, *What Works: William J. Bennett's Research About Teaching and Learning.* (See reference and discussion on page 66)
> * *Billy Graham Evangelistic Association (BGEA).* Good, clean family movies: *billygraham.org/videos/cat/movies.* Also excellent paper publications
> * *CuriosityStream* – A low cost subscription service with commercial-free documentaries and programs on history, the arts, science and technology. *www.curiositystream.com*

---

[148] Access the *Parents Magazine* list directly at: *www.parents.com/kids/education/home-schooling/best-homeschooling-resources-online/*

➤ *Parents Television Council* – Movie and TV show ratings and news for parents who care what is being fed into their children's developing minds – www.parentstv.org

➤ *Khan Academy* – More than 20,000 free, close-captioned online video lessons and practice sessions from this non-profit organization. Many different subject areas for individuals or classroom groups – for young children's early schooling, also for pre-college and for undergraduate students. Advanced Placement (AP) sessions available in several subject areas. Analysis and classroom management tools for teachers and parents. Available in 11 foreign languages and currently being translated into many more – *www.khanacademy.org*

➤ *Universities and Colleges* – If you want your children to consider a school with academic rigor and high standards, consider a list of *The 20 Best Conservative Colleges in America* – Website: *thebestschools.org/rankings/20-best-conservative-colleges-america*. A number of these colleges are also strongly Christian-oriented in their discipline, college life and teaching. If you are looking for a college that is faithful to Catholic Christian teaching and life, consider the Cardinal Newman Society's recommended list of 18 colleges – Website: *cardinalnewmansociety.org/recommended-colleges*. You'll have great difficulty finding 'snowflakes', 'safe spaces' or 'trigger-warnings' at any of these colleges and universities

➤ *Newsmax* – Balanced, but conservative family-oriented news magazine and *Newsmax TV* channel – *www.newsmax.com*

➤ *AMAC – Association of Mature American Citizens* – A rapidly growing alternative to the very biased and left-leaning AARP, with similar benefits – Website: *amac.us* (Note: the suffix is '.us', **not** '.com' or '.org').

N.B. – Any Internet addresses, QR codes and telephone numbers in this book are offered as a resource. They are not intended in any way to be or to imply an endorsement, nor does the author vouch for the content of these sites, numbers or references.

5 – Governance and Politics

THINGS FALL APART

The Failure to Educate

Our political system is fractured, our inept Congress is held in the lowest esteem, mobs roam the streets to assault political opponents, famous entertainers suggest the assassination of our President and millions of our youth now believe we should become a socialist nation.

The decline and fall of the Roman Empire was prefaced by the decline of moral values and we are seeing similar decay that is spreading, not at the slow pace of an American version of the poet Ovid, but at the Internet speed of light.[150]

We no longer teach our children the origins and reasons for the creation of this long-lasting republic. Author, historian and sociologist James Loewen expresses this with painful clarity in his fascinating book, *Lies my Teacher Told Me: Everything Your American History Textbook Got Wrong.*[151]

Loewen's in depth analysis of 18 high school history textbooks details outright false information, but more importantly the mind-numbing, boring way history is presented in these required books and its absolute failure at encouraging the teaching of any semblance of questioning, critical analysis or thinking about how America came to be in her present form.[152] The result is generations of citizens who are destroying something of which they understand not a whit and who are totally unprepared to vote for a government that will survive much longer.

Our public educational system has failed us. It has succumbed to years of greed and incompetence. Instead of being a system that helps children, it has been turned into a scheme run by adults primarily for adults and their labor unions.

The previous three chapters discussed family, faith, and education. In just a few short decades those three aspects of our life have changed dramatically. Our families are falling apart. Our faith in God has diminished and our educational system has failed us in so many ways that many of us have little knowledge or understanding of our history and little hope in an immediate future. We have lost faith in our fellow man, have no hope or faith in the Creator of the Universe or in his healing or his mercy, and too often treat one another in ways that would make a barbarian blush.

The Problem of Divisive Factions

Civility and Disagreement

Some of our forefathers – the founders of this great democratic republic – had doubts that the republic would last. In fact in less than two years, President George Washington came under strong attack on a financial matter. But the republic survived, as it has to this day, because most citizens remained "a moral and religious people," as John Adams had so aptly cautioned.

---

[149] (With thanks to Chinua Achebe for appropriating the title of his famous book.)
[150] Ovid, Roman poet famous during the decline of Rome. His poetry was the equivalent of today's pornography.
[151] Loewen, James W., The New Press, 2018
[152] Most of these high school history books are more than a thousand pages in length and very heavy. One of them weighs over seven pounds. The author talks about a group of chiropractors and others who are concerned about the effect on students who must carry them in backpacks.

In his great witness of the American Republic, Alexis de Toqueville stated,

> *Liberty cannot be established without morality,*
> *nor morality without faith.*[153]

A number of countries have tried to imitate our constitutional success. On average they have lasted only 19 years.

We have had a time in this country during and after its founding when the main weapons of internal disagreements and attacks were letters, speeches and pamphlets. But now, as we slowly lower our national standards of discourse into the slime of limited vocabulary and contentious ignorance, we use verbal insults and even physical weapons to harm those with whom we disagree.

Preventing Factional Disruption

Our founders were anything but naïve about our lesser human natures. This great republic was created with a very deep understanding of human failings and weaknesses. There was no intention to create an Utopia, but rather a system that would balance the needs and the greeds – the goods and the bads – so that we could continue to update, modify, iterate – go back and forth from something that didn't work well to something that worked a little better, all the while staying on the straight road of a system of laws and moral behavior delineated by a hard-won Constitution.

The men who sat down together to pen the Declaration of Independence and the Constitution and later the Bill of Rights knew well the avarice in the human soul and they set up a self-correcting system of checks and balances.

Their valiant efforts did not attain perfection. Rather we have had to reconsider many topics over the decades. For example the rights of women and African-Americans. It takes time and cultural shift to move away from the sins that all mankind inherited from the past – things that those of us who have studied history can understand – but of which most of the current foam-at-the-mouth rioters have no understanding. No thanks to their inept public school history lessons.

But these founders – many of them – had been students of hard work, learning several foreign and ancient languages – not so they could speak them, but so they could study and understand the wisdom of the ancient Greeks, the wisdom of the Romans, the wisdom and foolishness of those who had come before. These 18th century founders of our American Republic sought to discover why some systems of governance worked and why other systems failed.

In 1787 and 1788 a series of essays, later called the Federalist Papers, were written to persuade the citizens of New York to ratify the Constitution. One of them, Federalist No. 10, penned by James Madison, warns us of the need to control divisive factions:

> *... a well-constructed Union [must] accurately develop [a] tendency to*
> *break and control* **the violence of faction**. *... The instability, injustice and*
> *confusion introduced into the public councils, have, in truth, been the*
> ***mortal diseases*** *under which popular* **governments have everywhere**
> **perished**. [Emphasis mine]

Maintaining Civil Order and Balance

Madison and the other founders understood that failure is always just around the corner, in every government and in any system. And they gave us, through the grace of God, a system of government

---

[153] De Toqueville, Alexis, *Democracy in America*, Vol 1, 1835

wherein we might live together, work together and bring in the many people from the face of this earth and unite us in common effort, so that out of *the many* we could become *one nation*.

This was no fantasy. This was an understanding, reaching back to the Scriptures, in John, Chapter 17, where Jesus prayed to the Father before his crucifixion that *all* his children would become *one*. He knew that there were many divergent opinions and interpretations among the Jews, Romans and Greeks. He knew there were many people who would not work together, but he foresaw a time when we might work together. And I believe so, likewise, did our nation's founders.

Our nation's founders looked at us in our deep human weakness and they said, in so many words, let us try this: This is the best we can do, from our knowledge and our wisdom. And with this Constitution, we give to our new nation, three branches of government, no single one having absolute power. But each being used to check and adjust and to admonish and correct, if necessary, the others to keep a civil order and legal balance.

Assisting Cultural Erosion

A more recent political depravity is buying the loyalty of large numbers of illegal immigrants in return for voting rights, as has been proposed in a couple of states. Democrats want immigrants to sneak into the country so that they will vote for them; Republicans want illegal immigrants so that their businesses will thrive by not having to pay them fair wages.

Too many politicians on the left and on the right have little concern that they are undermining the foundations of our republic, as they bring in unskilled workers who, in a few years will likely become unemployed as more automation takes their jobs – farm and factory jobs and other hourly-paid labor.

Nor do these politicians have any visible symptoms of distress about bringing in people who have totally alien and disruptive cultures[154] – or those who have difficulty assimilating. This is the case of many Muslims, whose culture and theology makes it almost impossible to assimilate and insists they eventually overthrow the American "infidel" system and replace it with Sharia Law.[155]

At present, the Muslim presence in the U.S. is only one percent of our total population. But their numbers are growing rapidly through immigration and very high fertility rates and this will become a problem for our children and our grandchildren.

We have a class of political leaders who seemingly don't give a second thought if they make our culture worse, partly because they reject that culture they never understood and because they relish the many worldly benefits from their current positions of power. But if we don't get culture right, nothing else matters.

If the eagle dies, how soon before the vulture takes charge?

---

[154] Santa Muerte, Voodoo, Santeria, Witchcraft – to name a few.
[155] Read more about Islam's Sharia Law in *Appendix B. Peaceful/Militant Islam* , and visit the index and bibliography references.

Challenges from the Political Left

Coloring outside the Lines

Dennis Prager is one of the more intelligent, thoughtful and courteous people you could ever encounter. Nine years ago he set up a YouTube channel, *Prager University* that makes videos on philosophical, social, economic and political topics. [156] Dennis Prager is a brainy conservative and everything he and his associates teach in short, high quality videos contains a reasoned analysis and conclusion. He never attacks a person, although he does go tough on many 'controversial' ideas. He is an intellectual in the best sense of the word.

Recently his YouTube channel has been 'shadow banned' by YouTube and Facebook. YouTube is owned by Google, a subsidiary of Alphabet Corporation one of the wealthiest companies in the world.

Shadow banning is where an uploaded video can no longer be found with the search function. An algorithm or a human censor removes most evidence of its existence and subscribers to the channel may no longer be informed of new postings.

Facebook rendered postings by *PragerU* invisible to Prager's three million followers *after* Prager filed a lawsuit against Google/YouTube.

Because Prager often talks about issues that upset people on the political left, such as 'diversity', 'gay marriage', 'terrorism' or 'Islam', YouTube's algorithms have designated his postings as "Hate Speech."

YouTube, Google, Apple (podcasts), Pinterest, Spotify (music), Twitter and Facebook all practice outright censorship banning or shadow banning of conservative content. Interestingly, every one of these companies is controlled by wealthy supporters of left wing politics. They are, every one, alarmed that Donald Trump could ever have won the presidency of the United States and they have been doing whatever they can to make sure he never wins a second term and that his current term is made as ineffective as they can render it. [157]

Facebook and Twitter recently banned Republican congressional candidate Elizabeth Heng's campaign advertisement which shared the story of her family being forced to flee from Cambodia. They said it was inappropriate and contained "shocking, disrespectful or sensational imagery" even though it was historically factual. After much communication (and public embarrassment) Facebook eventually approved it, but Twitter apparently has not.

In December, 2018, Facebook tried to punish Franklin Graham by removing a 2016 post and banning his activity for a day. Graham, the son of famed evangelist Billy Graham and president of several organizations that aid the poor, starving and homeless around the world was wrist-slapped for voicing support for a North Carolina law (H.B#2 – the "bathroom bill") that prevented men from using women's public restrooms. After Graham protested, Facebook restored the old post and 'apologized'.

Many other conservatives have been similarly either completely censored with their content removed or shadow banned. Leftist organizations and individuals who actually do promote hating of people on the political right – or physically harming or killing them – this content normally remains, such as the postings by the violent fascist *Antifa* mob, or the anti-Semitic rantings of Louis Farrakhan.

---

[156] *PragerU* is not a university in the true sense in that it offers no degrees, nor does it hold classes.
[157] For example, Jeff Bezos, CEO of Amazon Corp., the world's wealthiest man, recently bought the *Washington [DC] Post* newspaper which has become a relentless critic of President Trump (and seldom tells readers of his successes.)

Are You One of Those 'Hate Group' People?

Imagine that you have dedicated decades of your life to researching American culture and that a private organization decides it doesn't like your work. They label your organization a 'hate group' and convince MasterCard® and Visa® to stop processing credit card donations which are a main source of funding for your conservative think tank.

That's what the Southern Poverty Law Center (SPLC), working with the George Soros-funded Media Matters organization recently did to the David Horowitz Freedom Center.[158] And the left wing of the Democrat Party supports these actions.

SPLC has become a nasty radical leftist organization that labels most conservative organizations as 'hate groups' and its ranks of lawyers work hard to make sure that organizations they don't like are denied banking services, credit card services or social media access.

The SPLC has classified the conservative Christian nonprofit group, The Family Research Council as a hate group for spreading "false and denigrating propaganda about LGBT people."

Funded by wealthy liberals it has become a hit group that targets legitimate individuals and organizations with labels such as "Islamophobic", "extremist", "anti-immigrant" and "racist."

Formed during the Civil Rights movement, SPLC once had a valid purpose. Now, it no longer suffers from poverty (It is reputed to have a cash value of nearly half a billion dollars) and it uses the law as a hammer and threatens lawsuits to disable almost anyone they dislike. With 250 staff members and offices in four states it is an organization worth watching.

If you become too visible, SPLC can drive you into oblivion, i.e., you might have to sell your house just to pay your legal bills.

How strange it is that our constitutional republic, powered by free market capitalism, has made these big organizations very wealthy and yet they now turn against the very goose that laid their golden egg as they push for more censorship and socialistic big government policies.

These elites use their wealth and positions of power and ability to control information to silence those on the political right with whom they disagree. They draw the lines of acceptability and insist we color within their lines or we will be silenced.

Coming Next – Public Utility Regulation

Imagine if your telephone company said you could not communicate with other people if the company disagreed with the content of your call? Or imagine if United Parcel Service or Federal Express refused to deliver packages from people they didn't like?

Free assembly (online and in person) and free speech are pillars of our free republic. When a public resource company that is so important to our communication and our very social existence becomes a giant monopoly that inhibits fair competition and censors us on the whim of a few elites it is time for legislative, regulatory or judicial action.

Congress should prioritize the regulation of social media and giant Internet companies as Public Utilities, subject to the speech and assembly rights granted all citizens by the First Amendment to our Constitution. We have existing federal laws that govern communication, interstate commerce and antitrust laws to prevent monopoly. Surely some clever congressional attorneys can find a way to apply existing law to make the system fairer without strangling Internet freedom.

---

[158] "David Horowitz: "Visa, Mastercard Cut Off Payments to My Think Tank Based on SPLC 'Hate Group' Label", *Breitbart.com*, August 23, 2018

Save us From our Suffering

"Big Government Will Save Us"

Government, especially big government is about suffering – without human suffering there would be little need for big government.[159] We human beings have been suffering or afraid of suffering since the beginning of time.

The Old Testament tells how, against the best advice of the prophet Samuel, the people of Israel demanded a king[160] to rule them and protect them from calamities and distress[161] even though they were warned of the severe adverse consequences of having an earthly king and forgetting to obey God.[162]

History shows that every human person goes through suffering at least once in their life. Out of this suffering different forms of government have emerged. In America we have a constitutional government which emerged out of suffering imposed from a foreign tyrannical king. The people who dealt with this suffering created a country that has endured for almost two and a half centuries.

But now there is another form of government that is sought by people to assuage or prevent their suffering and that beast is the source of most of the political and social problems that we are seeing today.

We have become a nation of wimps – people who cannot endure the slightest discomfort without seeking redress. Every problem is seemingly caused by someone else and the government or a law firm is seen as the road to repair.

We demonize one another as racists, haters, bigots and worse because talking to people we disagree with is just too much work. And our mutual bigotry is fed by a constant stream of biased news media populated by so-called journalists whose perpetual commentary feeds the national fires of distrust, judgement and bias as they convince the masses that "the other side" is the cause of all our suffering.

We have come to the unpleasant point in time when, instead of looking for the sources of our problems we too often seek to identify the people who supposedly have caused them – people to blame and punish. Personal introspection and critical thinking are nowhere to be found.

Some say this is a result of our highly legalistic mind set. We have more lawyers per capita in America than almost any other country in the world.[163] Whenever there is a disaster, whenever there is a common problem, whenever something doesn't go quite right, a committee is formed, a report is written to identify who caused the problem and what legal actions should be taken.

Every committee has a few lawyers. Only in the case of technical disasters, like airplane crashes do we see a forced need for more technical people – aeronautic engineers, chemists, structural engineers, etc.

We have created a society in which people believe the government has a major responsibility to relieve our suffering and keep us healthy, feed us and take care of us in our old age.

Meanwhile we ignore the creeping decay from within.

---

[159] Approximately two-thirds of the U.S. Federal Budget is for mandatory spending (cannot be altered) almost all of which is for social and medical programs,

[160] *1 Samuel 8:4,5*

[161] *1 Samuel 10:19*

[162] *1 Samuel 12:14,15,25*

[163] In the 113th Congress (2013-2015), 59 percent of the Senate and 42 Percent of the House of Representatives were lawyers. In 2014 there were 450,000 lawyers in America, three times as many as any other common law nation. Twelve percent of our lawyers are employed by the government. (Trial lawyers are an important major source of funding for the Democrat Party.) According to the American Bar Association the number of lawyers in Congress has been decreasing as they are replaced by the rise of a permanent 'professional political class' of former "campaign aides, lobbyists, members of think tanks and employees in public interest jobs." (Debra Cassens Weiss, *abajournal.com/news*, Jan. 20, 2016)

The Laboratory of Eternal Life

Some of the extremely wealthy among us are working hard at living forever. Planning such unusual things as having their brains or their whole bodies cryogenically frozen in hopes of future scientific resurrection and complete restoration of health. Some are building self-sustaining underground villages in anticipation of whatever apocalypse they imagine – global warming, high altitude nuclear pulse, global financial disaster, nuclear war or a Donald Trump second term.

When you can't imagine anything better beyond living the jet-set life with every earthly desire met at the snap of a finger it is no wonder many of the very rich are heavily investing in living-forever research.

Even though the common man can't afford the luxury of underground living or cryogenic resurrection, it is natural to want to live as long as possible with as little pain and suffering and as many toys and goodies as possible. That is the new goal of a disturbingly large plurality of American citizens.

Nobody wants to die because the new religion of the masses on the political left (and some on the right) says there is nothing after death. So, even if we can't afford cryogenic resurrection, let's get everything we can now and we want the government to soften any intervening pain. We insist on a government that keeps us from suffering.

On the Road to a Fully Socialist America

It is virtuous to help people in need. But the socialist-leaning leaders of the current U.S. government have committed us to give away money we don't have and those advocates are proposing to give away even more money for things like free college tuition and free health care – *and even free cash* – that will absolutely bankrupt the country in a few short years.[164]

Our national debt has doubled in the past decade. Our previous administration (President No. 44) added more to our national debt in eight years than all our previous presidents combined. We have a financial crisis in our federal government, in our states and in our own wallets which we'll talk about in more detail in the next chapter.

One quarter of all Americans have *nothing* saved for their retirement. Nothing. Zero. Why? Because they are confident that the government will look out for them. This is new. This is not the way things were fifty or sixty years ago but it is the way things are now and the Social Security system is on the verge of bankruptcy, the Medicare system is at the edge of bankruptcy, our nation is on the verge of bankruptcy and many of our cities have already declared or are on the edge of bankruptcy. (The city of Detroit Michigan is currently in Chapter 9 of bankruptcy proceedings.)

According to U.S. Census Bureau data, 52 percent of all Americans under the age of 18 are living in households which receive 'means-tested assistance' from the government.[165] That's another word for 'welfare'.

We are running out of money. To some people it seems reasonable to look to the very rich among us, tax them, take their money and use that to pay our debts and debt service expenses.

But regardless of what we may think about free enterprise, free markets and how these people became so wealthy in the first place, a little bit of back-of-the-envelope calculation shows that if you

---

[164] One estimate proclaims that free health care will cost 33 trillion dollars over ten years and that personal and corporate taxes will have to *double* to pay for it. Free cash is being proposed and promoted by several wealthy Silicon Valley tech elites who have expressed concern that their artificially intelligent machines and robots will put too many people out of work. (Of course these brilliant people are not proposing that *their own* personal money be used.)

[165] This includes Supplemental Nutrition Assistance Program (food stamps), Medicaid, public housing, Supplemental Security Income, the Special Supplemental Nutrition Program for Women, Infants and Children (WIC), Temporary Assistance for Needy Families, and the National School Lunch Program.

were to take **ALL** the money from these wealthy ones – the richest in America – it would not even begin to solve our national financial problems much less pay off the national debt.

But sadly, many of our students who have recently passed through high school and college, (I shudder to use the word 'graduate') – those who have gone through our educational system – most of them are provably incompetent at even the basic tools of mathematics and finance. The *Atlantic Monthly* reports that *three quarters* of American school children about to complete high school (ages 15 to 16) are not proficient in math.[166]

We have produced a weak generation that presumes it will be taken care of, that expects to be fed, that looks to be mothered by a great utopian vision of a country that will watch over them, that will alleviate all their fears that will prevent or remove any pain. And if there is any real suffering it will be diminished or abolished by the government. There will be a doctor somewhere, or a lawyer somewhere, or someone somewhere, paid for by the government who will stop the suffering. And if not, a committee or a judge or a jury that will find out who caused the pain, blame them, so that we can feel a sense of revenge if not justice and recompense.

Things are the way they are because they got that way, while we slept.

Addressing Crises – Two Approaches

Sudden crises often demand quick responses. Not always required, but often demanded by a people who cannot handle a little pain or prolonged inconvenience.

Every big problem is best conquered by one of two approaches: *Command and control* by capable leaders or *voluntary self-organization* by the people themselves. The choice depends upon such constraints as urgency, resources available and capability and willingness of the governed or controlled masses.

In the first approach, very capable, intelligent, properly trained and tested individuals will direct the masses and tell them – even force them – to execute decisions from above. All involved are required to participate. Every successful military unit operates on this command and control principle for obvious reasons. This is how armies are organized to win wars. It is how disasters such as hurricane and earthquake evacuations and recoveries are best handled. Personal freedom, privacy and safety may suffer for the sake of speed and efficiency. But it solves the current problem and eliminates suffering but does little to unite the people.

The second approach leaves the masses to voluntarily congregate, self-organize and work out their own solutions. There may be more than one competing remedy and this less-efficient approach usually takes longer to attain useful results. But it often can do a great deal to unite the people, who bond as they set aside differences to attain a common objective.

Sometimes combinations of these two are appropriate but for purposes of discussion we consider these two alone because they are the most common.

Urgency – The Excuse for Government Intervention

Most of the socialistic changes in our government have come about through a sense of urgency, real or imagined. The Great Depression of the '30s needed immediate solutions to overcome massive unemployment and potential starvation. The Second World War required sudden changes in our manufacturing, our farming and every aspect of commerce. The 'command and control' model was essential. Then when the war ended, there were thousands of wounded soldiers returning and the

---

[166] Ryan, Julia, "American Schools vs. the World: Expensive, Unequal, Bad at Math", *The Atlantic Monthly*, atlantic.com, December 3, 2013.

government built veterans' hospitals. Veterans were given free tuition for college and many other benefits.

Now, in peacetime, many of these social benefits remain and few can fault us or our government for continuing to help in these ways.

Socialism Creeps In

But today, we see more creeping socialism as politicians create false senses of urgency, often through threats, such as recent threats (false) of reducing Medicare benefits, of scare tactics where 'new' statistics are promulgated showing how many children might be without health care. And the recent awareness that 10 percent of students are unable to pay off their college student loans (and thus, the politicians say, the government should do something – forgive the loans, and/or pay for free college for everyone.)

The list goes on and on.

But the real problem is that we, as a morally and socially weakened people, can no longer endure any kind of suffering and we insist the government rapidly respond and help in almost every matter. This becomes an invitation to more big government control and socialism.

President George W. Bush endured a 'beating' by the press for the lack of preparedness and slow response of the Federal Government (FEMA) to the devastating Katrina Hurricane in 2005.

Every time there is a national (or large local) crisis, we would be given to believe that private, religious and charitable organizations aren't enough to handle the urgent needs and so the government steps in. FEMA, the National Guard and other state and federal agencies take over. (See discussion of faith-based organizations in hurricanes on page 52 where private organizations out-performed the federal government.)

It wasn't always that way.

Citizens Responded to the Great Johnstown Flood

In the great Johnstown, Pennsylvania Flood of 1889, when more than 2,000 people died, the newly founded American Red Cross sent 50 nurses. Citizens and businesses from all across the country came in to help in the recovery. 18 foreign countries sent money. Pennsylvania's Governor sent out Army National Guard troops to prevent looting (and several looters were subsequently shot or hanged on the spot.) Towns and cities across the region formed committees of citizens to assist and send supplies and volunteers.

But there was no FEMA and no demand that the federal government step in, apart from urgent requests for some medical materials. (The Surgeon General of the federal government was asked for and sent several railroad cars of disinfectant.) This recovery was a mutual response by volunteers, state and federal government, but much of the organization was ad hoc by the local and regional volunteers themselves. Those were the days when travel of any distance took time and local communities came together to help one another in times of need.

Certainly the Johnstown Flood made people aware of the need for better communication, quicker response for emergencies and help in rebuilding. But it did not lead to a call for big government intervention.

(Unfortunately this disaster was pivotal in moving our legal system toward the current concept of *strict liability*, where you are responsible even if you meant no harm or ill intent.[167, 168] The Trial Lawyers Association[169] absolutely *loves* the strict liability 'gold mine'.)

---

[167] The dam that burst was privately owned and the owners were sued, but ultimately, and against common sense, they prevailed in court.

Avoiding Permanent Bureaucracies

We will always have these two choices before us – let the government do it, or encourage the citizens to band together and do it. Depending upon the urgency and resources needed, we may have no choice. But we do have a choice in making sure that those federal agencies, set in motion to handle temporary problems, do not become permanent bureaucracies that suck up our national resources and discourage personal responsibility with unnecessary red tape and out-of-date regulations. Sunset provisions are one way to handle this.

And we need to make sure our own personal resources and time are not so overcommitted that we have no energy to dialogue and work together. The Devil – the great divider – wants to discourage us from working together and we need to be always on guard.

MORE STATESMEN; FEWER POLITICAL HACKS

The Cultural Peril of a Permanent Political Class

Many political leftists among us want to create a new form of government. Indeed, we have already created much of it. To alleviate suffering or the fear of suffering we have a government that feels free to take from those who have, without their consent and give to those who do not have, "whatever the cost!" Who among us can deny the crying needs of the 'do-not-haves' – those who are poor, those who are weak, those who are in trouble, in sickness and in agony and in need?

But some of the crying ones include the lazy – those who *could* work and support themselves and their families, but who choose not to work, out of sloth and greed or an acquired sense of entitlement.

We are in a situation where many of our ruling class – those who govern us – work at their political jobs as a career. Our founders never intended such a thing. Nearly every one of our founders had a separate trade or profession.[170] Politics was not their career and they never envisioned that the likes of a Nancy Pelosi, a Charles Schumer or the late Strom Thurmond – and many others – would come into power and remain in power forever and that political elected office would become their only lifelong job, their only career.

Today we have politicians who will use the money that they take out of people's pockets – 'legally' of course – and give it to others, not so much out of a concern for those others, but in order to acquire their loyalty and their votes. There is no polite way of stressing that this is unembroidered stealing of one person's money to buy another person's integrity. They steal money to buy the votes of people they hope will keep them in power and give them yet more power. Sadly, buying a few votes is an antique political evil but its new modern version is directed at a mass market.

---

[168] For example, if your cute little puppy dog bit the person who trespassed on your property, or your neighbor fell in your swimming pool or in the hole you just dug – it matters not what you intended or did not intend, the penalty is on you because something you owned (or manufactured) caused harm. You are liable for damages. Strictly. (And 'emotional harm damages' are often added to actual tangible damages.) There are limits and proportionalities and a host of other things that apply to actual cases.

[169] A few years ago this organization was given a friendlier, softer-sounding new name: "The American Association for Justice." They and their members continue to be major financial contributors to the Democrat Party which has helped protect their interests for decades.

[170] In fairness, there were a few founders, such as John Adams who made an intellectual career of studying the philosophy of war, politics and civilization.

Term Limits

The Need and the Impediments

History shows that the longer a politician stays in office, the more they raise large sums of money to pay for reelection staff and expenses. The bulk of this money flow comes from, or under the control of, the wealthy upper class. Studies show that as time goes on, these politicians become more in the pocket of their wealthy donors and less inclined to support the priorities of their middle class constituents. (See discussion on page 103 of related Princeton and Northwestern study.)

How do we free ourselves from the tyranny of permanent politicians and decades of one-party rule in ALL of our large American cities, which have become politically immune to oversight and correction? Some observers have proposed limits to the number of times a politician can be re-elected to office. But for that to become law, those same affected politicians must vote for it. That is about as practical as asking a pig to go on a diet. Don't hold your breath.

For years legislatures and states have debated term limits, a few states and localities have actually enacted half-hearted, weak laws, but there is always opposition, some of it reasonable, most of it emotional. And where citizens have demanded term limits and laws have finally passed, career politicians have pushed for repeal.[171]

The purpose of term limits is to give the people a chance to look at new candidates and to decide who is best to serve them. There is also the hope of changing government to represent ALL the people.

A 'Smoother' Approach

Here is an alternate suggestion. Instead of absolute term limits, after which the politician is **out**, why not require that those who wish to run for more than, say three consecutive terms, must take one term of *sabbatical absence* before running again.

Preferably, during that sabbatical term, they would not work in or have influence over the same domain as their current political service. They might work in a non-political private or community service job, such as a think tank or an NGO (Non-Governmental Organization).

This proposal would offer another alternative option to the sabbatical absence. Occasionally there may be a congressman or senator who, through experience or other skills, has an absolutely essential and critical temporary role to play. The required sabbatical term could be cancelled, and the politician would run for one last and final term after which s/he would become permanently ineligible for that position again.

A sabbatical would give everyone a little breathing room, and yet, those politicians who truly serve, and who are experienced and respected by their electorate could be elected for one more term.

The deal might be sweetened by letting incumbent politicians be exempt and by providing some additional financial or benefit retirement perquisites to those who accept. Clean and pure? No. Pragmatic? Maybe.

Encouraging Good Candidates to Run for Office

The Salivating Tabloid Media

How do we get good people to run for office? How can we encourage competent people to offer themselves for public service? We need to do a great deal of self-examination on how we as individuals may impede this.

---

[171] Jacob, Paul, "When Local Lawmakers Won't Take No for an Answer", *Wall Street Journal*, November 2, 2018

Endless negative news 'investigations' and spurious reports dissuade many good candidates from running. When someone is running for office or elected to office or nominated for an important position that requires affirmation by Congress or by state legislatures, how often do we titillate at all the dirty news that is dug up – often alleged but unverified – about these people, their wives, husbands, their cousins, grandfathers, etc. in an attempt to disparage them and destroy their candidacy. And we can only blame ourselves because without customers – us – the mainstream news media would have no reason to report on these sensational rumors. Yes, we can blame the media – they do a wonderful job at destroying candidates and lives. But it is we who keep buying their salacious product.

One only has to look at what has happened with President Trump – how the media has disparaged him, attacked him, his children and infant grandchild, his family, in-laws, father, mother and everyone around him in an attempt to destroy his candidacy and later his presidency. And they do this with every single candidate whose values they dislike.

The Kavanaugh Circus

And then there was the disgusting travesty of what was done to Supreme Court nominee Brett Kavanaugh in October of 2018. The Senate Judiciary Committee Democrats, a group of people who demonstrated that they didn't give a second thought about him or his family, descended to the gutter of public character assassination. They made it clear that they only wanted to be certain another conservative would not join the Supreme Court and overturn their right to kill babies.

After Kavanaugh had gone through weeks of vetting and hearings and provided hundreds of thousands of pages of requested information; after dozens of people who had worked for and with him had given very favorable support and *the day before* the Senate Judiciary Committee was to refer him to the full Senate for affirmation, the committee Democrats 'found' a woman from 37 years ago who said he tried to rape her when he was 17. Then they produced another woman and then another. It was clearly a planned hit job. Since then, at least one of his accusers has admitted she lied.

Kavanaugh said, "My name and my family have been permanently destroyed by vicious and false additional accusations." He called the allegations directed at him a "grotesque and coordinated character assassination" that will "dissuade competent and good people from all persuasions" from serving the country in the future.

Clearly, no competent person in his or her right mind will ever again submit their name as a Republican nominated candidate for a U.S. court. Thanks to this and previous charades, we will likely get the less capable among us to serve as our leaders and judges.

========================

More could be said about how Kavanaugh was adjudged guilty without a trial and it will be amplified *ad nauseum* by others who focus on political misbehavior. But the purpose of this book, while not ignoring the vagaries of human foolishness, is to understand what we can do to repair and strengthen the republic.

The Market for Bad Ideas

Part of the problem is our willingness to listen to and tolerate salacious, emotion-heavy stories. The other part is our inability to deal with them in a rational manner. But just like drugs – if nobody bought or used them there would be no drug runners, no drug dealers. There would be no drug problem. No drug-related crimes.

We – you and I – we are the free market for bad ideas. We are the free market for *newscrap*. And until we sit down and say, "I'm not going to read any more of that." "I'm not going to put that bumper sticker accusation on my car." "I'm not going to repeat gossip and spread rumors about people I know little or nothing about." "I'm not going to do that. And I'm only going to listen to sources that tell me 'facts'. And if I can't get sources that tell me the real facts I'm going to seek them out."

"I'm going to be part of a group that represents a NEW MARKET that the media cannot ignore. I'm going to be their best customer when they start accurate, non-salacious reporting." And then we are likely to have more, decent and capable people running for office and taking difficult leadership jobs if we are to turn this country around.

"I'm going to stay informed, but I'm not going to read all the tripe – I'm not going to listen to it on TV and in fact the sooner I cut the cable on my TV and support my local newspapers and news magazines, the happier and better informed I and my family will be. The stronger my family will be and the stronger my community and my nation will be."

If we want good people to lead us, we have to stop discouraging them from offering themselves and their lives to us. It is time to re-institute some standards of civility and reason.

Personal Physical Safety

Why do we have so many Secret Service agents walking beside almost every visible leader in our country today? These are men and women who are armed and trained to throw themselves in front of the leaders they protect or to shoot anyone who would harm them.

Why have we come to this?

There have always been people who rebel against authority. The First World War started when Archduke Ferdinand was assassinated by anarchists. James Wilkes Booth who assassinated President Lincoln was another such man – an active, violent anarchist. He was a prototype of the modern day Antifa terrorists – domestic anarchists using violent fascist tactics to silence their opposition.

Encouraging good people to run for office is almost impossible. It's difficult to run a government office like a business because of all the red tape and bureaucratic hurdles and the pay is way less than they often can make in the private world. Then there's the loss of privacy and the non-stop harassment from the hostile media, mentally ill individuals, and people on the political margins – including constant death threats.

Many years ago, my father, Almerin O'Hara, Sr., was appointed by then New York Governor Nelson Rockefeller to serve as his Commissioner of General Services – basically that part of the state government that does most of the purchasing. This job entailed handling many grievances – out-bid contractors, construction site union difficulties and all the normal state-wide personnel problems. Dad received, on average, more than one death threat a week, but could not publically reveal it because that would have encouraged copycats. Instead, this army veteran with three and a half years of combat experience always wore a suit jacket – and known only to a few confidants – with a shoulder-holstered .38 handgun. He also had several rifles and an automatic machine gun in the trunk of his car. He wasn't paranoid; rather he was an emotionally stable, cautious realist. His situation was typical of all high profile public servants and none of them talked about it. And that was almost 50 years ago in the 1970s. People I talk with tell me the situation is much, much worse today.

Media Profits and Political Weeds

We will never completely eliminate these dangers but today's mainstream news media continuously fans the divisive flames of hatred which incites a few, disturbed, dangerous and unstable people to emerge and do horrible things. Irresponsible journalists will shrug and point to their immunity in the First Amendment. Their editors and publishers face increased competition and falling profit margins and too many will do almost anything to sell their wares, and likewise reject any notion of responsibility. Sadly, after a while it may all seem to be 'normal' journalism.

Too frequently this environment discourages capable people from running for elected or appointed office. Instead we reap too much of our legislative and administrative harvest from a crop of second-rate political weeds.

Recognizing Capable Candidates

We could use a few more candidates who can speak to us in the same words as that young woman who was just elected as the youngest member of Montana's State Legislature. Her name is Sarah Joy Laszloffy:

> *I grew up with the model of servant leadership that Jesus modelled throughout Scripture and I firmly believe that public office should be just that. Servant Leadership.*

Why can't we look for and encourage more candidates like that? Why can't we respect them and why do we have to dig, dig, dig for dirt if we disagree with them? Why can't we disagree with candidates based on the positions that they take in matters of law, governance and policy? Why do we have to personally disparage them and their loved ones?

Part of the reason is, again, our educational process has failed us. Too many in the opposition often are limited to four letter words, not having ever learned the full use of the language or the ability to study, analyze, discover, question and reason critically. And we have become a coarser, less civil society.

Impatience, arrogance, agnosticism, even atheism. This is where we are and when a good candidate for leadership comes along, how will we recognize such a person? Will the media tell us? Maybe not. Will we hope someone else tells us?

Maybe not.

A successful business hires capable workers, not by random chance but by applying interviewing and hiring skills whose wisdom comes from experience and by matching the prospective employee to the vision, needs and values of the company.

Maybe we need to go back to our traditional values and the Scriptures which are the foundations of our faith and learn the language of discernment and goodness – learn the language that Jesus and the writers of the Proverbs tried to teach us – put this into our hearts, put this into our minds, put this into our souls and take that language and use the wisdom that comes from it so when we hear a candidate speak we won't depend entirely upon someone else's analysis to guide us. We will have our own analysis tools.

Then we may be able to 'hire' more leaders who will lead us and a government that will guide us according to the rules and the laws of our land and our Creator. A public order and mutual respect we should all desire.

NATIONAL POLITICAL RENEWAL

Addressing a National Solution

The Source of All Law

In a nation of people where hearts would be governed by the laws of love and whose paths are guided by the teachings of Jesus, governance becomes more internal and personal and less necessary from far off marble buildings full of experts. God gave us Ten Commandments and Jesus gave us an eleventh, all simply expressed in just a few words. The amendments in our first ten Bill of Rights comprise only 462 words. Yet, every year in America our legislatures and government agencies crank out an estimated 50,000 *new* laws and regulations,[172, 173] every one of which is provably descendant from and dependent upon the few laws given us thousands of years ago.

---

[172] We must be careful about complaining when our legislatures take too many vacation days and weeks. Some of us hope they will take more. There's an old saying, "No man's life, liberty or property are safe while the Legislature is in session!"

We have become a people that have forgotten that God is the Founder of our free will and Liberty, that he is the Creator of all that is Good and Beautiful, that he is the Creator of each and all of us and that we, his people, need to pause and take time out. Turn off our electronic screens – our iPhones, tablets, TVs and computers – and get down on our knees and pray that he will guide us through these difficult times as we foolishly poison our public life and destroy our nation and as we govern ourselves in ways that he never designed, that our Founders never intended, with all the consequent adversity we have brought upon ourselves.

And we need to ask Him for forgiveness, mercy and renewal.

Strength in Numbers, Weakness in Numbers

The challenge ahead is not for weaklings. Sometimes we feel overwhelmed. Despite all our modern electronic toys, we have less free time today than many of our ancestors. Centuries ago the Church enforced mandatory work-free Sundays and holidays and kings and princes could do little to object. By one economist's estimate, peasants in 14th-century England worked no more than 150 days a year. Today, America leads the world in hours worked and we are the only advanced country with no national vacation policy or compulsory holiday time. The problem is exacerbated by fear of job loss and weak or corrupt labor unions which encourage extra work.

Small towns across America are having increasing difficulty finding volunteers to serve on local civic committees, volunteer fire departments and rescue squads. Working people are just totally exhausted most days after commuting to and from a full day of work. When they do come home, young men and women are finding they have to take their children to extracurricular school activities. There is little time for rest, much less for adults to congregate and face the nation's problems or even to get out and vote. Even Sunday church attendance continues to decline and part of the reason is called "soccer practice" and "lawn mowing" and "ESPN" and "total exhaustion."

Consequence of Failing to Vote

As documented in an earlier chapter, an avowed hardline socialist recently unseated a six term Democrat in a primary election when only 13 percent of eligible (Democrat) voters bothered to show up at the polls. This socialist won a congressional seat in November, 2018 in her traditionally Democrat district where that 13 percent amounts to *only four percent* of the total community population. *96 percent of the people let four percent decide how they will be represented.*

Avoiding Community Atrophy

We are all too busy. When we don't or cannot set aside unplanned time, when our days are totally booked seven days a week, we make no allowance for life's emergencies, much less the public service activities that need conscientious Americans to change the course of our seemingly rudderless ship of state.

If we find that we are feeling exhausted and only have time to complain or listen to others describe the problem but we ourselves can't get involved, we have begun to dig a one-way tunnel to civic darkness which our children and grandchildren will inherit.

It may be time to re-prioritize our personal and family time. Not because it will make us less tired, but because we absolutely need this to survive. We each need to set aside and announce times when our coworkers know our phones will be turned off. Times when the shades are drawn, the phones and other

---

[173] Many creative solutions to this plethora of laws have been proposed in the past. One city-state in Ancient Greece decreed that any politician who proposed a new law should appear in the assembly with a rope around his neck and if the vote failed, he was to be hung. For 100 years no new laws were proposed. (According to Ripley's *Believe-It-Or-Not.*)

electronics silenced and we can spend interactive time with our families and teach our children this new survival technique.

We shouldn't need the excuse, "I'm away on vacation," to take time for ourselves, our families and our communities. If we don't schedule these times they will never happen. My wife and I have, for years, refused to do any physical work on Sundays. That is re-creation and family day.

If our bodies are weak, some of us go to the Gym and exercise. If our minds are weak some of us do crossword or Sudoku puzzles. But what do we do when our sense of civic responsibility has shriveled and become so weak by lack of use that it atrophies beyond repair?

Strength through Civic Exercise.

We can form groups of like-minded believers who pledge to take some time off from the rat race to make this country just a little bit stronger. Whether that amounts to getting people out to vote, joining the local fire department or a women's auxiliary or some other regularly-meeting or working-together group. Just do it. And don't wait until you are retired. We need the wisdom and hard work of the retired folks but we also need the strength and energy of the younger folks as well. And we'll all suffer a bit together without the government's help, for the good and promise of our enduring nation.

> *If you want to change the country, politics won't work. Talking*
> *sports won't work. Only living an authentic, consistent life,*
> *reflective of the teachings of Christ will work.*
> Congressman Trey Gowdy

Encouraging Civility in Politics

A Civic Experiment

In October, 2001 I did a political experiment in our town which some people say was at least partly successful. We had disruptive politicians who were fighting each other and the townspeople. Civility had taken a back seat to hostility, name calling and open verbal warfare. Local newspapers published editorials condemning our dystopian town government. We were on the threshold of our local November town election.

I created a *civility pledge* and asked each of the 15 candidates for the seven open positions to sign the pledge. Road signs (picture on right) were posted all over town. Every public bulletin board had a posted notice. Press releases were sent out. The results were then advertised on a special website for all to see.

```
10 of 15 signed the

BEEKMAN CIVILITY
PLEDGE

DID YOUR CANDIDATE
SIGN IT ???     Find out at:

www.CivilityPledge.com
```

Ten people signed the pledge and five refused. Five of the signers won office. Two of the refusers also won, one of them, a man who everybody knew was decent and honest claimed his 'libertarian' right to not self-encumber by signing.

Although there was no way of enforcing the pledge, those who signed it, *publicly agreed that they would voluntarily resign if they could not keep their pledge*. The complete text of the pledge is in *Appendix E* on page 151.

The result of this election was a new group of people who led our town to an extended period – years – of civility, peace and good governance.

A Basis in Scripture

The idea for this experiment came from reading the *New Testament, Matthew, Chapter 18, Verses 15-17*, I noticed that Jesus gave a formula for handling disagreements. Instead of talking behind someone's back to third parties, instead of shouting the offense in public, try first to deal with the situation just between you and the other person. If that person won't listen to you then bring one or two others with you and try again. If he still won't listen, take your concern to the "congregation" – in this case, the community. The fourth and final step – if he *still* won't listen to you, have nothing more to do with him, "Treat him like a gentile and a tax collector." (History has never been kind to tax collectors!)

Chapter 7 following, is about getting people to work together with civility or suffer the alternatives.

A Vision for Political Renewal

> *But of a good leader, who talks little,*
> *when his work is done, his aims fulfilled,*
> *they will all say, 'We did this ourselves.'*
> *Lao Tzu, Chinese philosopher, 5th Century BC*

As we begin to re-focus and address these concerns, here are a few potential actions to consider:[174]

Local & National Policy

➢ Insist that our schools teach how this country was created and how it works according to the Constitution and make this a requirement for high school graduation
➢ Make available to the average person, guidance for contacting their local and national political representatives (e-mail, websites, postal addresses, phone numbers for main and local offices)
➢ Encourage people to contact their representatives, with advice on what works best
➢ Petition your state legislators to back legislation to call a national Constitutional Convention to pass Term Limits and Parental Rights amendments to limit government interference in our families. (See section on this topic on page 41.)
➢ Term limits – A high priority – In the US Senate and House of Representatives
➢ Begin a real national debate on campaign finance reform.

Foreign & International Policy

➢ Consciously articulate and export the better parts of our culture
➢ Encourage and reward the exportation of ***decency*** (See related discussion beginning on page 24.) Most residents of foreign lands have no idea who we Americans are, our values or how we actually live. They only see our lives through the ugly, warped lens of 'Hollywood'
➢ Place some 'Hollywood' exports on the same forbidden list with WMDs – Weapons of Mass (Mental) Destruction. This includes perverted music as well as some performance art videos. Internet videos should have a warning (advertisement) in more than one foreign language
➢ For those exports that do make the cut, charge an export duty in proportion to the degree they undermine foreign policy. (How to do this constitutionally will require some clever thinking.)
➢ Reinstate & privatize Voice of America (VOA) – export real news about good things
➢ Encourage NGO medical teams, US and others
➢ Support CARE and other volunteer groups
➢ Spread the good news, as in the comment regarding Mosul by Dr. Elliott Tenpenny in *Decision Magazine* (see footnote)[175]

---

[174] N.B. – Any Internet addresses, QR codes and telephone numbers in this book are offered as a resource. They are not intended in any way to be or to imply an endorsement, nor does the author vouch for the content of these sites, numbers or references.

> Beware the military-industrial complex (Cf., Eisenhower's farewell speech) Greed, Big Business and their customers dine together
> Take note of how our businesses impact foreign countries – esp. in Central America where big businesses, our meddling government and the drug market have combined to destroy whole countries which are now run by criminal gangs
> Stop trying to export democracy – it doesn't work. Acknowledge foreign need for their own forms of government
> Fix the U.N. – remove some committees
> Re-align foreign aid to reward good behaviors.

Prayer for the Nation

A Prayer for the Protection of Religious Liberty can be found in *Appendix D* on page 150.

Governance and Politics Resources for Change

Help is available but knowing where to look is often the first problem. Here are some starting points that others have found useful.

> *Choosing Good Leaders for Tough Times* – A two-session DVD project from *American Family Association*, focuses on conservative principles of limited government, strong national defense and traditional family values and choosing leaders with vision, commitment to principle, consistency, boldness and integrity. Available at *afastore.net* or 877-927-4917.
> *Essential Partners* – (*See p. 115*) An aid to civil dialogue. A non-profit organization which offers a free publication, *Reaching Across the Divide* for improving productive dialogue between political parties. *whatisessential.org*
> *Communispond* – A company that offers communication skills development courses for professional development and public events – *www.communispond.com*
> *Dale Carnegie Training* – Courses and seminars, especially on leadership training and how to communicate with diplomacy and tact – *www.dalecarnegie.com*
> Public speaking training – *Toastmasters International* – A group that probably meets in your area and helps shy people feel more comfortable speaking in public. *www.toastmasters.org*
> *Constitution of the United States of America* (Online at): *www.senate.gov/civics/constitution_item/constitution.htm* or you can download a printable booklet at: *constitutionbooklet.com/constitutionbooklet.pdf*
> Thomas Jefferson had a lot to say about our current situation, *famguardian.org/Subjects/Politics/ThomasJefferson/jeffcont.htm*
> *Declaration of Independence* (Online at): *www.constitution.org/us_doi.pdf*
> FOIL or FOIA – Freedom of Information Law/Act – Information available to politicians and government employees is generally available to the public also, at the federal, state, and local level. Exceptions involve personnel-related and confidential or otherwise classified information. There is usually a nominal per page charge for copies. Every citizen should be aware they have a right to see what their elected representatives are doing. Ask your representative for information relevant to your locale and political district.
> (Check also the suggested resources in other chapters in this book.)

---

[175]"Healing for Mosul's Suffering People", *Decision* magazine, May, 2017, pp. 32-33, [This article examines how the Iraqi sympathizers to the enemy forces, brought into their volunteer-staffed field hospital are seeing something that doesn't fit – that what they've been taught all their lives must be wrong as they are treated carefully and decently by Christians at the field hospital. Quote:"I want people here to understand the contrast that is being witnessed there between the suffering, chaos and war, and the love of Christ that is being shown."]

6 – Finance

There is nothing wrong with men possessing riches.
The wrong comes when riches possess men.
                    Billy Graham

SUCCESS AND FAILURE

In our civilization everything always boils down to money. Some have enough, others have too little. Families suffer without enough to pay the bills; governments fail for lack of it. Citizens may revolt and overthrow governments when prices soar,[176] A stable family seeks to maintain adequate resources and a stable government seeks to keep prices and employment numbers stable. Without this financial stability personal and national success becomes difficult or impossible.

In this chapter we will explore being broke and being poor, at both the personal and the national level and effective and ineffective proposals to prevent, reduce or solve these problems.

At the national level we will briefly explore some of the ways certain political beliefs create and encourage poverty or financial success.

At the end of the chapter there are some resources for analysis and improvement of personal financial issues and some hopeful ideas of how we might begin to address our national finance problems.

Personal bankruptcy – that awful word – sometimes it is inevitable due to job loss, business failure, extended sickness, natural disaster – there are many causes and if it hits you, you will need certified professional help – possibly a counsellor, a lawyer, and/or an accountant.

Governmental bankruptcy – at the city and state level is a more difficult problem that will affect everyone in the U.S. before long.

Success

Success needs a goal. There is an old saying, "If you don't know where you are going a roadmap won't help." If success means carrying the football to the goal line make sure you don't run the wrong way and score for the other team. If you fumble the ball, try to retain control.

But is success about winning? Does individual success mean that someone else must lose? Or can one person's success help another to succeed?

How can we define financial success? Whom does it affect and what are the consequences?

In the preceding chapters we talked about making family, faith, education and governance successful.

A politician might regard success as promoting and passing new legislation. A teacher can look with pride on a student s/he rescued from the pit of ignorance and brought to the peak of enlightenment. A pastor will be pleased when the congregation is growing and people are living in the Word. A father and mother will rejoice when their child graduates and takes that first job.

In this chapter we discuss financial success – that which is necessary and sufficient for our families and our nation.

---

[176] Some say the final death knell of the old Soviet Union was when the price of bread rose so rapidly that families could no longer afford it and the people revolted.

Successful people almost always have goals, stated or implied, and financially successful people seldom strive only for money.

My late father encouraged me to follow my talents and ambitions without regard to pay. He cautioned me, "If you want to make money, work toward what you love and the money will follow. If you work only for money you will succeed only at being poor and you will be dissatisfied with your life." This from a man who learned the hard lesson early as he was forced to take many menial jobs to support his mother and siblings during the Great Depression after his father had died.

One definition of financial success: having sufficient stable income that lets us raise strong, capable and godly children in a strong and godly family.

Spreading the Fruits of Success

In Chapter 3 we discussed tithing and alms giving among the religions of the world. In 2010 Warren Buffett and Bill and Melinda Gates, created what they call *The Giving Pledge* wherein a number of individuals and families – billionaires – pledge to give at least half of their total wealth to philanthropy or charitable works during their lifetime or upon their death. To date, 168 billionaires and many other wealthy families from around the world have signed the pledge which is approaching a trillion dollars total.[177]

Philanthropies include efforts to alleviate poverty, aid refugees, promote arts and culture, environmental causes, criminal justice reform, education and health issues and medical research.

Malaria kills more than a million people every year, mostly in Sub-Saharan Africa. Although 100 million dollars was being spent to conquer it, most of that was being spent for the military. Larry Page (Google Corp.) and Bill Gates (Microsoft) have now pledged millions into research to alleviate the cause and curse of malaria. In fact, of the 3,000 species of mosquitos in the world, only three carry most human diseases. The goal is complete eradication of this disease that kills mostly very young children.

In the previous chapter we describe how the majority of foreign aid from America comes not from the federal government, but from millions of individual ordinary citizens who contribute to hundreds of Non-Governmental Organizations (NGOs) and causes such as Oxfam, CARE International and Doctors without Borders (Médecins sans Frontières) which is currently fighting a deadly spreading Ebola epidemic in Africa.

Failure

Our country is in massive debt and we owe tremendous sums to many of our adversaries. Too many Americans live from paycheck to paycheck and have little saved for emergencies, much less for retirement. How do we dig out of the hole of financial failure, both for ourselves and for our nation?

Poverty – especially in our cities – is highly correlated with family breakdown, drugs, street gangs, violence and high prison incarceration rates. People without moral values prey on one another and the strong take from the weak and all semblance of civilization – beyond the visible material artifacts – disappears.

What is cause and what is effect? Politicians on the Left proclaim that racial bias and poverty cause these societal problems and they demand more government money and jobs to fix the problem. But considered analysis shows it is the other way around. Broken families are the first cause of the poverty and moral breakdown and our well-meaning governmental programs were a primary cause and continuing them only exacerbates an already out-of-control problem.[178]

---

[177] Clifford, Catherine, "These 14 billionaires just promised to give away more than half of their money like Bill Gates and Warren Buffett", www.cnbc.com, May 31, 2017

[178] Parker, Star, *Uncle Sam's Plantation: How Big Governemnt Enslaves America's Poor* and *What We Can Do About It*, WND Books, Nashville, TN, 2003

Poor vs. Broke

There's a difference between being poor and being broke. Broke is lack of money; poor is lack of money and hope. Wretchedly poor is being broke, poor and at the edge of despair.

I have been broke several times in my early life, once without money or food. I've never been poor and can only imagine the fear and hopelessness, especially for an abandoned single mother with young children to feed, and possibly living in a dangerous neighborhood.

America is Broke

When America is about to run out of money, America prints more money. That's legal for the Federal Government but impossible for states. For you and me it's called counterfeiting, with up to 20 years of free housing at a federal prison.

When America doesn't have enough money, America also borrows money. For years we have been borrowing from unfriendly and hostile countries, such as Saudi Arabia and China.

Since the 2016 Presidential election our country has been trying to get its financial act somewhat together, but the demands of preexisting social welfare programs – 'entitlements' – make any real progress almost impossible

For years both congressional parties – Democrat and Republican – (but mostly Democrats) have been giving away money to combat poverty, all the while *increasing* rather than decreasing the problems of the poor. But once such a commitment is made, it becomes almost impossible to reverse, since people come to depend upon and feel 'entitled' to these government handouts.

As we discussed in the previous chapter, 52 percent of American children under 18 years of age are living in homes that are on one form of welfare or another and 70 percent or more of all Americans rely for part or all of their income on the Federal Government.

PERSONAL FINANCE

A man with a surplus can control circumstances, but
a man without a surplus is controlled by them and
often has no opportunity to exercise judgment.
Marshall Field

Things We Want, Things We Need

There's Another New god in Town

Technology has been become our god and *this* god always delivers. We know our prayers have been answered when the glowing image of FedEx or UPS appears. We offer our prayers and supplications at the altar of *Laptop* or *Smartphone*. *PlasticCard* accepts intercessory prayers and requests a tithe of ten percent or more, depending on the word of *FICO*, a prophesy of *Equifax*. The occasional sin of *LatePayment* is forgivable but when repeated too often, a larger tithe is required. Cumulative offerings to *PlasticCard* require us to disengage our families, atone for past sins and work overtime to pay our tithes.

Our Material Appetites

Our appetites for material things are driving many families to the brink of economic distress. Our children demand expensive toys and electronic gadgets which keep them from breathing outside fresh air and cause enslavement and permanent changes in their brains.

Grandparents and some parents are amazed at how many young children insist on having expensive Apple smartphones, many of which cost $1,000.00 or more, when inexpensive ones can be purchased for a small fraction of that. These are the same adults whose most expensive childhood 'toys' probably cost only a few dollars. The demands of children for material things – game consoles, large screen TVs, high cost footwear and clothing is driving many parents nuts. But when every other child in the neighborhood gets what they demand, it's hard for some parents to say "no."

Total U.S. household debt is of the same order of magnitude as our national debt.[179] We are all living on the edge and the false god of technology is pushing us over that edge. An Apple iPhone may cost $1,000.00 but when mom and dad pay for it with the credit card the monthly amount doesn't initially seem like so much.

We are spoiling our children, big time. When they finally leave our nests, their expectations may exceed their abilities to meet them. That's when the dysphoria begins. If they are dumb enough to shack up with some girl and procreate before they have an education and a job, the odds are they will become members of the angry poor. Or at least the pregnant girl and her child will become one of the government-dependent poor.

Conquer Now and Survive

Families that realize in time and take preventive steps can cause a little suffering now and prevent a whole lot of pain and suffering later on. The first step is – for both mom and dad – to learn to easily say the word, "no" with gentleness and firmness and age-appropriate explanation. When a child is very young, the only explanation needed is, "That's the way it will be." But if we don't start that when they are young, it will become near impossible to say and enforce later. And unless we are the heirs to unlimited cash, our fate will be financial stress – which is one of the main reasons marriages fail and families fall apart.

Government Impact on Family Finance

Even though many states offer some relief from property and school taxes to the elderly, if you live in one of the 'blue' or Liberal Democrat high-tax states, such as New York, California or Illinois, you can be sure you will be making the annual decision either to paint the house or pay the property taxes to avoid losing it to foreclosure. School taxes rise almost every year but studies show the quality of children's education stays level or decreases. This author lives in one of those states where everything is taxed. Even our dog has to pay an annual tax.

Remember the famous words, "Read my lips." And then the more famous ones, "If you like your health care plan you can keep your health care plan. Your health insurance premiums will go down." Oh well, who believes politicians anyway. Everyone I know has had their health care premiums rise, some have risen astronomically and most have had to leave their previously adequate old health care plan.

Social Security and Medicare are eventually going broke and we will all have to pay for this mismanagement by our federal government.

Every time some Democrat or Republican politician finds another underfunded special interest group to put on the dole, our taxes go up to pay for it.

Wouldn't it be nice to have a responsive, responsible, representative government that was seriously concerned about the finances of the middle class, whose taxes pay the government's bills. Our families need financial stability and our representatives don't do enough to ensure it.

---

[179] In 2018 total household debt was $13.3 trillion. The largest segment, mortgages, accounted for 68 percent according to the N.Y. Federal Reserve's household debt report.

Planning for the Future

A family budget is essential, especially when the first child appears and new, unfamiliar expenses occur. Life insurance is a must for young couples, for both partners, but especially for the breadwinner(s).

And it is never too late to have a will, to prevent the government from deciding where your property goes if you should die unexpectedly.

There are many useful references available to guide new parents toward successful family finance; some of the better ones are in the category of "Christian Finance." Some references are given at the end of this chapter.

NATIONAL FINANCE – GOVERNMENT OF THE PEOPLE

Why Congress Spends So Much

For many years our elected politicians have been writing bad checks on an empty national bank account for health care, pensions, and a host of welfare entitlements. The advertised cost is nearly always underestimated for political publicity reasons. The Congressional Budget Office tries to accurately estimate expected costs of new legislation but tricky political finance games often obscure actual results. And since the federal government doesn't employ modern accounting methods it is easier to obfuscate and hide political intent.

How We Pay For It

Our founders fought the Revolutionary War and we left the British Empire partly because of unfair, excessive taxes. Today we pay taxes on just about everything imaginable to every branch of government. Taxes in America tend to be lower than some European countries but still the typical American pays more in taxes than for food and clothing combined. A popular list that's been floating around on the Internet shows the great creativity of politicians to tax everything imaginable.[180]

There was a time in America when people went to prison for gambling. That was until politicians found they could legalize it and bring more money into the public coffers to pay for their pet projects. New York State, and others, legalized the 'numbers game' and called it the Lottery, telling the people the proceeds would be used to fund education. Millions of new dollars flowed in but money is fungible and the schools saw little or none of it. Politicians diverted it to other pet projects.

Similarly, police no longer need to raid as many gambling dens because legislature-approved casinos are now legal in many states. 'Recreational' marijuana is now legal in some states (your state may be next). Usury is now legal; it used to be called 'loan sharking' and people went to jail. No more. Credit card companies can charge outrageous interest rates – 20 or 30 percent. And all of these previously forbidden things are now legal. Behold! Our legislatures have the amazing power to legalize sin!

---

[180] A *partial* list of our taxes: Building Permit Tax , Commercial Driver's License Tax , Cigarette Tax , Corporate Income Tax , Dog License Tax , Federal Income Tax (Fed) , Federal Unemployment Tax (FUTA) , Fishing License Tax , Food License Tax , Fuel Permit Tax , Gasoline Tax , Hunting License Tax , Inheritance Tax , Inventory Tax , IRS Interest Charges (tax on top of tax) , IRS Penalties (tax on top of tax) , Liquor Tax , Luxury Tax , Marriage License Tax , Medicare Tax , Professional Licensing Fees , Property Tax , Real Estate Tax , Service charge taxes , Social Security Tax , Road Usage Tax (Truckers) , Sales Taxes , Recreational Vehicle Tax , School Tax , State Income Tax , State Unemployment Tax (SUTA) , Telephone Federal Excise Tax , Telephone Federal Universal Service Fee Tax , Telephone Federal, State and Local Surcharge Tax , Telephone Minimum Usage Surcharge Tax , Telephone Recurring and Non-recurring Charges Tax , Telephone State and Local Tax , Telephone Usage Charge Tax , Utility Tax , Vehicle License Registration, Tax , Vehicle Sales Tax , Watercraft Registration Tax , Well Permit Tax , and Workers Compensation Tax.

Neither are there any more required store closing hours or days in most states – once upon a time stores were closed on Sunday. Then only Sunday morning. Politicians saw the light and finally laws were changed and stores could stay open seven days a week. More business hours means more sales tax and employee income tax collections.

Every one of these legislative legalizations have been shown to exact a heavy price on the lives and financial health of the poorest, weakest and most vulnerable among us and their families.

Problems in Front of us Now

Homelessness – the word evokes images of mental illness and drug usage. But the real facts are that, although 20 to 25 percent of homeless people are mentally ill, the vast majority are not and they are *homeless for financial reasons.* In 2017 there were 553,742 homeless people in America according to HUD statistics.[181, 182] One third of all homeless were families with children. A large number of homeless are people who are working – they just cannot afford a place to live. Approximately one third of U.S. homeless sleep in unsheltered places such as in back of buildings, out in the woods, in cardboard boxes, etc. For others there may be temporary nightly shelter provided. An accurate homeless count is available for every county and large city in the country.

Bankrupt Local Governments – Many of our large urban areas are struggling with underfunded pensions and debt service expenses. As populations age, people move away and retirements increase, more cities will face bankruptcy and the federal government will likely be needed to bail them out. So this becomes a problem for every one of us, whether we actually live in one of these cities or not.

Problems Lurking Around the Corner

Minimum Wage Law Destroys Economy – In April, 2015, Seattle, Washington passed an ordinance which will progressively raise the minimum wage to $15 per hour by 2021. According to a study by the National Bureau of Economic Research which has been called "very credible," one year later it has already killed over 6,300 jobs at single location firms and *the average low-wage employee's wage fell* by $125 per month. The report states, "Low-wage workers lost $3 from lost employment opportunities for every $1 they gain due to higher hourly wages."[183, 184]

The whole idea of minimum wage was originally designed for entry level jobs, even though there are some families who depend on it for their main income.

Seattle's law amounts to nothing more than an unfunded mandate on small businesses and actually shrinks the job pool as employers try to make ends meet. Employers have reacted by cutting payrolls, deferring new hiring and reducing hours or letting workers go. In the end it encourages more automation which creates even more unemployment. As one left-oriented national newspaper remarked, "Bad News for Liberals."

Meanwhile in Venezuela, strongman and Socialist Dictator Nicolás Maduro recently decreed a minimum wage increase of 3,500 percent to take place at once. Two weeks later 40 percent of Venezuelan stores closed, probably forever.[185] So much for Socialism. Their only hope now is either a coup by the military or for the Chinese to come in and buy half the country (and its vast oil reserves) and

---

[181] *The 2017 Annual Homeless Assessment Report (AHAR) to Congress*, The U.S. Department of Housing and Urban Development , December, 2017

[182] Several years ago the U.S. Department of Housing and Urban Development established a very sophisticated and accurate system for measuring homelessness throughout the U.S. which relies on local social services organizations using special database software and a yearly "Point-in-Time" actual street count.

[183] Jardim, Ekaterina, et. al., "Minimum Wage Increases, Wages, and Low-Wage Employment: Evidence from Seattle", *National Bureau of Economic Research*, June 2017, www.nber.org/papers/w23532

[184] The report estimates a loss of about 10,000 jobs when multiple-site firms are included, ibid. (p. 29)

[185] Delgado, Antonio Maria, "Maduro's huge salary hike deals fatal blow to 40 percent of Venezuelan stores", *Miami Herald*, September 14, 2018

force them to change their ways. (I believe the latter is more likely and news reports suggest it is already beginning.)

Subprime Automobile Loan Bubble – Ever since the subprime housing bubble that started the Great Recession of 2007-2008, in which banks loaned money to people who couldn't afford to repay, auto dealers have been doing likewise for several years and some economists are predicting another possible recession when these chickens come home (in their new cars) to roost.[186] The auto bubble is much smaller than the 2007 problem but there would be a significant ripple effect throughout parts supplier and associated manufacturing industries.

Why do so Many of the Wealthy Lean Left?

Many people question why so many wealthy people vote Democrat and hold extreme politically left of center views on financial topics like Socialism, world government and welfare.

In the 2016 presidential election, *every one of America's 493 wealthiest counties voted for Democrat candidate Hillary Clinton*. These were almost exclusively in cities and urban areas. The remaining 2,623 counties voted for Donald Trump. Most of those counties comprise small-town or suburban areas.

Much has been written about this seeming conundrum and there seem to be three leading reasons:

First is *self-reinforcing isolation*. Many of these wealthy individuals[187] get almost all of their information from left-leaning sources and from one another. Several years ago a *New York Times* study of reading habits of the political Left and the Right, based on Amazon's recommendation engine data confirmed part of this theory. It showed two separate isolated cohorts of books, one demonstrably liberal the other demonstratively conservative. People who read one liberal book read another, but never read a conservative book (as I remember it, there were only three exceptions) and the reverse was true for the conservative readers who clustered around one another's books but didn't read any on the Left.

Professed liberal Bernard Goldberg wrote as far back as 2002, in his best seller, *Bias*, that most news media is overwhelmingly left-biased.[188] Many of them, well-educated but so socially isolated that they are truly unaware that there could be another, opposite and equally valid point of view.

The second reason, similar to the first, is *lack of exposure*. Many of the comments from urban liberals during the 2016 election cycle show only a superficial understanding of the other half of this country – those folks who work on farms and in factories and small businesses.

There exists an almost hostile and haughty dismissal of working class people. Then-Senator Barack Obama at an April, 2008 fund raising speech to wealthy donors described these working people: "… they get bitter, they cling to guns or religion or antipathy to people who aren't like them …" This was his attempt to "explain working class culture to a much wealthier audience," according to *The Huffington Post*.[189]

The Stockholm Effect has not yet touched many of these urban liberals whose understanding of the other half of America consists of mostly twisted, late night TV caricatures and biased news reports.

The third reason is **demonstrable financial preference**. That is, many on the Left point to more favorable treatment of their financial business concerns by Democrat politicians.[190] There was a time when Big Business and Wall Street were 'owned' by the Republican Party. That has shifted significantly over the past decade.

---

[186] Gutscher, Cecile, "Subprime Auto Debt is Booming Even as Defaults Soar", *Bloomberg.com*, February 2, 2018

[187] Wealthy: generally defined as the top 4 percent, or those earning in excess of $200,000 per year.

[188] Goldberg, Bernard, *Bias, A CBS Insider Exposes How the Media Distort the News*, Regnery Publishing, Inc., Washington, DC, 2002

[189] Fowler, Mayhill (blog), "Obama: No Surprise that Hard-Pressed Pennsylvanians Turn Bitter", *The Huffington Post*, 11/17/2008

[190] Edsall, Thomas B., "How Did the Democrats Become Favorites of the Rich?", *The New York Times*, October 7, 2015

Our Wobbly Federal System

Our National Appetite is Out of Control

Big Government has been killing our economy. Our national debt is currently around 20 trillion dollars. That's $20,000,000,000,000.00. That amounts to $165,000.00 per federal taxpayer – you and me. Just to put this number in perspective, the nearest star in our universe is Alpha Centauri. At the speed of light it would take 4.3 years to travel that far. This star is 25 trillion miles away. If we could buy a mile for every dollar of debt, we'd be almost there by now!

If this debt isn't bad enough, figure that, as the Federal Reserve Bank decrees further raises in the national interest rate, the annual payments on this debt will soon rise accordingly increasing our annual federal budget.

No one expects the United States to have a balanced budget soon, if ever again. But if we did, and – it's a big IF – if by some miracle we could produce a surplus of 50 billion dollars every year, it would take the next 400 years to pay off this enormous national debt. But it won't happen – no self-respecting, liberal politician can be expected to sit idly by when there is 50 billion dollars in unallocated funds!

Every special interest has its hands in Uncle Sam's pocket. And almost every request for funding has its advocates who propose the end-of-the-Universe-as-we-know-it if their special request is not funded. Students want free tuition. Patients want to live forever with free medical care. Public employee unions want more retirement benefits. And the list goes on.

A new book by John Cogan, *The High Cost of Good Intentions*, presents a history of entitlements, many of which were begun with the best of intentions. But once they were established, Congress fattened them, year by year, to serve a wider and wider audience of voters until the costs skyrocketed. [191]

So, as long as it's so easy to spend other people's money, expect the national debt to continue to increase until something drastic happens. And maybe then it will wake us up.

That 'something' might happen very soon in the form of another very, very big financial crisis. Already the seeds have been planted. For example, the State of Illinois is on the verge of bankruptcy. At this writing, the state *owes* more than 14 *billion* dollars to its creditors. And its pension system is vastly underfunded.

And Illinois is not alone. Other states and municipalities have similar problems. California, by all measures, is in serious trouble with a total debt of *more than 170 billion dollars* and four of its cities are already bankrupt. Something like that could precipitate *the* trigger event.

The question we should be asking is, "If our national appetite doesn't decrease, how will we survive as a nation?"

We currently have 120 million federal taxpayers funding 164 million people who receive federal benefits. We borrow money from China and other countries so we can pay pensions to our own retirees. Thinking this can go on forever is a delusional fantasy.

Hit the 'Pause Button'. Forget for a moment about Iran and North Korea and China and Russia and ISIS and the rest of the hostile world out there. The real enemy is right here. Behind the hypothetical, proposed border wall.

In the famous words of Pogo, "Yes, son, we have met the enemy and he is us." [192]

---

[191] Cogan, John F., *The High Cost of Good Intentions – A History of U.S. Federal Entitlement Programs*, Stanford University Press, 2017.
[192] Words of *Pogo* by cartoonist Walt Kelly, *ibid.*

FREE MARKET FACTS AND SOCIALIST DREAMS

"Where you stand depends on where you sit," to strangle an old metaphor. If you sit in a country that has seen the economic rape and pillage of unbridled, unregulated capitalism your stand will likely be negative. One such person is the Jesuit priest, Jorge Mario Bergoglio from Argentina, who became Pope Francis. Argentina is an example of how the favored few, the 'grandees' have taken advantage of the people for decades. The Pope has condemned 'capitalism' in many forums, speeches and homilies. He feels that capitalism enslaves people. That is his personal opinion and is *not* a proclamation of the Catholic Church.

In fact, free market capitalism has been successful almost everywhere in raising the masses out of gut-wrenching poverty into a successful economic middle class.

Almost seventy years ago a lesser known priest, Father Joseph Beausoleil, a missionary in the mountains of Bolivia, used capitalism to bring hundreds of farmers and laborers out of poverty.[193]

His Andes Mountain parish was an agrarian society, stuck in subsistence poverty. Fr. Beausoleil started a small, primitive credit union where farmers could pool and share their limited monetary resources. This repository, owned by the people it served, then made short term loans to one another.

For example, if a farmer needed to purchase seed or sheep shears or start a handcraft business and needed more money than he possessed, he could borrow and later pay back his loan, plus interest, from his eventual profits. The credit union grew and hopes and crops of the poor farmers grew with it.

Initially there were eleven farmers. Years later that credit union grew and gave rise to a federation of 80 such credit unions in parishes, factories, communities and labor unions throughout the country of Bolivia.

Fr. Beausoleil had used simple capitalism to free people from the bonds of poverty.

Sensible economists believe that any modern form of free market capitalism needs some degree of regulation within the rule of law. But many are appalled at the current regulatory overreach of our U.S. government agencies.[194] President Trump and the U.S. Congress have recently begun removing some of the more onerous regulations.

It is capitalism that has grown the middle class around the world and made life livable for millions of third world citizens. History has clearly demonstrated that Socialism has only one destination and that is a demoralized work force, eventual massive poverty and tyranny and loss of freedom.

A functional, civilized society can develop ways to minimize out-of-control capitalism and greed, while maximizing its benefits.

Free Markets and the Illicit Drug Problem

On the down side, the free market can be very successful in areas we would rather avoid. The illegal-drug market is an example. The illicit drug business is an active and vibrant market system, composed of growers, cartels, a distribution system and political enablers, and lastly the customers, many of whom are so-called respectable U.S. citizens.

All attempts to control the flow of these drugs have failed for one simple reason. Our leaders have either been unaware of or ignored the powerful market forces at work. Politicians try to keep us focused on their great *solution du jour*: controlling supply (destroying crops) or stopping distribution

---

[193] "Priest Builds Credit Union Into Empire", *The Desert Sun (Palm Springs, California)*, Feb. 6, 1964, p.11 (This story was also reported in a feature article in *Reader's Digest*.)

[194] Friedman, Milton and Rose Friedman, *Free to Choose, op. cit.*

(intercepting shipments), disrupting and seizing payments (monitoring and controlling the flow of large sums of money) and/or pursuit and incarceration of big suppliers and cartel leaders.

None of these has any permanent effect, other than to become increasingly more expensive and encourage suppliers and dealers to become ever more creative and evasive. Drug runners have exhibited extreme creativity including the construction of mile-long trans-border tunnels, complete with railroad tracks and cars, and in the ocean, specially designed, difficult to detect drug smuggling submarines.

When we destroy *organized crime* we usually open the way for *disorganized crime*. Incapacitate one visible target and what remains morphs into a panoply of dozens of visible and invisible new targets, like the hydra of ancient mythology. Yet the market *demand* still exists and the illicit products will eventually find their way to the *customer* as long as that demand continues.[195]

America's national 'war on drugs' has been a tremendous failure. We have been fighting the wrong problem. (Elsewhere in this book, we discuss major reasons for this demand among children, adolescents and adults.)

Our failure to break this market has encouraged massive amounts of crime and absolute social disruption and chaos in parts of Mexico and Central and South American countries and is destroying normal life in many parts of the U.S. The great refugee caravans approaching our southern border attest to this intolerable chaos in parts of Central America.

Successful change to any market requires us first to understand and then address the customers and their needs. Anything else is a foolish waste of resources, time and human lives.

But that does not imply free drugs for addicts or legalizing and de-criminalizing them, as some have suggested. There are many other alternatives when a compassionate, caring, faith-oriented and united country puts its whole heart, soul and brains to the task.

Socialism – Success <u>and</u> Failure?

> *For every complex problem*
> *there is a simple solution*
> *and it is wrong.*
> Umberto Eco

For some folks the quick fix of Socialism seems a lot more reasonable than waiting for the free market to work. Or, as nescient detractors preach, waiting for a 'trickle down' effect. Socialism has produced economic disaster in every country that has tried it. But for some reason that doesn't stop politicians from endlessly repeating the mistake. Perhaps because socialist solutions sound simple and offer the quickest fix for serious problems.

The economist Friedrich Hayek, among others, has pointed out that Democracy eventually leads to socialism, which eventually leads to dictatorship and tyranny. His work explains how this happens.[196]

In its simplest form, command socialism answers the call when the democratic process cannot respond rapidly to crises. Demands of the people for strong leadership can mutate into authoritarian control and thence to tyranny. A careless and unwitting people can fail to forsee the change.

Free market capitalism is more complicated to understand and explain but leads to a higher standard of living for everyone. But few suffering people can wait for the growth of free markets to assuage their suffering, so they opt for the quick – and often irreversible – fix of Socialism.

---

[195] Recently some states have begun unintentionally increasing the criminal drug market by reducing criminal penalties for use and possession. One can expect bigger demand for illicit drugs in those states.
[196] Hayek, Friedrich, *The Road to Serfdom*, op. cit.

Venezuela is a vivid current example, where Socialism has metamorphosed into oppressive and now violent tyranny and basic human needs are no longer being met in the marketplace and the people are starving. The majority wants to rid itself of the Hugo Chavez legacy and Nicolas Maduro's iron-fisted tyranny but it is too late, short of a violent revolution or an army coup.

Closer to home, the island of Puerto Rico was ill prepared for an electrical power grid emergency following the September 2017 hurricane Maria. The socialist government had long ago taken control – ownership and careless management – of the island's electric generation and distribution system. A year after the hurricane, large areas of Puerto Rico – tens of thousands of customers – were still without electric power. *This is one of the fruits of socialism and its breeding partner, one-party corrupt government.*

The Fallacy of Redistributing Wealth

Free health insurance, free food, free college – on and on – the Socialist promises run deep and wide.

One goal of Socialism is to make sure everyone has enough of everyone else's money that no one will be poor. Advocates love to disparage the wealthy – the 'one percent,' or the (fill in the number) other percent.

No discussion of economics is complete without a discussion of the discoveries of the Italian sociologist and economist Vilfredo Pareto and what is called the 'Pareto Effect'.[197] He studied the distribution of wealth in different countries and at different times in history and found that there was a common shape to the distribution curve (graph.) He discovered there were always some very rich people and some very poor and there was a smooth distribution of increasing (or decreasing) wealth between the extremes.[198] Everywhere, in every country and every time in recorded history.

===

One oft-repeated misperception, "The one-percent control 99 percent of the world," is a provably false political-economic statement, although there is some truth that many very wealthy people exert tremendous power over society.

For example, in a pre-Trump era, 2015 *NY Times* article, Thomas Edsall quotes a Princeton & Northwestern study that nails it: "… policies popular with the middle class but not with the affluent rarely win enactment." [199] He goes on to quote, "Conversely, policies opposed by the middle class but backed by the affluent …" go on to be adopted. Understanding of this is one of the reasons that Hillary Clinton's "deplorables" got agitated and elected Donald Trump in 2016.

Disruptive Innovation

Now we have a 'Silicon Valley group of *nouveau riche* billionaires who feel more comfortable with the Democrat Party. Many of them are actively working to suppress and censor conservative news and conversation on their giant social media websites. Witness the alleged political manipulations of ultra-wealthy tech elites such as Jeff Bezos, Sergey Brin, Jack Dorsey, Bill Gates, Larry Page, Thomas Steyer, Mark Zuckerberg and the master manipulator of all times, George Soros.[200]

These very capable folks are determined to see a Democrat president and Congress. If they eventually get their wish, America will be dominated by the socialist agenda. History shows that Socialism – forced redistribution of wealth – ultimately only produces more poor people and a much

---

[197] Pareto's law is also (incorrectly) called the "80-20 rule." This misuse of his findings states that 80 percent of an effect is due to 20 percent of the cause.

[198] Pareto found a slight leveling in the middle of the graph in countries where there were established trade unions.

[199] Edsall, Thomas B., op.cit.

[200] Horowitz, David and Richard Poe, *The Shadow Party: How George Soros, Hillary Clinton and Sixties Radicals Seized Control of the Democratic Party*, Nelson Current, publisher, 200

poorer society. Yet some of these very intelligent, technologically-educated and history-ignorant elites will continue to try leading us down that road.

Free Money?

One of the more recent 'brilliant' ideas to spring from the cocktail parties of the filthy rich, guilty, tech-smart, would-be oligarchs is to give *free money* to everyone. This dazzling idea is to alleviate the expected suffering when their new artificially intelligent (AI) wonder robots start putting everyone out of work and we mere peons will need cash for food, climate-change raincoats and other essentials. A few of their more intellectual think tank supporters have proposed that free money will actually save on current welfare spending and *increase* personal motivation and make everyone better off and more responsible. (Seriously!?!)

Take a deep breath. The first time I heard the shrill panic call that computers were going to put everyone out of work was about 60 years ago. What actually happened is that new jobs were created and workers were retrained and entered new, previously unanticipated careers.

This scenario is more than likely to repeat; many jobs will be displaced, just as happens with every new technical revolution (where did all the thousands of telephone operators go?). But then a new wave of employment and job growth will follow (think about the thousands of wireless and fiber optic communication jobs that have been created). Challenged, the people of this country are tremendously creative.

The only thing that could decelerate or derail rapid adaptation is 'help' from the government. We should probably anticipate having to deal with the interventionist wisdom of a few elite leaders. They will be there to save the panicked labor unions.

No one knows in advance what skills will be required but the best preparation for training will be the ability to be open to new ideas and continue one's studies for the acquisition of new job skills. Unfortunately our current test-focused public educational system does little to prepare future workers for *learning to learn*.

With every major invention, the panic cries sound anew. But who knows? Chicken Little just may be right this time – we may all be out of work soon. But don't hold your breath.

And don't start counting your free money yet.

═══════════════

Just one question for these unquestionably bright tech geniuses: What robot is going to take care of all the lonely, the elderly, the sick and the orphaned? Will these people simply need more money? That's what many Progressives have been saying about our inner city poor for decades, "All they need is money; They need jobs and money. The reason they have problems is they have no money and no jobs." Meanwhile progressive social engineering and welfare projects continue to undermine the proper functioning of families and communities where the real need exists. Government money doesn't raise healthy, responsible children who get up and go to work on time every morning; stable families do that.

Notice that these same folks who can only see a money solution are the same who seldom dirty their own hands by helping to bind the festering sores of the poor or picking addicts out of the gutter or helping to raise a street child or visiting an abandoned prisoner or a confined mental patient. And Heaven forbid they would have ever served in the U.S. Military to defend and secure our country!

═══════════════

In January, 2017 Finland began a two year trial, giving free money to 2,000 randomly selected unemployed people. The Finns recently decided not to continue the program.[201] Preliminary analysis indicates the scheme will increase rather than decrease income inequality in their already high-welfare

---

[201] Goodman, Peter S., "Finland Has Second Thoughts About Giving Free Money to Jobless People", *The New York Times*, April 24, 2018

country. This and other variations of the free money idea, including 'negative income tax' and 'universal income credit' are being tried or proposed in San Francisco, Ontario Canada, Great Britain, Italy and the Netherlands. One stated objective is to simplify existing welfare systems.

Many objections center on the potential for demotivation. For example, the problem of young uneducated adults who would sit around and play more computer games all day.

Hasn't anybody noticed that the more handouts the government gives to the able poor the less they do for themselves? Encouraging idleness only increases poverty, and the worst poverty is poverty of the unchallenged mind. It's called *de-motivation*!

Oh, and everyone gets *two guesses where all this free money will come from.*

RENEWING OUR FINANCIAL PRACTICES

A Vision for Economic Renewal

Personal and Family Economics

Money doesn't create peace but financial instability invites the Devil. A family with financial stability is more likely to be a family at peace. Statistics show that mother and father are more likely to stay together. Separation and divorce does irreparable damage to children and creates poverty – both financial and poverty of the spirit.

Wherever possible our personal priorities and community energies and our government policies should encourage one parent to stay home and raise the young children.

Every family should have a savings plan, however small, and stick to it. Consider using the services of a *certified* financial planner.

Too many kids spend their summers "hanging out" on the streets or in the local mall. It would do a world of good for them to get summer jobs but with current minimum wage laws, few businesses can afford to hire them because of their inexperience. We need to change these employment laws to allow teenagers to work as apprentices, paid below minimum wage, as was the case just a few decades ago. This will get kids off the street in the summer and begin to teach them responsibility and the dignity of work. (This author got his first full-time job – way below 'minimum wage' – at the age of 16 and learned a trade. That would be almost impossible today because of union-sponsored and forced minimum wage laws.)

School tax relief is essential for parents who send their children to private or church or parochial schools. Private schools add value to the nation in many ways and it is unfair for parents to have to pay twice to educate their children.

Finally, if you are struggling with debt, consider renegotiating the terms of your debt, whether it's with a bank or credit card company. Sometimes lower interest rates and different ways of paying off loan principal amounts can be negotiated to everyone's benefit. Note holders want to get their money back and will often bend over backwards to prevent a default. And consider renegotiating the rates your cellular service provider charges. Don't wonder. Ask.

National Economics

It may be time to start to mind our own business and stop with the wars. And cut back on duplicate government programs to reduce taxes. Let's oust the Keynesian economic philosophers,[202] once and for all – and stop printing money and stop borrowing from our foreign adversaries to pay our bills.

In every country that has tried it, capitalism has created the largest and strongest middle class prosperity of any economic system. Of the three competing viewpoints, Hayek (capitalism and free markets), Keynes (government control and bailouts) and Marx (Communism and total government ownership), Hayek's philosophy has created the best results. (See comments and footnotes on pages 170 and 102.) When government gets out of the way – just a little – the economy soars – as has happened in the past few decades in China and India.

We need to change U.S. Tax policy in many areas including the inheritance tax – the so-called 'death tax' – that penalizes asset-rich but cash-poor family businesses when the father or owner dies, thus preventing inheritance and continuance of the business by the children. People who have worked all their lives to support their families cannot leave these businesses to their rightful heirs – they often must be sold to pay the inheritance taxes. Recent increases in the taxable threshold are a good start, but more change is needed.

Wealthy corporate executives seem to be inordinately involved in lobbying Congress for favorable laws and regulations. Simpler and more stable corporate tax laws could help to de-motivate corporate interference in politics. There have been proposals in the past to eliminate *all* corporate taxes and tax only shareholder income and dividends. That Congress would agree to this is likely fantasy, but serious economists have long proposed it.

A consumption tax – value-added tax – would throw the burden of running the Republic on those who have the money to make purchases. A loaf of bread is one thing but a 100-foot yacht is quite another and should pay a consumption tax. Many industrialized countries successfully use this value-added (or consumption) tax instead of an income tax.

Where welfare assistance is needed and provided, government policy seems to do everything possible to discourage marriage. Benefits in food stamps, public housing assistance, and health care (ACA "Obamacare") can be abruptly reduced or totally cut when low income people marry. The government incentive is then to discourage marriage. For the sake of stronger families and their children we need to change this.

Resist at all costs the Left's new push to create a guaranteed income for all – The 'Universal Basic Income' (UBI) for all Americans.[203] The supposed problem – we are all going to be put out of work by robots and artificial intelligence. The solution is worse than their cure. Paying people for not working removes the incentive to create and the very dignity of work itself. More baloney and apple pie from our 'betters'. The problem these elites are trying to solve will be solved by a free citizenry, left to its historic creativity and unfettered by an elite-run federal government.

Finally, the proposed Constitutional Convention is seeking to pass a Balanced Budget amendment to the Constitution (See Convention of States Project, on page 41).

---

[202] Keynesian Economics – A theory developed by John Maynard Keynes after the Great Depression. Keynesian economists generally advocate a government role during periods of recession and inflation, through central bank intervention, as was applied to our great national recession that started in 2007. Monetary rates set by the Federal Reserve Bank went close to zero. Personal savings investments then essentially stopped returning any interest growth, requiring retirees to live off invested principal rather than interest, unless they had invested their money in growth stocks and other circumventions.

[203] For the other side of this story, see a current article, "As Poverty Surges in Italy, Populists Propose a 'Citizens' Income', by John Follain, *Bloomberg Businessweek*, August 30, 2017

Economics and Finance Resources for Change

Rather than trying to 're-invent the wheel', there are many existing, already tried solutions to many financial problems. Here are a few for your consideration.[204]

Personal Finances

➢ **Financial planning** can be complex. Consider looking for a financial adviser or financial planner (licensed and/or certified) to help plan for your family's future. A good planner will ask about the kind of lifestyle you want, your fears and concerns for the future, the important people you want to provide for (e.g., children's education), your special interests and your vision for a happy and healthy retirement

➢ **Personal Finance Lessons** – The free online training website, Khan Academy, has a series of personal finance lessons for adults and recent college graduates. *www.khanacademy.org* (search under the topic, "College, careers and more")

➢ **Money management** – Many not-for-profit organizations, such as *Focus on the Family* help people whose spending has gotten out of control. Contact one of these organizations if you need help budgeting. *www.focusonthefamily.com* (Beware of lesser-known organizations that may charge you excessive fees.)

➢ **Medical expenses** – *Liberty Health Share* is one of several ACA-exempt Christian health expense-sharing organizations – *www.libertyhealthshare.org*

➢ **Christian Finance** – A financial website by a blogger, Bob Lotich, contains a lot of useful ideas, planning tools and references to other financial websites. One quote from the author, "Financial success is a lot more about minimizing stupid decisions than making smart ones." Look for, "The Top 20 Christian Financial websites," at: *christianpf.com*

➢ **(See also,** related suggestions in previous chapters.)

National and State Finances

➢ **Truth in Finance** – We need to start accounting for federal income and expenditures like a business. Only small businesses use *cash accounting* methods but our federal government – the largest 'business' around – uses this primitive method that records cash when it is *received* and expenses when they are *paid*. The cash accounting method makes it much easier for politicians to play tricky, deceptive political finance 'games'.

    All serious businesses use the *accrual accounting* method which measures income and expenditures *when they are committed*. Moving our federal government to the accrual method would give the people a much more accurate picture of proposed and actual expenditures and would be one significant step toward more responsible budgeting and expenditure.

➢ **Deficit Budgets** – I haven't got a clue what to do about a 20 trillion dollar national debt and our 4 trillion dollar annual [1/2 trillion dollar deficit] budget, other than to make some real changes in our national appetite and spending spree: Throw out the bums who are passing all these deficit budgets and bring a new set of bums? Repeat after me, "*Term Limits*."

---

[204] These are suggestions only. Use them at your own risk. Never make important personal financial decisions without professional advice.

7 – Effective Dialogue

THE GOAL

Civility, Respect and Progress

Effective dialogue has broken down in our society, especially in our politics, as each side seeks to demonize the other. Much energy is wasted, opponents become increasingly polarized and little good gets accomplished.

Effective dialogue sometimes proceeds under duress. For example, in the *Book of Luke*, Jesus proposes that an outnumbered king might wisely avoid battle by negotiating with the enemy:

> *Or what king, when he sets out to meet another king in battle, will not first sit down and consider whether he is strong enough with ten thousand men to encounter the one coming against him with twenty thousand? Or else, while the other is still far away, he sends a delegation and asks for terms of peace.*
> *Luke 14:31-32, (NASB)*

We can assume such a decision is colored by an element of fear – a fear of losing. The weaker king may be interested in saving his and his subjects' lives and as much else as possible. The opposing enemy probably is interested in avoiding outright war and losing warriors, yet gaining as many spoils of war as possible. Both are interested in avoiding mutual destruction. Jesus' comment suggests they consider discussing their mutual interests.

Mutual Interests

Roger Fisher and William Ury in their best-seller book, *Getting to Yes, Negotiating Agreement Without Giving In* popularized the idea of dialoguing about *mutual interests* rather than hard and fast – and often, polarizing – *positions* where one's success often depends on the other's failure. They give the example of two sisters who, trapped in a snowed-in cabin, fought over possession of the last remaining orange. After much angry argument they finally compromised by cutting the orange in half.

But one sister was hoping to make orange juice while the other sister was about to bake a cake and wanted only the rind to flavor it. Each sister might have been able to use the whole orange, had they bothered to determine each other's' *interests* instead of their opposing *positions*.

Working Together

In this chapter, we discuss dialogue under different forms of motivation, from the most altruistic, where each party is deeply concerned about the other – to the dystopic environment of mutual fear, where one party seeks to totally crush the other.

The opposite of love is not hatred but fear. Somewhere in the middle we can hope for better results through mutual civility and respect.

In the public square and especially in our government, we need to challenge some of our elected officials to act more like civilized adults.

Working Together
A Hierarchy Of Behaviors And Their Motivations
○ **Godly Love** – Voluntary Altruism
○ **Brotherly Love** -- Bonding
○ **Respect** – Common Humanity
○ **Civility** – Common Interest
○ **Submission** – Need to Yield Power
○ **Fear** – Brutal Domination

THE BEST IS RARELY SEEN

Godly Love – Voluntary Altruism

Agape, or Godly Love – At the top of the list are those people whose work is offered freely because of an overwhelming common philosophy which transcends self-interest.

This level of loving cooperation is called by the ancient Greek word *agape*. A definitive description of *agape* love is given in the Bible:

> *Love is patient, love is kind and is not jealous; love does not brag and is not arrogant, does not act unbecomingly; it does not seek its own, is not provoked, does not take into account a wrong suffered, does not rejoice in unrighteousness, but rejoices with the truth; bears all things, believes all things, hopes all things, endures all things.*   *1 Corinthians 13:4-7, (NASB)*

Saint Mother Teresa comes to mind, a person who dedicated her entire life to helping the destitute poor and outcast of India. Godly love transcends tribalism and selfishness and is rarely witnessed on this planet.

Brotherly Love – Bonding

Brotherly Love – Where people have bonded, through familial ties or while working toward an important, even dangerous common goal. We see this especially in Police, Firemen, and war veterans: Army, Marines, Navy, Air Force and Special Forces, among many others. Battles against a common enemy tend to create strong bonds among survivors. Many of these, though unrelated, call themselves and act like brothers.

One example comes to mind – the August 1958 Jehovah's Witness International Assembly in Yankee Stadium in New York City was attended by more than 123,000 people from all over the world. During the assembly talks, there was absolute, respectful listening and silence. When the convention was over the attendees, without leadership direction, cleaned up everything and the entire stadium was left spotless. Each person saw the need to do their share without being asked. I have spoken with people who were there and they were amazed at how such a large number of people worked together so successfully and smoothly like one large, peaceful family.

ATTAINING THE POSSIBLE

Respect – Common Humanity

Respect happens when we see our common humanity in other people, despite our differences. The deference with which we treat one another is called 'respect'. Too often today we are forced to deal with or witness tremendous disrespect. Disagreement is no excuse for disrespect.

In preparing this book I have asked many friends, acquaintances and strangers, what is missing, what must we be doing to bring this Nation back together again? A common answer: we need to restore respect back into our personal and national dealings and discourse. Even though we may strongly disagree with our leaders, even our President, respect is essential to continued productive dialogue. We seem to have forgotten that you don't have to love or even like someone to treat them with civility and respect.

Disrespect

Disrespect has become a way of life for many adults and children alike. That's how it used to be in more *uncivilized* and barbaric times, hundreds of years ago, when hostile families, clans and nations set themselves above their neighbors. Then, world wars, famines and mass tragedies – common challenges – brought survivors closer, and for the most part – we began to act in more civilized ways – both in our small groups and as a nation.

But now we have lost much of this mutual respect. Inter-group hostility is everywhere. Our language has a new word: '*dis*' which has replaced '*disrespect*,' The longer word apparently takes too much effort to pronounce.

So we see individuals and groups '*dissing*' each other. Blacks *dis* whites; conservatives *dis* progressives; Fox News *disses* CNN; The New York Post *disses* the Daily News, and Donald Trump *disses* nearly everybody.

Disrespect is not new – it is just more common today. In 1959 a popular folk group, *The Kingston Trio* had a satirical, tongue-in-cheek hit song, "They're Rioting in Africa" that expressed the growing sentiments and fears which came on us full force during the Cold War and in the societal breakdown that began in the 1960s. Some of the words:

> *... The whole world is festering with unhappy souls*
> *The French hate the Germans, the Germans hate the Poles*
> *Italians hate Yugoslavs, South Africans hate the Dutch*
> *And I don't like anybody very much!* [205] *...*

Stockholm Effect and the 'Deplorables'

A casual study of history and human psychology confirms that people tend to treat members of their 'own kind' better than 'outsiders'. And evidence suggests that when we spend time working with others to solve a common problem we bond more closely.

The 'Stockholm Effect' was named after a hostage-taking situation in Sweden where initially the hostages lives were in grave jeopardy. But the hostage-takers spent days with the hostages and got to know them and began to regard them more as human beings than 'objects. And eventually they willingly gave up their hostages and surrendered to the authorities.

Maybe if we spent more time getting to know and understand those 'deplorables' that presidential candidate Hillary Clinton once mentioned, we might live more peaceful lives.

Restoring Respect

Reversing the trend is going to require a fresh outlook. First, we need to convince ourselves there are common ideals we must work for or else we will die as a country. Much of this book is devoted to those topics.

As hard as it is, we have to work with opposing individuals and groups to convince them of the need for civility and respect. In truth, there will be some who will never be convinced.

---

[205] A commentary on our changing, increasingly more complex society – I wanted to include more of the lyrics and did my 'due diligence' of trying to get publication permission but was stymied when I got the run-around for several days. It turns out that TWO different companies own the publication rights to this song and the complication wasn't worth the bother. However, you can find the entire lyrics in several places on the Internet where they are *legally published without permission*. (See "How Technology Has Been Killing Art, Music and Video" in Chapter 1.)

Teaching Respect

Young Children – The very young need to be trained at home by their parents. And their parents need to be reinforced (and not sabotaged) by those who create the rest of their children's environment. Don't send your kids to a day care environment that tolerates any kind of disrespect.

Totally kill the TV until your children are at least five or ten years old – They need to wait for Sesame Street. And they will not learn respect by watching ball players yelling at sports officials. The rest of us waited and we grew up more or less OK.

Few parents can monitor 24/7/365 what their children see on TV. You wouldn't leave attractive yet poison food lying around for their stomachs. Why give them access to rotten material that permanently warps the mind and the soul?

One family I know had no TV available for the children until they were each almost eight years old. Instead they had an 'un-cabled' TV with a set of parent-selected videotapes that the children could watch at selected times. The three children loved the system and they all grew up to be responsible adults.

To the best extent you can, instruct your children. Show them the duties, dangers and blessings of family and community life and give them instructions on how to perform these duties, avoid the dangers and secure its blessings. Show them by daily example and slowly let them develop on the path you set for them until that path becomes fixed and habitual.

> **Do TV Commercials Affect Young Children?**
>
> "Currently there is an ad for a travel company featuring a teacher who is ready for vacation. The kids in the classroom are tearing up the place. One kid is in the fish tank. Others are beating the furniture with bats and sticks. I have seen a commercial in which two girls are kicking in the sides of an air conditioner because it broke down. There is a commercial in which two young boys who are being baby-sat by their uncle destroy the house. They jump on all the furniture, tear up feather pillows. Grandma calls and asks, 'Are we having fun yet?'"
>
> *From a reader, writing to advice columnist Annie Lane, Published June 28, 2017.*
>
> (Reproduced by permission of Annie Lane and Creators Syndicate, Inc.)

TV, the Internet and video games contain the most family-hostile material imaginable. Keep these from your children *at all costs*. Baby sitters – no TV around the children. Relatives – Grandma, Aunt Tillie, etc. – no TV around the kids. No Christmas or Hanukkah video game gifts for them. None. Take control of these little plastic minds while you can and before the job becomes much, much more difficult.

Pre-Teens and Teenagers – It's much harder to teach respect if it is missing at these ages. But it is possible. One middle school teacher recently told me of an incorrigible kid who was unusually disrespectful to her. She tried by showing total respect to him but nothing worked. Finally she took him aside and told him what was expected of him and announced that from now on, she was going to talk to him the same way he talked to her. This went on for a time and soon, he came to her crying. He changed after he saw and felt what he was doing to her. This is probably a one-off example, but it worked for him.

Respect needs to be taught at school as well as at home. Not just insistence for respectful behavior, but the reasons and consequences. Of course in today's environment, many teachers are reluctant to try anything that might get them in trouble. And many schools have so many incorrigible kids the job is virtually impossible for the average teacher.

That's where the un-average teacher comes in. There is a lot of positive anecdotal evidence about success using male teachers for older grades. And male and female teachers with military backgrounds fare very well with disruptive kids. But teaching real respect is still a next – and very difficult – step.

There are highly effective programs that teach teenagers respect. And there are private organizations, which work to change behaviors, such as Teen Challenge,[206] and so-called boot camps. These are tough ways and are reserved for the lost youth. Then there is the U.S. Army. I've met and worked with many formerly disrespectful 'tough guys' who have come out of military service with advanced respect abilities.

Starting when I was about 60 years old I started to notice a number of teenage store clerks who would act as if I wasn't even there as I checked out. They wouldn't greet me, they wouldn't talk with me, and if I asked them a question, all I got was a grunt or a very distant answer as if I didn't really exist. These are kids who have never learned to deal with older adults.

Then there are the teenage clerks who are just the opposite. They and I may have little in common but they make eye contact, and are civil and polite. We need to support and encourage these young people and the parents who raised them!

> You are a child of God and worthy of **respect** and **love**.

Adults – If an adult is disrespectful there is little we can do, other than to be as respectful as possible and hope they will follow. As strange as it may seem, research shows that self-confident people are less likely to be disrespectful. I often feel a bit sorry for those disrespectful ones who may be masquerading their inner feelings.

But a *caveat* – try to be as respectful as possible in the face of 'in-your-face' disrespect, but don't appear weak. That is an invitation to let them misunderstand your civility and respect. They will learn nothing and regard you as an ineffective 'wimp'.

Unfortunately, for many adults – including some in our government who call themselves adults and yet act like petulant children – there is little hope. But I have witnessed changes, even in adults, where all others have given up. Sometimes a change of scenery is all that's needed: A term in the Armed Forces (not applicable beyond about 35 years of age), and as mentioned above, private boot camps. Prison and other forms of incarceration can change people also.

Sad that we need to even think this way. Let us hope and pray that our young people will grow up more respectful than some of our current crop of disruptive and combative adults.

Civility – Common Interests

If we can't rise to respect, let's try for civility. Civility is the way people treat one another when they want to work together for the common good.

Civility breaks down when what's good for one is absolutely no good for another and the attitude devolves to, "You don't have a ghost of a chance to convince me to give up anything to get you to work with me. What's mine is mine and you are a nincompoop without a clue."

Being civil doesn't mean we're going to sing *Kumbaya* together and it doesn't mean we like or even trust the other person. It means we are going to try to keep the heat down and listen to one another and postpone judgment as long as we can to hear and try to understand the other side. And maybe trust can slowly develop.

Civility is the bare-bones minimum way we need to treat one another. This is the opposite of the aggressive, combative way that's become too much of our national culture and that we are flooded with on too many TV shows – and in the nightly TV news reports.

---

[206] *www.teenchallengeusa.com/about*

(How one town's government was successfully encouraged to become more civil is described in *Chapter* 5 – Governance and Politics, on page 90.)

The struggle for civility is often a challenge to avoid something worse.

═══════════

PAINFUL ALTERNATIVES

Submission – Yielding to Power

At the extreme end of the behavioral hierarchy are submission and fear. Submission may be voluntary or involuntary, such as one sees in many types of employment. Any of us who have ever held a job knows that the boss is the authority and we need to yield some of our time and effort in exchange for pay and benefits. Some bosses are easier than others.

Douglas McGregor described the 'Theory Y' organization where employees are internally self-motivated – morale and productivity tend to be high.[207] He contrasted that with the 'Theory X environment' where work gets done only under management watchfulness, pressure and duress. In a Theory X environment morale is usually much lower.

(In the McGregor context, Islam is a Theory X religion, especially for women. The word 'Islam' in Arabic means 'submission'. A follower is motivated by external force or the threat of it. Converts can be won by the sword and the threat of death.)[208]

═══════════

Fear – Brutal Domination

Used in warfare, fear can get an enemy to react to the advantage of the oppressor. It is frequently employed by tyrants and sometimes needed in prisons and other places where violence rules and few of us want to tread.

> *Be polite, be professional, but have*
> *a plan to kill everybody you meet.*
> *Retired Marine General James (Mad Dog)*
> *Mattis, Former U.S. Secretary of Defense*

Thankfully General Mattis' admonition applied only to the Marines he led into battle, but he is highly respected, both by our own troops and – in a much different way – by our enemies.

When General Mattis was asked, "What keeps you awake at night?" He replied, "Nothing. I keep other people awake at night."

Those terrorists out there are trying to motivate us. Why shouldn't we sleep-deprive them?

═══════════

---

[207] Management 101 – the idea of Theory "X" and Theory "Y" was developed by social psychologist McGregor and is a part of every basic management training program.

[208] Contrast that with what Jesus taught. Jesus might be called a Theory Y teacher. A devout follower is motivated from within and needs no sword hanging over his head, nor does s/he need to be monitored and punished by 'religious police'.

HELP FOR BETTER RESULTS

Opening the Door to Productive Dialogue

There was a time during the Cold War that we began cultural exchanges between The USA and the Soviet Union. We sent performance artists like Louis Armstrong. The Russian people absolutely fell in love with his music when he performed a jazzed-up version of their beautiful folk song, "Moscow Nights."[209] Slowly there was a thaw between our two nations and the beginning of productive diplomacy. Some of us remember that the seeds of diplomatic relations were planted between China and the U.S. only after table tennis (ping pong) matches between the two countries began. President Nixon and Secretary of State Kissinger then worked with China to bring them into the society of world nations.[210] All of these things served one purpose – first to get to know one another and build trust and then to enter into productive dialogue on important mutual issues.

Even so, some neighbors don't want to get to know us. Some extremist Hindu and Muslim groups and nations don't want us spreading our religious or cultural ideas much less our perverted 'Hollywood' culture. Some of them have already judged us and will have no more to do with us. Others have decided to reject us *a priori*, without a first word.

We have a lot of 'those others' right here in our own country. Dialogue needs to begin with simple, unemotional things until we get to know one another.

"Five Meetings"

An interesting, somewhat related opinion article by Andy Kessler in *The Wall Street Journal* suggests a process for bringing two sides together in agreement in exactly five meetings. He cautions that fewer than five can result in failure and more than five means you have already failed. The first, a short meeting he calls "the sniff." Then, "the story," then, "the data," followed by, "the ask," and finally, "the close." Supported only by anecdotal opinion it still makes interesting reading and gives one pause to think about the need for a process for beginning an effective dialogue.[211]

Professional Help

There are a number of ways to bring groups together to productively dialogue with civility and respect. Sometimes professional help is required and many such organizations are at the ready. One such organization is *Essential Partners.*

Essential Partners is a non-profit organization in the Boston area that seeks to enable proponents to get to better understand one another. They provide workshops for individuals and client services which encourage dialogue without taking sides, so opposite viewpoints can be heard and discussed calmly.[212]

The claim their methods were designed using the best practices from family therapy, neuroscience and mediation to help people feel understood and to better understand one another.

---

[209] Подмосковные вечера (Podmoskovnia Vechera) – On YouTube, the original folk melody: *www.youtube.com/watch?v=KairmsARpyo*

[210] After these ping pong matches got wide publicity, President Richard Nixon and Secretary of State Henry Kissinger were able to start diplomatic relations. China had been an isolated world community. A good summary article can be found at *www.history.com/news/ping-pong-diplomacy.*

[211] Kessler, Andy, "Anything Good Takes Exactly Five Meetings", *The Wall Street Journal*, November 18, 2018, *www.wsj.com/articles/anything-good-takes-exactly-five-meetings-1542578334*

[212] This organization is one of several which offer similar help and is noted here as an example and not intended as an endorsement.

They reportedly have clients in 38 US States and 15 foreign countries where they work on problems as diverse as environmental policy, classroom disruption, racial divides and inter-religious issues.

An interesting pamphlet/booklet on their website, *Reaching Across the Divide*, focuses on bringing people into more respectful political dialogue. This 12 page booklet illustrates many of their techniques which are applicable to other areas of difficult human interaction.

Essential Partners website: *whatisessential.org*.

━━━━━━━━━━━━━━━━━━━━

N.B. – Any Internet addresses, QR codes and telephone numbers in this book are offered as a resource. They are not intended in any way to be or to imply an endorsement, nor does the author vouch for the content of these sites, numbers or references.

8 – America's ReAwakening

America's reawakening will have its most profound effect on the children and young adults of the next generation. Consider the positive effect on our common culture as we start to re-think and repair some of these ways we live and work:

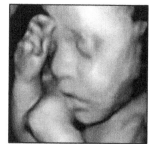

Tsiaras TED Talk

Pre-born Children

- Compassion should be our first reaction for the woman who seeks an abortion. What are her motivations? Each of the several reasons can be addressed separately and where possible to offer help and to logically and rationally reduce the incentives and need for abortion (see footnote).[213]

- Make it illegal to force religious organizations to handle adoptions for situations contrary to their religious beliefs. Several highly rated Catholic organizations that previously handled large numbers of adoptions have been forced to close because of this.

- If a future session of the Supreme Court should repeal Roe vs. Wade that could be the worst possible thing for the pro-life agenda, depending on the decision. Each of the individual 50 states would then be free to pass their own pro-abortion laws. Then, instead of fighting one federal court decision the battle would be against differing laws and rulings from many states.

  The only hope for true repeal is to have the Supreme Court recognize that pre-born children are *persons*. The U.S. Constitution would then guarantee them *life* and make it impossible for states to permit (or regulate) abortion. Stay tuned.

  The sidebar describes a vivid TED[214] Talk video that should leave no doubt that an unborn 'fetus' is a very much alive hu-

---

The Miracle of Life

Only within the past two decades have we been able to see 3-D pictures of the developing fetus inside a mother's body.

An amazing video in the TED series on YouTube describes the development of the human child from conception to birth. Mathematician Alexander Tsiaras presents this short very interesting animated micro and macro MRI.

A single cell can divide into two, then into four, then eight and so forth and each division becomes more and more specialized. As Tsiaras explains, at one point new cells are being created at more than a million per second.

He explains that there are over 60,000 miles of blood vessels and capillaries in the child at birth.

Twice in the presentation he refers to the process as the result of some kind of divinity. And confesses that even though he is a mathematician, there is no way we can understand the process it is so marvelously complex.

(Scan the QR code to see the video.)

---

[213] Biggs, M Antonia, et.al, "Understanding why women seek abortions in the US", *National Institutes of Health*, July 5, 2013, *www.ncbi.nlm.nih.gov/pmc/articles/PMC3729671*

[214] TED is owned by a private nonprofit foundation whose goal is to foster the spread of great ideas, usually in the form of short, powerful talks of 18 minutes or less. It began in 1984 as a conference where Technology, Entertainment and Design converged, and today covers almost all topics, from science to business to global issues, in more than 100 languages.

man being.[215] (See *Appendix J. Using QR Codes in This Book*, on page 177 for information on scanning QR codes.)

Infants & Small Children

- Research shows that children who spend their first three years with their mothers are less inclined later to suffer mental illness and depression including ADHD and they are significantly better prepared to handle the problems of life.[216]
- A universal family leave program is needed to enable working mothers to return to their employers after several months of being with their newborns. State and/or Federal government law should support this. (See *Paid Family Leave*, page 40.)

Developing Children

- Research shows that young children who are given and taught to handle age-appropriate responsibilities grow to be more responsible adults. Parents take note.
- Too many parents kowtow to the whims of their children, so that the children effectively run the household. Too many of these children grow up to be poor partners in marriage and business and unprepared, self-centered citizens. Children don't have a "right to be entertained" and their place should be second to parents and family until they can independently support themselves.
- Too much of our religious education – Protestant and Catholic – indoctrinates the mind rather than the heart. Years later we see children-become-adults without the strength and courage that comes through faith. Too much cultural tradition and not enough basic Christianity.
- Public schools generally do a poor job in preparing children for adult life. Education is much more than being able to recall endless streams of facts. Many children never develop their individual God-given talents in these test-preparation factories. As long as public schools exist, children should be kept out of them until grade 8. New laws should make universal school choice possible, permissible and affordable for parents.
- Where possible, eliminate public schools, as has been done with amazingly positive results in New Orleans, Louisiana.[217] Charter schools, private and parochial schools and home schooling should become standard for elementary education in America.
- Likewise, eliminate the absurdity of teachers' tenure for pre-college public schools and substitute individual contracts. (A recent Supreme Court decision will now encourage public schools to lean in this direction.)

Adolescents and Emerging Adults

- Several decades ago labor unions successfully lobbied Congress to require employers to pay minimum wage to kids even when they have no applicable experience. Consequently, hardly anyone hires them for summer jobs anymore, so they spend their time being bored, creating mischief, roaming around shopping malls, getting zero work experience, and unable to help with family expenses. It's time to change the law to make it legal to hire high school kids for summer, holiday and part time work at below minimum wage. Why not let employees – the kids and their parents – decide whether or not it is a fair wage, rather than big unions and government?

---

[215] *https://www.ted.com/talks/alexander_tsiaras_conception_to_birth_visualized*
[216] Komisar, Erica, *op. cit.*
[217] Leonhardt, David, "How New Orleans is Helping its Students Succeed", *The New York Times*, July 15, 2018.

- Similar to the above, few employers can train apprentices without paying government- or union-approved wages. As a result there is a shortage of workers in certain trades and only the fortunate few with union connections can normally get into those trades.
- The classical American liberal arts college idea has become a complete and expensive failure in its mission to provide a true liberal education on many campuses. We need a new concept of college education if we are to train a generation of responsible, competent citizens. Changes are coming and we need to be aware and support those universities and colleges that adopt them.[218]

Families

- Children of single parents, especially in the poor and black communities have a paucity of caring adult male role models which have been proven to be essential for development of young adults. There are already many volunteers and organizations that help, such as Big Brothers Big Sisters of America. What is needed is more private and government support to make it easier for competent adults to mentor young men.
- Every child has a special and unique ability or talent that needs to be developed. The happiest people on the planet are often those who have been able to discover and develop their talents and were given the opportunity to apply them to their lives and communities. Too much of our public educational system is like a factory which tries to turn out uninspired identical parts. Children get bored, lose interest in their own education and personal development and seek entertainment, while they satiate their senses at the expense of their minds and souls. Look no farther than the country of Finland to see a very different and successful approach to education, a few parts of which we might adopt. Finnish students are number one in the world in test scores.
- Too much television and screen time (smartphones, tablets and computers) is provably warping the hearts and minds of our children. Parents: consider 'cutting the cable'. Pay attention to what your children are doing with their toxic new gaming and social media toys and take control. Their souls depend on you.
- The news media's *BREAKING NEWS!!!* brouhaha carries endless, fearsome stories of child abductions and other atrocities, so we are given to believe that letting a child outside without at least one helicopter overhead is tantamount to abandonment and child abuse. There are certainly instances of child abuse and abductions but nowhere near what the screaming 24/7/365 national news media loudly proclaim. Children need to be made to put away their electronic toys and get out of the house once in a while to breathe fresh air and grow in their own age-appropriate activities. Parents have become too over-protective. Many of our children are becoming socially stunted and unable to fend for themselves. They drift off to college and become sensitive, easily upset 'snowflakes' unable to cope with conflict or interpersonal reality.
- Spare time is in short supply. All of the things that we need to do to reawaken America's spirit may sound good but busy people are often *too* busy to have the time. Individuals and families should consider a new habit of setting aside a few unscheduled hours every week from normal work and related interruptions for family and community. As a society we need to encourage *real* spare time for everyone. (God gave us 14 percent of our week to rest, but how many of us actually observe and practice Sabbath rest?)

---

[218] Treadgold, Warren, The University We Need, Reforming American Higher Education, Encounter Press, 2018

Government

- Begin the process of amending the U.S. Constitution to give parents first rights in the upbringing and education of their children. This would force the government to demonstrate, by appropriate evidence, that it has a compelling interest where it may attempt to intervene in family matters. (See *Convention of States ProjectConvention of States Project*, page 41.)
- Lifetime career politicians of both parties hold the government hostage to their own selfish, personal ambitions. It is no surprise then that the U.S. Congress has a public approval rating of around 16 percent. The longer these ossified politicians stay in office the more powerful they become and the less they work for the common good of the people and the country. We must press hard for congressional term limits.
- Buy them out? How about we offer free money (and everything else) – golden parachutes – to politicians who agree to vote for term limits and then retire. At first glance this may seem too expensive. But look what these career politicians have done to raise our national debt to astronomical levels. Buying them out might prove to be a real bargain. Those who refuse the monetary offer would reveal themselves as power hungry and they could be the hardest to get out of the government.
- Even though Congress has an approval rating lower than Pepé Le Pew the skunk, it is amazing that 90 percent of politicians who run for re-election still get reelected each year. One reason? Voters who complain to pollsters are too darn lazy to actually get out and vote and so a small, active, unrepresentative minority re-elects them time and again. Solution? Get off our duffs, organize, and encourage one another to vote!
- There are a great many selfless, competent people in America whose service could improve our government but they reject the option of political office because of the overwhelming personal cost. Money is the least of it. Almost every visible politician has to deal with death threats, nasty media attacks based on rumors, and the public humiliation of black-sheep family members or decades old juvenile sins.

  But the worst problems are having one's family and children 'disassembled' by the irresponsible tabloid media in the most vicious ways, and having to deal with radical groups attacking their homes, loved ones and children. Most officials I have spoken with say they seldom publicize these threats because doing so only encourages mentally unstable copycats.

  Partial solution: Amend existing law to make it a more severe federal/state crime to physically threaten, harass, assault or harm any federal/state candidate, politician, official or member of their family, or to incite others to do so.

9 – Stories from the Heart of America

STRANDED! UNTIL A STRANGER CAME TO HELP

Sometime around 1985 I was driving home from a very long and tiring day at work when, around 11:30 at night, my aging car died. It was a lonely country road and there was zero traffic. A little moonlight, but no other, way out in the countryside. Home was still another 25 miles away. Steam was pouring out of the engine compartment. And I was very tired.

I opened the hood and saw that a radiator hose had burst. I was able to cut off the broken part of the hose near its end but could not re-attach it since the existing hose clamp had rusted beyond salvage. I was right next to a stream where there was ample water to refill the radiator. But I couldn't fix the problem without a hose clamp.

This was before cell phones and there was no one nearby where I could make a phone call. And if I could call, who might help? Every repair shop was closed for the night.

After only a few minutes of mumbling about my bad luck, a lone car pulled up in back of me. A middle aged man got out and asked if he could help. I showed him the problem and half-joking, inquired if he happened to have a hose clamp. He shook his head, "No," he said, "but I do have one back at my house in Kingston." Now Kingston was ten miles back in the direction from which he had come.

Without a pause he continued, "I'll go back and get it." I was dumbfounded. This was a complete stranger. I didn't even get his name.

He turned his car around and disappeared into the night.

Almost an hour later, as I was sitting in my car contemplating my fate, he pulled up in back of me and said, "I got it!" He handed me the unexpected, greatly desired object that would let me go home.

In five minutes I had installed it, filled the radiator with water from the stream and was ready to go. I asked him if I could pay him for his trouble and he refused, smiled, got back in his car, and before we could talk more, he disappeared down the road toward wherever he was going at that hour of the night.

Hose Clamp

A complete stranger helped someone he didn't know with an unlikely effort. Why did he do this? Who raised this man to be the way he is? What are his values? I will never know, but I have seen so many others like him in America that I am no longer amazed at how helpful and decent people can be when they encounter someone in need.

A FATHER TAKES HIS SONS TO AFRICA

Mike is a pleasant, unassuming middle aged guy. I first met Mike two years ago at my local car service garage where he is friends with the owner. I looked at him and thought, "This is a person who must have been a teacher or lived a quiet life somewhere near a factory." Recently we got into a conversation as we were leaving a church service and I invited him for a cup of coffee. Unassuming is his middle name.

Mike has worked all over the world. Now in a second career, he is an electrician who specializes in fiber optic systems for buildings and large institutions. He is also a certified pilot who has flown just about every kind of airplane from 747s to crop dusters. And he is very devoted to his family.

Priorities

Not long ago a major airline company made Mike an offer. Come back to us and we'll pay you a comfortable, six-figure salary for flying a 747 again. The only hitch, he would only get back home four days a month. Mike is not a wealthy man, but he turned down the money and the job so he could be with his family.

Back before the kids came along, when Mike was flying all over the world, he would often take his father with him. They spent a lot of what Mike calls "windshield time" together – his dad imparting wisdom and Mike taking it all in. Mike's dad passed away a year ago. They were very close.

Greeting Strangers

About a dozen years ago he decided to take his dad and his two oldest boys, 10 and 11, to learn about a foreign country. A friend who is a priest from Ghana suggested they visit his home. They flew to Africa and stayed one night in Accra, Ghana's capital. The next day, they drove inland to Wenchi, a city in central Ghana where they stayed with the family of their friend.

They spent the next three weeks going from village to village, meeting many people – from the village elders to the common people. The kids immediately noticed how differently the people lived. Economically poorer, but much happier, whether playing the national sport of soccer or just being with one another.

Upon entering a new village, absolutely the first thing one does is to observe a centuries-old cultural protocol. All the village elders line up to greet and welcome you. The newcomers shake hands down the line, from left to right, and each elder asks, "what is your 'mission'." Mike said his mission was to meet the local bishop.

This idea of 'mission' began long ago when someone from another region would appear in a village, perhaps escaping from persecution or war, and everyone wanted to know why he was there.

Cultural Lessons

Everywhere they went the boys noted the tight bonding and respect for families – strong extended family ties are everywhere. A child's aunts are called 'mothers'. Children always have a 'mother' available. Everyone works together for the family.

It is rare for a person to be alone. Such a person is regarded as a very sad and unhappy person.

Ghanaians have great respect for elders. Mike's father was about 70 at the time. One morning the head of the house asked him, "How did you sleep last night?" "I slept fine, but the rooster woke me up early," Dad replied, matter-of-factly. Not as a complaint, only a comment. No one mentioned the matter again, but the next morning there was no rooster crowing. That day, again without comment, the rooster appeared at the dinner table, cooked in the traditional festive way.

A few days later, the local church held a special worship service in an outdoor tent-like structure. It was praise and worship, with talks, and music and dancing. The praise and singing and worship reached a joyful crescendo and soon everyone was up and praise dancing. There was so much dancing, Mike said you could actually see a slight haze of dust rising. The service normally lasts an hour or two but in their honor, it lasted five hours.

Mike's dad, as the elder of his family, was asked to get up and address the congregation. But as he was a bit shy, he turned to Mike and said, "You do this one." Mike had about three seconds to prepare, but it went well.

Justice

In another village, they were stuck in traffic when a man on foot raced frantically past them. People behind were yelling something in their local dialect. Their driver said the man had just robbed someone. But the people ahead heard the 'charges' and convened an instant 'jury' and 'judge'. By the time their car reached the bottom of the hill, the man had been caught, the sentence had been executed. He was beaten and released to go home in shame. There was no lengthy trial or appeals process. The tightly bonded community had spoken.

'Graduation' Day

Mike's kids discovered a new outlook on life. Things you can't get out of a book. I thank him for sharing this story and hope it may inspire you also.

No question that the people of Ghana are poor by western standards, but they live much happier lives. Not everything they do is appropriate to adopt here in our multi-cultural society. But we can learn a great deal from them about the importance of family. Strong extended families that America used to have and is losing much too rapidly.

Mike came home with a case of malaria; his boys came home stronger and indelibly transformed.

FINDING THE SOUL OF AMERICA ON A MOTORCYCLE

This is a story of the Heartland of America and how people treat strangers and one another. Same as it was 50 or 60 years ago. Many of these people were able to renew their culture after the great disruptions of the 20th Century because they had the stability of family and community to lean on.

George is an unassuming, late middle age man from upstate New York. But for his friendly face and an awesome, full salt and pepper beard you might not notice him in a crowd. It must take quite a while to grow a beard that long. I had to suppress my first impression, unspoken, as I thought, "Moses would be proud of you."

Surrounded by his family and grandchildren, I met George on a bright July day at a memorial service for his cousin, Bob. We got to talking for quite a while. He, like so many others, is sincerely concerned about America and where she is headed. We exchanged thoughts about the many different people who make up this country.

The conversation soon turned to a recent journey. You see, he has a son in Los Angeles and he decided it was time to go visit him. On his motorcycle.

A Hardworking Man

Before we get to his story, let me introduce you. George has always been close to the land and its people. He grew up on a farm with the usual animals and all the responsibility that entails – feeding the hogs, tending the cattle and tilling the fields. There he discovered his talent for machinery. Talent is an understatement. Love is a better word.

I had heard about George's reputation a few years ago. He is comfortable with anything that is made of wood or metal. Any kind of machinery, big or small, simple or complex is his comfort zone. He can weld things together or take them apart and make something altogether new.

He soon realized that he has the gift of vivid visual perception and memory. It serves him well in his trade.

Welders use a near-opaque eye shield to protect their eyes from the intense light of the torch. When the hot torch strikes the metal, you can be temporarily blinded. A vivid mental picture of where that torch and welding rod are going is essential.

When George is welding, whether it is ordinary steel-to-steel or the more advanced specialty-welding, done in an oxygen-free argon atmosphere, his four years of specialized schooling has paid off and he is recognized as an expert. If you need it created or repaired, George can do it.

Back Roads across America

George rides his Triumph motorcycle on sunny off-work-days, but business is brisk and he doesn't take much time off. Three years ago, while he still felt youthful enough, he decided to make the cross-country ride. So he and a friend got on their bikes and off they headed across the country to see his son in California.

Now there are two ways to enjoy any journey. In our busy way of life, most of us focus on getting there, and ignore the in-between. But George and his buddy planned to enjoy the journey, as well as the destination. So, skipping the Interstates, they traveled the back roads and saw America. And the adventures began.

Fresh Coffee

It was late one morning with the rising sun behind them, and the flat, straight, open Kansas highway ahead – time for a break. The small town had one diner – maybe diner is too big a word – it was a mom and pop coffee shop.

Across the empty restaurant was a lone woman, busily working on a grill. "Hello," she welcomed, "here's a cup of coffee. It's on the house. We always welcome motorcycles! Sit anywhere you like."

Thanking her, they had no sooner sat down than a few locals ambled in the door. "Passing through?" one of them said. "Yes, we're on our way across country." The local folk all pulled up chairs and sat around them and the friendly conversations began. If you've never been out in the real country, this is Middle America at its best. You can't buy this kind of hospitality – it's a gift.

Two thousand years ago, Jesus mentioned something we seldom do anymore – He implored us to lovingly welcome strangers. He said even the tax collectors and foreigners do that.[219] For those uncomplicated folks in that little Kansas town, it long ago became a joyful, deep-rooted habit.

Some other patrons arrived and joined in and they were soon surrounded by a friendly and pleasant crowd. The conversation went on for quite a while until the two needed to get back on the road. Bidding goodbye, they set off down the road. Just ahead was the next surprise for these two wanderers from New York.

Moses? In Kansas?

Leaving the restaurant they headed west along that straight country road. The land was flat and the road was straight as an arrow, from one horizon to the other. When you're on a bike, you're close to the ground, you see things you overlook from a car. Little animals scurry out of the way, brilliant desert flowers blooming everywhere, tumble weed racing the wind.

Two miles ahead, they spotted the unexpected. A pickup truck had pulled off the road and furniture and clothes were scattered in the road and everywhere.

As they approached, a woman was struggling to get a mattress and mattress springs back on the truck. It wasn't working. She wasn't strong enough for the task, and she had become exhausted in the fast warming desert sun. Meanwhile her two small grandchildren were clambering around in the cab. The man who had loaded the truck was already miles ahead, unaware of her plight. Even if she had a phone, there was no service in that barren desert.

George and his buddy pulled up to offer help. As he removed his helmet, his improbable beard unfurled and the woman did a double take. Who knows what she was thinking?

It took them only a few minutes to load the furniture and other things and tie them all down. The woman was practically in tears with gratitude.

---

[219] *Matthew 5:46-47*

She had a strange foreign accent and George's friend asked her, "Where you from?" She mentioned she had recently come over from Israel.

Then, with typical Middle-Eastern hospitality and overflowing with gratitude, she invited them to come to her new home where she would cook them dinner! Strangers helping and welcoming one another in a strange land. Distant cousins, maybe? At least, descendants of Adam? Or just human beings with a common sense of humanity.

Although they declined the invitation, these indelible memories, in the middle of America, will always remain with them.

A FAMILY'S TERROR AND RESCUE FROM DROWNING

Ocean beaches with breaking waves can produce deadly rip currents. A rip current occurs when the wind blows water off the tops of waves, toward the shore resulting in a strong flow of water away from shore that can challenge the strongest swimmer. An estimated 100 people die each year in the U.S. from being caught in these sudden currents. A rip current is not to be confused with an undertow, which is much weaker. A majority of lifeguard rescues are of swimmers caught in these overpowering currents.

80 person human chain saves a family
Courtesy Northwest Florida Daily News

Recently, a pleasant day at a Florida beach almost turned into a major family disaster. A mother was leaving the water when she noticed her sons were not with her. Turning she saw them far from shore and heard their screams. The whole family rushed into the water to try to save them, despite warnings from people not to go in. According to a news account, the entire family – all nine of them – were soon in 15 feet of water and being dragged out to sea.

One alert young woman earlier had found an abandoned child's boogie board. When she realized someone was drowning, she jumped in with the board and began swimming toward the family. Then her husband and a few other men formed a human chain to pull everyone back to shore.

Differing news accounts claim the chain grew to between 40 and 80 people and was between 70 and 100 yards long. All nine of the family were rescued, and although the grandmother suffered a massive heart attack in the process, she was saved, taken to the hospital and survived.

Occasionally we hear of people in trouble and onlookers – just on-looking – doing nothing. This situation shows what ordinary people do to help strangers in need. There was no government committee, no circulated petition, no police call for volunteers. People just stepped in and did what was needed.

I have no doubt that the people in the human chain were men and women from many places, races and religions. I would not be surprised to find atheists, Muslims, Jews, Christians, Buddhists and others. This is America and helping one another in a pinch is what we do.

AN UNCLE'S WISDOM

I want to share part of a letter I wrote, responding to and attempting to calm a dear cousin who had written after the terror strikes of 9-11-2001, expressing her great fears about what horrible attacks and wars were now on the horizon: 9-11 had awakened her, as it did the rest of us from a relatively peaceful 'sleep':

Dear Cousin,

Luke 21:9 says, "When you hear of wars and revolutions, do not be frightened. These things must happen first, but the end will not come right away." (Think 1812, Antietam, Gettysburg, WW-I, Spanish Civil War, WW-II, Korea, Vietnam, Desert Storm, Rwanda, Bosnia, etc.) By the way, in the war of 1812-1814, we lost the Capitol, the White House and the Library of Congress, all burned to the ground by (our friends) the Brits.

Part of the coming battle will be a battle of ideas guided by compassion and love for our fellow man and will be fought by communicating. We must do that, for they are unable. We are strong. Now we must be resolute. The battle will take a very long time and it must be fought.

I want to share a memory with you — a memory of your father. It was about 1959 during a family discussion about nuclear blackmail, nuclear catastrophe and apocalyptic stuff in general. Much of the conversation I have forgotten, but I can still picture your father, sitting on your living room couch, perfectly at ease, calmly listening. Finally, your father put the whole conversation in perspective (which I paraphrase): "If they drop the bomb on you, you are going to die, and you cannot do anything about it. But it is highly unlikely that they will. And so you will spend the rest of your life consumed by your fear, and then die a natural death. *You will have wasted your life.*" His words made a profound effect on me and have guided my thinking ever since.

WHERE TO GO WHEN ALL HELL BREAKS LOOSE?

"New York City, in a heartbeat." That's what a friend said to me recently. This is a guy in our weekly men's prayer group. No, he is not delusional and he is not a dreamer, stargazer or Pollyanna. He is a practical, experienced guy who has witnessed how people in the Big Apple have come together during past times of crisis – He mentioned 9/11 and an earlier major power outage. People who were total strangers suddenly came together and helped one another.

Oh. sure, there were the looters and the riff raff who taxed the police, but they were in the minority. But they got most of the press coverage.

The media pours out the bad news because they need attention in order to make money. But if we pay too much attention to bad news we lose our perspective. Most people are decent at the core and ready to help one another when the chips are down.

Try this. Cut your cable and save lots of money. Read books. Turn off the iPhone and talk with one another.

AN AMERICAN FABLE

A Native American grandfather was talking to his grandson about how he felt. He said, "I feel as if I have two wolves fighting in my heart. One wolf is the vengeful, angry, violent one. The other wolf is the loving, compassionate one." The grandson asked him, "Which wolf will win the fight in your heart?" The grandfather answered, "The one I feed."

10 – Unanswered Questions

We will need to come together with concerted efforts and commonality of purpose to address some of these issues. There are many more, but here is a sample:

- **Culture**: How do we prevent a recurrence in America of the 'decline and fall of the Roman Empire" by reining in our Hollywood *Ovids* and their trash and filth, while still retaining our First Amendment right to free speech?
- **Family**: How can a broken family (or 10 million of them) repair itself and give hope to future generations? (Consider the obstacles set forth in Samuel Butler's classic, *The Way of All Flesh*. – a story of brokenness as the sins of the fathers propagate through four generations.)
- **Family, Education, Culture** – What message do we send our children when we say we love them but yet they soon learn we value life so little that we permit the violent killing of unborn babies simply because they are inconvenient.
- **Faith**: How can we encourage faith groups – churches and synagogues – to perform more works of charity such as when they started most of America's hospitals and schools?
- **Faith**: How do we convince churches to rid themselves of excess property to avoid the inevitable future taxation that will start another, unnecessary cultural war?
- **Faith, Culture**: How do we deal with new waves of migrants – e.g., Islamic – who refuse to integrate and actively want to change our Constitution, our laws and our culture?
- **Education**: How can a poorly educated and unprepared teacher prepare a capable and gifted student and why do we even permit it?
- **Education**: Question: Why are so many college kids dominated by emotional reaction and provably unable to discuss or hear alternate points of view? This might be a subject for some serious research:

    Hypothesis: Beyond a certain age, perhaps 10 or 12, it is too late for their developing brains to master the skills of critical thinking, reason or debate and this is attributable to some failure of parents and school.

    Alternate research paths:
    - a) They are indeed unable to master these skills past some critical age and they are permanently disabled
    - b) They are simply ignorant and/or unaware. All that is needed is more or different education
    - c) Something else.

- **Education**: How do we keep big mega-businesses from disproportionately influencing the education of our children?
    - ✓ Textbook writing and production are big business monopolies
    - ✓ Testing companies make big money developing and pushing common tests
    - ✓ Computer games accustom kids to violence and anti-family values
    - ✓ Social media is addicting our children and inhibits healthy socialization
    - ✓ All these companies spend millions of dollars to convince us and our politicians that they are not at fault and any problems are caused by something else.
- **Education:** Author Anthony Esolen in his book, *Out of the Ashes – Rebuilding American Culture*, suggests that we completely throw out our K-12 public education

system and start over.[220] But how do we do that, given all the political capital and big money involved in our current systems?

- **Governance**: How do we get the Political Left and the Right to listen respectfully and work with one another?
- **Governance**: What is the proper balance between 'big money' and free speech in light of the *Citizens United* Supreme Court decision?
- **Economics**: How can we deal with our National Debt in a way that minimizes the damage to the next generation(s)?
- **Finance**: How can families begin to finance their own lives and balance their budgets without government aid?
- **Culture**, **Governance**, **Education**, **Faith**, **Finance** and **Family**: How do we finally bring the heavily left-biased media back to a balanced respect for *all* American values and beliefs?

Perhaps the answer to some of these questions will come from strengthened families. Success stories illustrating strong and positive role models can give hope and encouragement and there are many such examples.

One robust example – Dr. Ben Carson and his brother, fatherless and living in poverty, with the passionate guidance and help of his illiterate yet strong-willed faithful Christian mother overcame their poverty and excelled in their education and careers. Ben Carson's story is worth repeating.[221, 222]

---

[220] Esolen, Anthony, *op.cit.*, pp.49-70
[221] Dr. Ben Carson is a retired brain surgeon and currently the U.S. Secretary of Housing and Urban Development (HUD)
[222] Carson, Ben, M.D., and Cecil Murphey, *Gifted Hands, The Ben Carson Story*, Zondervan Press, 1996

11 – An Open Letter to My Children

My Dear Children,

I have a gift for you, a gift that will help you live in this world more abundantly than you could ever imagine. The riches I have for you were given to me; this inheritance I turn now over to you:

Some people will offer you earthly comfort and riches. Be vigilant and careful. Just remember that the Devil offered the same to Jesus. But Jesus told us to be *in* this world, but not *of* it. Others will say to you, "follow me" for your "salvation." But remember what you have been taught – Jesus alone has the path to salvation.

With your love and gifts, remember the poor, the hungry, the lonely, the stranger, the sick and the prisoner. Look and you will see Jesus in them. Don't reject him; find *caritas* in your heart for them. In the blink of an eye they could be you.

Show your love of God with gifts of love, freely and faithfully given, and remember faith is important but without works of affirmation faith is dead. Study the trials of the rest of the world and see that America is a unique gift from God. Understand its origins. Participate in its protection. Regarding earthly leaders, pray to God for the discernment to know whom to follow and whom to question. Do not be distracted by nasty politics but support and vote for those who will *protect and defend* this republic and what it means to us and the rest of the world.

Tough as it may be, try to love those who disagree with you. Show them the truth by your loving actions. Pray for them. If there are not many of them you may be doing something wrong or you are too fat-dumb-and-happy-comfortable.

Pray always. But balance your prayer. It is OK to petition our Creator in difficult and in bad times. But remember also to praise him for the sunrise of the new day. And when bad weather and storms come, remember that the sun is *always* shining only two miles away – *always*! *Straight up*! Believe in what God has done but your eyes cannot see.

Remember, you can read in *Genesis* that God created *everything* and that it was *good* (not "some of it good and some of it bad" – but "*good*" – *all* of it!)

Pray always. With humility and a contrite heart admit your weaknesses and God will give you strength. Give thanks for your blessings. And remember to thank God for your trials and sufferings! They are like pumping spiritual iron. He will guide you through them and you will become stronger as you walk with him.

Give thanks. Do not compare your gifts with those of your worldly brothers and sisters. Nor should you compare your trials to those of others. Jesus told us, "[His] burden is light and [your] yoke is well-fitting." Each of us has been given the gift of a custom-fitted yoke to carry life's burdens. We just need to remember to unwrap the package and use it.

When you suffer, do not accuse God. He is not a God of suffering but of healing. Bear your burdens and pray for his strength to get you through the suffering. One day or one minute at a time.

Our faith is not complicated. Two things you must do always: Love God; Love your neighbor as if he is one with you. Resist the temptation to argue one with another over fine points of theology. Leave those distracting discussions to your teachers. One cannot argue over a fact but one can get de-railed by an opinion. A fact is a fact and the truth is the truth. Pray for occasional glimmers of the truth and for increasing wisdom. Now we see only dimly, but when at last we see God face to face, only then shall we see the whole truth. Be patient with the growth of your own understanding.

Pray sometimes without words. Place yourself before the Lord and ask him to empty your mind of the turmoil of the moment and in the silence of your heart let him fill you with awe and wonder. Take five minute pilgrimages to the Lord. But take care that when you empty your mind that you always pray first in Jesus name, that the Devil will not try to fill the empty space. And if you can't find five minutes then you may be too busy. So pray about that.

Meditate on the glory and goodness and wonder of God. Meditate on that which you can see – a bird – a butterfly – a flower – a dead leaf – an ancient stone. Meditate on that which you *cannot* see – the host of the heavenly unseen – the distant universe – pure love itself. Pray always. Let everything you do be done prayerfully. Praise your Creator always.

Protect all life. Pray for the unborn. Pray for the dying. Pray for the joyful. Rejoice in one another's successes and accomplishments. Never be jealous, for God has given you a *great gift*. But first you need to search for it, unwrap it and use it.

Study the Word of God. (Hint: don't start with *Genesis* but, like Mahatma Gandhi, I recommend *Matthew* chapters 5, 6 and 7.) Meditate on it. Pray for the strength and courage to be humble. Find holy teachers and listen to them, but reject the glitzy, worldly and ostentatious ones.

Never try to debate the Devil; run from him. He is smarter than you and will win every argument. He always plays *zero-sum* and you will lose. Pray for the discernment to know what is right and holy. Pray always in Jesus name as he taught us.

Finally, my children pray and work as did Jesus for the unity of his people (*John 17*) that we might all be one in him.

I love you. I pray for you daily. My love is with you and your loved ones always.

Your dad,

Almerin O'Hara, Jr.

Epilogue

"[Brothers and sisters:] I, a prisoner for the Lord, urge you to live in a manner worthy of the call you have received, with all humility and gentleness, with patience, bearing with one another through love, striving to preserve the unity of the spirit through the bond of peace; one body and one Spirit, as you were also called to the one hope of your call; one Lord, one faith, one baptism; one God and Father of all, who is over all and through all and in all."

Saint Paul's Letter to the Ephesians, Chapter 4, Verses 1-6, (NAB)

==========

"Let us not become weary in doing good, for at the proper time we will reap a harvest if we not give up."

Saint Paul's Letter to the Galatians. Chapter 6, Verse 9, (NIV)

==========

Through many dangers, toils and snares, I have already come;
'Tis grace hath brought me safe thus far, and grace will lead me home.

Amazing Grace, Verse 3

==========

The past
cannot be changed;
we have inherited it;
The future is for our heirs;
The present is ours and will change that future
depending on our choice today:

Participant?
Spectator?

==========

Do you think your efforts won't count? Remember,
Amateurs built the Ark
Professionals built the Titanic;

Appendix A. Out of Slavery – The Struggle of Black America

Chronology

From bad to better and then to worse, this is a timeline of the Black family tragedy in America.

- 1619 – Twenty African slaves brought to Virginia to work tobacco fields
- 1794 – Cotton Gin patented by Eli Whitney – This created a strong European demand for cotton which caused a massive increase in slavery in southern states
- 1857 – Dred Scott Supreme Court decision, ruled that African-Americans could not be citizens of the United States. (Majority of the judges were from the South)
- 1861 – Civil War, started by seceding southern states objecting to the newly formed Republican Party's anti-slavery stance. The North initially fought to re-unite the Union, and then by 1863 the North was also focused on freeing the 4 million slaves.
- 1863 – President Lincoln's Emancipation proclamation
- 1865 – Civil War ends. 620,000 soldiers died -- white men fought white men to decide if Black slavery should continue
- 1865 – Slavery legally abolished (13th Amendment)
- 1868 – Civil rights & equal protection granted (14th Amendment)
- 1870 – Right to vote granted (15th Amendment)
- 1945 – WW II ended; Blacks fought for America
- 1947 – Jackie Robinson joined Brooklyn Dodgers
- 1954 – School desegregation decision (Brown vs Board of Education)
- 1961 – Affirmative action (Pres. Kennedy Executive Order 10925)
- 1964 – Civil Rights Act passed in Congress
- 1964 – Poll tax eliminated (24th Amendment)
- 1965 – Affirmative action (Pres. Johnson Executive Order 11246)
- 1955 - 1966 – Massive Urban Renewal projects destroyed 'slums' in 1,000 US cities, resulting in widespread destruction of the extended family structure in black families.[223] Soon followed by an upsurge in fatherless, family-poor children, drug use, crime and street gangs
- 1974 – Beginning of national imprisonment upsurge.

    Approximate numbers (combined federal and state, black and white):*

    1958 – 200,000 in prison
    1974 – 200,000 in prison
    2015 – 1,500,000 in prison.

    * See detailed graph of *U.S. Prison Population by Year*
    earlier in this book on page 15.

---

[223] *Lost Rondout, A Story of Urban Removal*, 2016, A video by Stephen Blauweiss and Lynn Woods, From the back cover: "In the 1960s, federally funded urban renewal projects destroyed hundreds of working-class urban communities across America. [This video] chronicles how one such project impacted the Hudson Valley city of Kingston, New York, demolishing 500 buildings and displacing thousands of people..."

APPENDIX B. PEACEFUL/MILITANT ISLAM AND AMERICAN CULTURE

Is Islam a Religion of Peace?

*The Sharia is coming to the UK – this black flag you see here, one day
is gonna be on 10 Downing Street. Our message is deadly, we are calling
for world domination, and the Sharia for the UK.*

Mohammed Shamsuddin, London Jihad apologist

I have known and worked with many Muslims and have nothing but respect for them and their character. These are, generally speaking, peaceful people who would rather not be involved in the turmoil we associate with current Islamic movements. Indeed, the average follower of Islam is no more or less like the follower of any religion in that their first objective is to attain for themselves and their loved ones the basic needs of life.

The problem appears after those needs have been fulfilled and the turmoil within the soul is fed by the words of an ancient warrior who sought to conquer and convert the world.

Islam is a 'religion of peace' only if we re-define the word 'peace', despite what some politicians have said in the past. The word 'Islam' in Arabic means 'submission'. Islam is a religion of peace for Muslims and will become so for anyone who submits and converts to Islam. Submit and you will have peace.

GOAL OF WORLD DOMINATION

The goal of the predominant proselytizing version of Islam today is total world submission and domination. Many Muslims await the return of a ruling Caliphate. The last one, the Ottoman Caliphate lasted more than 400 years and ended in 1923. [224] But not until they nearly conquered much of Europe, had they not been stopped at the Battle of Vienna. There, they were overwhelmed by forces armed with superior science and weapons. Earlier Caliphate warriors had fought more than 500 vicious battles, in the 7th and 8th Century to conquer Spain, Portugal, lower France, Sicily, lower Italy, Turkey and many other regions.

There are two major branches of Islam, The Sunni majority branch and the minority Shi'a. The 'orthodox' Wahhabi sect of Sunni Islam started in India in the 19th Century and got its big growth spurt in Saudi Arabia following the collapse of the Ottoman Empire. The Wahhabi goal is to 'purify' Islam and it seeks to renew the Caliphate as do recent outgrowths of this movement such as Al Qaida, ISIS and several others throughout Africa and Asia.

The Shi'a minority version of Islam, which comprises about ten percent of all Muslims, has a different world domination idea. Their 12th Caliph, the Mahdi, is said to have disappeared and they expect him to return and rule the world. They believe that he, their messiah, will be revealed on earth as he establishes his global Islamic kingdom, ruled by Sharia Law.

The Sunnis have a similar idea and both branches believe we are in the end of times and that when their messiah returns, so will Jesus who Islam recognizes only as a prophet. They believe that Jesus is not the Son of God and Savior, as do Christians, but rather will return as an officer in the Mahdi's army.[225] They teach that his job will then be to force non-Muslims to convert or die.

---

[224] Led by a Caliph, who is the successor of Mohammad. He is the ruler of all things civil and religious for the entire people. Four different Caliphs ruled during the early wars that spread Islam with the sword throughout the Mediterranean region and destroyed and replaced Christianity in Northern Africa.

[225] Referring to Jesus as "The Son of God" will often evoke a furious response from Muslims because the 'revealed truth' of their Holy Koran unequivocally states that "Allah has no son."

APOCALYPTIC ISLAM

Both Sunni and Shi'a believe that soon, the world must be totally destroyed in apocalyptic chaos and carnage. They believe that Allah is definitely on their side, and recent ISIS gains in the Middle East and Africa, and the 2015 nuclear agreement with Iran reinforce their certainty that the worldwide caliphate is soon to arrive.

It is an understatement to say that Sunnis and Shi'ites do not like each other. Indeed, in 2011, an agent of Shi'ite Iran tried to assassinate Adel al-Jubeir, the ambassador to the US from Sunni Saudi Arabia. Because he is a Sunni, he is, according to their book, an unbeliever. Orthodox Muslim believers of both groups are not only permitted, but are encouraged to kill unbelievers by following specific instructions in their holy book, the Koran.[226]

But regardless of their 1,400 year intense dislike for each other, *they will fight, and have fought their common enemies together*.

Sunni ISIS is a critical short-term problem, but Shi'a Iran and its allies, including Syria and Lebanon's Hezbollah (Shi'a Islamist *Party of Allah*), is a more critical problem for the longer term. Iran is a highly developed country with well-trained scientists and engineers and an established, stable, authoritarian system of government that can produce atomic, biological and chemical weapons. ISIS on the other hand is more akin to the barbarians of the Middle-Ages.

ISLAM IS ONLY PARTLY A RELIGION

Islam is a political way of life, unlike any other major world religion. Islam's holy book, the Koran specifies a reverence and devotions to their god, Allah, but also specifies the allowable and required form of government and all permitted and forbidden rules of commercial, economic, societal and personal conduct and interaction.

Also, interestingly, every major religion in the world has a version of the 'Golden Rule' which applies to everyone – "Do unto others as you would have them do unto you." Every religion except one – Islam. Throughout the Koran one is instructed to treat non-Muslims very differently from Muslims. Their 'golden rule' applies only to other Muslims.[227]

In many countries, failure to obey Islamic rules is punishable in accord with the dictates of their holy book, the Koran. These punishments are taken literally. For instance, the punishment for theft is to have one's hand cut off. The punishment for 'insulting' Allah's prophet Mohammad is death. The punishment for teaching Christianity to a Muslim can range from a long prison term to death.

The punishment for converting to Christianity is the same in the four major branches of Sunni Islam and the three major schools of Shi'a Islam. A decree of Death.

In many Islamic countries these punishments can be carried out by any devout Muslim in the name of Allah, without any civil oversight or admonishment.

In some Muslim countries it's easy to insult Allah. In 2009, a Pakistani court sentenced a Christian woman, Asia Bibi, to death because she – a "filthy unbeliever" – insulted Allah by offering a jug of water to some Muslim women, who then dragged her to a police station claiming she had confessed to blasphemy. In October, 2018, after years in prison, a courageous three-justice panel of the Pakistani Supreme Court overturned her death sentence, claiming insufficient evidence. Religious hard-liners were enraged and will kill her if they find her. She has not been permitted to leave Pakistan and is in hiding in a safe house in Pakistan. Her lawyer is now in hiding in the Netherlands, in fear of his own life.

---

[226] For example, see *Surah 9:5* in the *Koran*: (Go throughout the land and dissolve any treaties with the pagans and) "... fight and slay the pagans wherever ye find them, and seize them, beleaguer them, and lie in wait for them in every stratagem (of war)."

[227] A version of this golden rule can be found, not in the *Koran*, but in the revered sayings of the Prophet Mohammad (*The Hadith*).

TRUE ISLAM CANNOT ASSIMILATE

The *Merriam Webster Dictionary* defines assimilation as "the process through which individuals and groups of differing heritages acquire the basic habits, attitudes, and mode of life of an embracing culture." America has always embraced foreigners and encouraged their assimilation. Indeed we are, almost all of us, descended from immigrants.

In the USA it is hard to understand how something like offering a cup of water could be an insult to the Muslim god. Unbelievably difficult to understand, yet just one of many issues that suggest Islam is unable to coexist with American culture. And why we need to be very careful about quickly bringing large numbers of people of any religion or culture who refuse to assimilate – but especially Muslims – into America.

History shows that of all faith groups – Christians, Jews, Buddhists, Hindus and Muslims – the ones that have the most difficulty assimilating into their new countries are the followers of Islam. As mentioned in the Introduction, friends who recently just returned from Ireland found that part of their ancestral small village in County Kerry had been walled off with signs forbidding entrance except to those who are Muslim. This pattern is repeated all over Europe and in parts of the United States.

A seminal study in the UK shows just how difficult it is for Muslims to assimilate. Trevor Phillips was a senior member of the government under Prime Minister Tony Blair, where he chaired the country's Equality and Human Rights Commission. Following the Blair era, Phillips had second thoughts about what immigration was doing to the UK's culture. In 2016 TV station Channel 4 contracted with him to produce a documentary on *What British Muslims Really Think*. Phillips hired a major surveying company, ICM Unlimited, to do in-depth interviews of over a thousand Muslims from all over the country. The results were startling. A surprisingly large number – one quarter – said they favored replacing the British legal system with Islamic Sharia law.

Terrorism was another concern. Phillips found that four percent (about 100,000 British Muslims) believe suicide bombing is OK to fight injustice. Only one third said they would inform police if they knew of a person who was preparing to support terrorism in Syria. This 47 minute documentary is available for viewing on YouTube.[228] (Click on QR Code to view it ➔)

**What British
Muslims Think**

WHAT ABOUT 'SECULAR' MUSLIMS?

Just like many other religions, there are some Muslims who believe, but do not practice – they are so-called 'secular' Muslims. But recent experience shows that their adherence to their culture and to the Koran has led many of their sons (and some daughters) to be later radicalized by Muslim pastors (Imams). Many of these young converts have then shown up on the battlefield – or the market square – to perform acts of violence and terrorism in the name of Allah.

Islam teaches that giving up one's life in the act of killing an unbeliever is an immediate ticket to Heaven and eternal life, full of material goods, happiness and peace, including an endless supply of sexual activity with virgins.

Their Sharia Law permits slavery, child marriage, polygamy and the brutal and demeaning subjection of women as second-class citizens. Islamic law also teaches that it is permissible to deceive and lie to a non-Muslim (an infidel) if the purpose is to further the goals of Allah. This tenet of their belief, codified in seven different places in their holy book, the Koran, makes it very problematic to

---

[228] Phillips, Trevor, "What British Muslims Really Think", *www.youtube.com/watch?v=xQcSvBsU-FM* , Published Apr. 15, 2016

believe in the validity of treaties and other agreements between Muslims and non-Muslims and their respective nations.

MUSLIM AND ARAB CULTURE

Not all Muslims are Arabs, although the religion began with Mohammad, an Arab and subsequently, his Arab followers.

Most Arabs are friendly and in their culture are very welcoming to travelers and strangers. The hospitality of the average Arab is renowned. This can be very confusing, given what a minority of their followers have been doing for centuries. For instance, you might want to research "Thomas

Jefferson and the Barbary Pirates." The Barbary Pirates were Muslim warriors and a major menace to our ships of commerce at the beginning of our republic in the 18th Century.

Family and community bonds are typically very strong in Muslim culture. Important decisions are made by authorities – religious leaders, family patriarchs and fathers. Questioning one's religion or one's family authorities is absolute taboo.[229] Authorities seek guidance from the Koran, the Hadith or religious leaders.[230] Critical reasoning, although understood, is seldom practiced and to disobey an authority brings shame upon the whole family. Honor and shame are the decision criteria for many actions. This is a type of reasoning that is very foreign to most Westerners and accounts for much East-West misunderstanding.

SIR WINSTON CHURCHILL'S COMMENTARY

Sir Winston Churchill was an Englishman who started out life as a soldier and journalist and went on the become the leader of Great Britain at the time of its greatest need and direst existential threat. World War II and Adolph Hitler were threatening the very existence of the entire continent of Europe and England itself. Churchill died in 1965 at the age of 90.[231] He was a great student of the world and understood Islam well. It was common at the time to refer to Islam as 'Mohammedanism'.

Here is a speech Sir Winston gave in 1899, regarding Islam.[232]

> How dreadful are the curses which Mohammedanism lays on its votaries! Besides the fanatical frenzy, which is as dangerous in a man as hydrophobia in a dog, there is this fearful fatalistic apathy.

> The effects are apparent in many countries, improvident habits, slovenly systems of agriculture, sluggish methods of commerce, and insecurity of property exist wherever the followers of the Prophet rule or live. A degraded sensualism deprives this life of its grace and refinement, the next of its dignity and sanctity. The fact that in Mohammedan law every woman must belong to some man as his absolute property, either as a child, a wife,

---

[229] *Koran, Surah 33:36* – The Koran forbids true believers from questioning Mohammad's decisions.

[230] Much of Islamic Sharia Law is based on the Hadith, the sayings of Mohammad, as well as the Koran.

[231] Personal note: I met Sir Winston once, by chance, in 1962 in the Piccadilly Hotel in London. He seemed alert with an air of dignity, but quite feeble, needing to balance on his cane with every step yet strongly determined to move forward.

[232] Sir Winston Churchill, *The River War*, 1st Edition, Vol II, London: Longmans, Green and Co., 1899, pp. 248-250

or a concubine, must delay the final extinction of slavery until the faith of Islam has ceased to be a great power among men.

Individual Muslims may show splendid qualities, but the influence of the religion paralyses the social development of those who follow it.

No stronger retrograde force exists in the world. Far from being moribund, Mohammedanism is a militant and proselytizing faith. It has already spread throughout Central Africa, raising fearless warriors at every step; and were it not that Christianity is sheltered in the strong arms of science, the science against which it had vainly struggled, the civilization of modern Europe might fall, as fell the civilization of ancient Rome.

How prescient. And he wrote this over a hundred years ago. As we reflect on Sir Winston's words, we might recall the words of a well-known professor who once said, "Those who refuse to learn the lessons of history are doomed to repeat them."

FURTHER THOUGHTS ON ISLAM

Unprepared Christians who think they can evangelize Muslims almost always fail. Many Muslims are well schooled to confront these well-meaning people and they have sophisticated arguments which are difficult to counter for the unprepared Gospel-toting Christian.

Potential evangelists would do well to read Nabeel Qureshi's book, *Seeking Allah, Finding Jesus: A Devout Muslim Encounters Christianity* to see the barriers that exist between our two worlds.[233]

Islam is not just a religion – it is a social and political system that seeks to undermine the very foundation of democratic government. Nowhere in the world is there any Islamic country that practices democracy. A core teaching is to take over and subjugate the world by force. It worships a god who allegedly gave this (Sharia) law through the Angel Gabriel and the subsequent sayings of Mohammad (The Hadith). We need to stop calling it a religion – it is a militant political and social-legal system that *also* has some religious overtones.

Islam's prophet Mohammad was a warrior who helped unite factions, clans and tribes with the sword and with his own leadership skills and charisma.[234]

Many in today's news media tacitly support (or at least do not condemn) Islam because,

- They are truly ignorant of its teachings, especially its laws allowing abuse of women
- They see and admire its strict political nature and many of them have animus toward Israel
- They are reluctant – afraid – to speak against it for fear of their own safety.

ISLAM IN OUR PRISONS

Today, Christian volunteers who attempt to do ministry in U.S. federal and state prisons are facing increasing difficulty as the rules for all religious outsiders have become more and more stringent. This has happened in part to prevent the teaching and promotion of Islamic violence and to avoid any appearance of favoritism of one religion over another.

While the Christian system speaks of world unity through faith, hope and love, the Muslim system speaks of unity through compulsion and a strong brotherhood that too frequently condones violence.

---

[233] Qureshi, Nabeel, *Seeking Allah, Finding Jesus: A Devout Muslim Encounters Christianity,* Zondervan, 2018, esp. Chapter 45

[234] Trifkovic, Serge, *The Sword of the Prophet – Islam, history, theology, impact on the world*, Regina Orthodox Press, Inc., 2002 (This book was strongly recommended to me as accurate by an Arab Christian who immigrated to the U.S. from an Islamist country)

Unscrambling?

Since the practice of Islam is much more than just a religion, might it be possible to separate-out its non-religious and violent messages so those could be restricted and the other, peaceful religious parts brought into the prisons. But how might these parts be detached? One wonders if the peaceful messages of Islam could ever be so isolated without upsetting the balance of the whole Koranic message. It's an interesting thought experiment that requires one to read and understand the Koran.

ISLAMIC WARS

Many leaders in the Arab world are waking up to the realization that they are in the midst of a civil war with a large number of extreme adherents of Islam. Iran's growing and dangerous regional hegemony with its nuclear and missile capabilities can only serve to alarm and strengthen its enemies.

Nor can America divorce itself from this struggle. We can't kill all the bad guys. But we will be forced to kill some of them who threaten and attack us. We must defeat their terrorist ideology if we are to preserve peace. But first we need to understand that ideology. Military officers are taught, "Know absolutely everything about the enemy before you engage him. Know more about him than you know about yourself." Yet few Americans have any real understanding of Islamic traditions and the Arab and other Muslim cultures.

In any given year, at any moment, there are between 30 and 40 wars, large and small, proceeding on the face of the earth. Crops and livestock are destroyed and famine follows each war. Almost every one of these wars is Muslim against Muslim or Muslim against someone else.

ISLAM'S PEACEFUL WAYS

The peaceful Sufi sect of Islam is a small minority. The Sufi interpretation of Islam is a very meditative practice. An online *Wikipedia* comment illustrates a key difference between Sufism and classical Islam: "While all Muslims believe that they are on the pathway to Allah and hope to become close to God in Paradise – after death and after the Last Judgment – Sufis also believe that it is possible to draw closer to God and to more fully embrace the divine presence in this life on earth." [235]

Among the adherents of Sufism are a husband and wife couple, Mazhar and Christine A. Mallouhi. Mazhar has studied the teachings of Jesus and without denying his cultural identity, has taught many Muslims about this way of peace. Several books by and about the Mallouhis are available for those who wish more insight into why modern missionary efforts fail in the Islamic world. [236, 237]

Unfortunately, peaceful Sufism is being annihilated in many places, including north-western Africa, by militant Islamic warrior groups who regard Sufis as infidels.

Ahmadi Islam, another relatively peaceful but small sect, is much closer in practice to orthodox Islam. But many thousands of their followers have been slaughtered by hardline 'orthodox' Muslims who consider them infidels. Nabeel Qureshi (mentioned above) and his family are members of this Ahmadiyya Islam sect.

Peace Initiatives

Despite a lack of media coverage there are leaders in the Muslim world who understand the need for peaceful coexistence in the light of our shared humanity and values. Many of them tread a very fine line between their peaceful and their hardline factions.

---

[235] *en.wikipedia.org/wiki/Sufism*
[236] Chandler, Paul-Gordon, *Pilgrims of Christ on the Muslim Road – Exploring a New Path Between Two Faiths*, Rowman & Littlefield Publishers, Inc., 2007
[237] Mallouhi, Christine A., *Waging Peace on Islam*, InterVarsity Press, Downers Grove, Illinois, 2000

King Abdullah II of Jordan is one such person. In 2004, he released a declaration known as the *Amman Message* which states that terror and violence have no place in Islam. In 2005 he gathered 200 Islamic scholars from 50 countries in what would become known as the International Islamic Conference. To date, many Islamic scholars have signed the Amman Declaration Mandate which asserts that only those with specified training in theology can proclaim a *fatwah* or Islamic legal ruling. Previously, any Imam, however untrained, could so proclaim, and many did so, often with chaotic results. This gathering may be a precursor to a more predictable and manageable world-wide Islam.

In 2007, King Abdullah founded another group in which distinguished Muslims and Christians might cooperate, based on the two principles of love of God and love of neighbor.[238]

Only time will tell whether this will produce true good will outside of the Muslim community between Islam and other faith groups.

Western Ignorance

One more note on so-called 'peaceful' Islam. An often-quoted verse from the Koran says, "If you kill one person it is like killing everyone in the whole world." These are the words of the Prophet Mohammad and are often used to 'explain' that true Islam does not believe in killing people. These words have been repeated on major news networks, such as CNN and ABC and many westerners have come to believe it.

The problem is, when this verse is read in context, Mohammad was *addressing it only and specifically to the Jews* of his day ("Children of Israel") and *not* to his fellow Arabs. The next verse in the Koran goes on to speak of killing and dismembering: ("… execution or crucifixion or cutting hands and feet off from opposite sides…").[239]

Eastern Ignorance

Many Muslims are ignorant of what the Koran preaches. Studies show that very few Muslims have ever read the whole Koran and their knowledge is often limited to what they have heard preached by an Imam or scholarly Mullah or their teachers or parents. In fact, almost every Mosque reads and prays from the Koran in Arabic – translations into local languages are strongly discouraged. Some years ago Muslims in Turkey started using a Turkish translation and the rest of the Islamic world made a mighty uproar in objection.

I recently read of one devout young Muslim who had *memorized the entire Koran in Arabic*. But he did not understand, nor could he speak Arabic. (Reminds one of some pre-Vatican II Catholics who memorized all the Latin prayers but understood little of what they were saying.)

This is cited as one reason many Muslims do not comprehend why it is that so many outsiders are upset with Islam.

Allah, it would seem is not bi-lingual and Islam is only a religion of peace for other (approved) Muslims.

---

[238] Catipon, Chiara, "A King's Legacy", *Living City*, December, 2018
[239] *The Holy Qu'ran*, (Translation by Abdullah Yusuf Ali,) [See Bibliography] Surah 5:32-33

APPENDIX C. MENTAL DIFFERENCES, LANGUAGE AND UNDERSTANDING

"It enriched my faith and it gave me words to understand and communicate my beliefs." Those are the words of a person expressing gratitude for his education at a Christian university. But why does he need words of a human language to *understand* his own beliefs and thoughts?

Why does an astronomer need the language of mathematics to explore and express his understanding of the changing structure of the Universe? Why does a computer programmer need a computer language to conceive and design a new application? Why does an artist need a canvas, paints and all the tools of his/her profession to fully develop and communicate an inner concept?

> *It's kind of like a dogma ... that language is basically a means of communication, and evolved as a means of communication. ... that's just taken for granted. It apparently is all false. It turns out that from the closer analysis of language, it's actually **a tool for thought**.* [emphasis mine] *It's a means of expressing thought, and on the side you can use it for communication, as you can use anything else for communication.*
> *Noted linguist, Noam Chomsky*

The fundamental message in this appendix is that our innate created human differences and our acquired and adopted ways make it very difficult for some of us to understand and talk with one another.

POLITICAL MANIPULATION OF OUR LANGUAGE

Changes in our language can subtly affect how we think about and decide important and complex issues. We live in a world where politicians and special interest factions constantly try to change the meaning of words to manipulate us. Words are hijacked to change our thoughts, our actions and eventually our culture.

The world of advertising knows this well. Ask any Madison Avenue advertising firm how they control the decisions of their clients' customers.[240] Warping the meaning of words is far simpler and more effective than promoting rational, logical arguments.

Just a few illustrations – words that have been hijacked in our culture over the past few decades:
- **Gay** – Formerly meant happy and care free; Now it is a polite term for active homosexual
- **Diversity** – Formerly referred to celebrating the music, food and traditions of other racial, cultural and ethnic peoples. Now the word has been hijacked to exploit differences and use them to divide us based on skin color, national origin or sexuality and to set one group against another
- **Save** – Once upon a time the word meant setting money aside for later; now it means spending less (e.g. "Our product was $20.00 now is only $15.00 – Buy it and save five dollars!") Save enough money this way and you can go broke.

We have entered an era when people who use the same words to interact, have increasingly different understandings – different meanings – of those words. Conflict becomes inevitable and civil dialogue nearly impossible, especially for those who assume they are talking the same language about the same topics.

Concepts expressed in the political and social subset of the English language have been wandering for some time. When the

So, what's a "no fly" zone?

---

[240] The public first became aware that advertisers were manipulating language to control our actions when Vance Packard published his seminal book, *The Hidden Persuaders*, in 1957. Chapter 3 discusses the new science of motivational research and its use of word triggers, symbolic communication and the manipulation of subconscious ideas through clever language, actions and other triggers.

political Left means one thing, the political Right insists on another meaning. A common example is the term 'health care'. To the Left, the term includes abortion – destruction – of an unborn baby; to the Right, 'health care' means encouraging good health and making a sick person well. The Left has developed a new understanding that an unborn baby is not 'alive' and so it is acceptable to avoid the guilt of murder that the Right insists.

The U.S. Constitution – to the Right it is a solid rock foundation; to the Left it is a malleable lump of clay to be molded, reshaped or ignored.

Many other less serious word meanings separate and divide us and the list continues to grow as we self-select into mutually antagonistic cultural groups – 'echo chambers' – whose civil interaction diminishes with each new contentious issue.

Words mean different things to different individuals. Different culture, schooling and life experiences each alter our associations and meaning of words. We think we understand one another, but that often is just a conceit. Even when people of good will try to work together, sometimes neither has a clue what the other is talking about.

And on occasion, good will seems remote or absent.

Is 'mankind' a Sexist Word?

Another side of this is the politically correct removal or changing of centuries old word meanings. One change, irritating to many, is the removal of the word prefix or suffix 'man', in its noun or pronoun, singular or plural forms. Such as 'mailman,' 'Congressman', 'mankind', or foolishly, some people even object to the term 'man-made'. Many of our English words are derived from German. Words containing 'man' are one example. This use of 'man' does not refer to male or maleness. Any half-educated person used to know this and it never was regarded as sexist until the radical feminists arrived looking for shooting targets. Shakespeare would have said, "Told by an idiot, full of sound and fury. Signifying nothing." [241]

(As in the German language, 'man' (one N) has one meaning and is the indefinite pronoun that means 'one', 'you', 'we', 'they', 'people' or 'persons'. In like manner, the English word 'mailman' means 'mail-person' and 'man-made' means 'made by people' and so forth. German language has a separate word for male human – 'mann' (two Ns.))

But ignorance proclaims its virtue in the streets, in our schools and everywhere between. Many of our culturally ignorant citizens haven't a clue how close we came 75 years ago to solving this and our other language problems by losing a war and becoming a German-speaking nation. (Google 'Adolph Hitler' and 'Zweites Buch' his late-published sequel to Mein Kampf, for more 'inspiring' details.) Achten Sie, meine schöne Schneeflocken!

New Words

Up until the rise of a new, vocal and culturally ignorant subset among us, including some militant feminists, Gen-Xers and Millennials, everyone knew these words referred to both male and female members of the human race. With the rise of Militant Feminism and Militant Homosexuality, one is no longer sure. Consequently there are now more than 60 different words for the politically correct to refer to gender, including such amazing newly invented gender-neutral words as 'Ze,' 'Zem,' 'Zir,' 'Eir' and others being popularized and actually taught at colleges and universities such as Vanderbilt University. [242] Who would have thought?

---

[241] Macbeth, Act 5

[242] Owens, Eric, "Overpriced Fancypants University Festoons Campus With Absurd 'Ze, Zir, Zirs' PRONOUN POSTERS, The Daily Caller, September 3, 2016

INHERENT HUMAN THOUGHT DIFFERENCES

Not Subject to Manipulation

Biological and neurological differences in human beings are *real* and *distinct*. Many are inherited and we cannot change them. We may have more control over the language we speak, the trades we practice and our opinions. But lack of understanding often runs elusively deeper. Some of these differences make us either stronger together or can weaken us when we disagree or fight. Some aspects of our understanding cannot easily be manipulated and are inherent in the inner structure of our brains.

In this part of the Appendix we illustrate, both by reference to research and anecdote, some of the very different ways the human brain comprehends paradigms, concepts, memes, ideas, etc.

Without such an understanding – at least an awareness – of these differences, one is likely to dismiss the thoughts of another person or group – or worse, to not even attempt to listen, much less to understand.

What follows is clearly incomplete and not at all 'scientific', yet should illustrate the basic premise that we need to *judge others less and listen more*.

AUDITORY OR VISUAL PREFERENCE? – A PERSONAL EPIPHANY

As a young child, my mother must have said to me a thousand times, "*Look* at me when I talk to you!" And I would consistently answer her, "Darn it Mom, I *hear* you!" After a while, I would obediently turn toward her but it felt very unnatural. I seldom smiled, even when I was happy. Many years later, on a trip to Paris, I had an 'Aha!' moment.

Passing by a bookstore window, a title caught my eye and I turned in and bought it on impulse. Two Canadian researchers, Raymond and Béatrice Lessoil, had written a book which asked the question, "Are you auditory or visual?" [243] The book opened my eyes (pun intended.)

Even though I think visually, I perceive best auditorily. Strange, I thought.

In the book, this husband and wife research team explains that while some babies look at you and smile, others seldom look and seldom smile. It's not a choice, but rather they believe it is innate, in the neurological formation of the child.

═══════════════════

That was a ho-hum idea until I read more and at last discovered the cause of my mother's problem! She fashioned me that way! Well, sort of – and unintentionally.

Sometime during the nine months it took me to get ready to lie in a crib my brain development took a turn. Apparently my auditory cortex became better connected than my visual cortex.

Not that I wasn't a cute baby – all babies are cute. In fact they looked at me and said, "He looks just like a little bumble bee! Let's call him Buzzy!" And so I had that silly, infantile nickname until years later when I worked as a door-to-door salesman and my manager refused to let me introduce myself that way. Bernie Blum changed my nickname to 'Al'. Thanks, Bernie.

Many people have asked me why I always seemed sad and didn't smile. It used to trouble me a lot. As a young adult I even seriously considered plastic surgery to force my face into a bit of a smile.

═══════════════════

Who doesn't love a cute little baby who goos and gurgles and looks right at you and smiles? Those researchers discovered that the reason some babies smile is because they are imitating what they see. They see you smiling and so they smile back. It soon becomes a habit. You talk to the baby, the baby

---

[243] Lafontaine, Raymond & Béatrice Lessoil, *Etes vous auditif ou visuel, Un concept de communication*, Marabout (Belgique), 1984, 224 p.

turns, you smile, and then the baby smiles. And the *visually-oriented* baby develops a new, lifelong habit.

But babies born *auditory-oriented* seldom look at you – they can be very aware – they just don't look, and they seldom smile and their faces eventually reflect that. I was one of those babies.

The Lessoils also discovered in their research that birth sequence often affects a baby's perceptual preference. If one baby is born auditory, the next is more likely to be visual, and so forth, alternating.

The take-away message from this research is, we ought to assume that someone is paying attention when they don't or won't look at us when we converse.

I've also wondered if more-successful, smiling politicians were born predominantly visual.

LEFT-BRAINS VS. RIGHT-BRAINS

Left Brains and Computer Graphics

An example from the corporate world – In the 1960s, IBM Corporation announced that it was hiring large numbers of programmers for the herculean effort of creating and building its ground-breaking operating system – OS/360® – for its new line of System/360® computers. Over a period of less than five years the company publicly announced it hired about 100,000 programmers. A senior corporate psychologist told me that almost every one of these new hires was screened first with the widely used DPAT test (Data Processing Aptitude Test.) This expert also told me that this test had only one single question that even remotely tested for 'right-brain' thinking, which is associated with visual thinking. All the remainder of the test focused on 'left-brain', logical, mathematical thinking.

Some say this is why IBM created so much excellent software but never excelled in its early graphical products and why eventually, Xerox PARC and Apple were able to create the first true user-friendly computer interfaces. The Apple II computer was the base on which Dan Bricklin created his Visicalc spreadsheet program – the first visual-oriented tool for performing calculations – which shifted the personal computer revolution into full forward gear.

The lesson from this is that, although there were a number of people in IBM who understood and demonstrated the need for this new kind of human interface, they were overruled by a widespread and different technical way of thinking about man-machine interaction. (Note: IBM's Research Division and a couple of product development groups did some interesting experimental computer graphics work, but most never led to formal company products.)

Left and Right, Butting Heads

Several decades ago there was a researcher who did an experiment with three groups of people. Each group had four men, selected according to their preferred mode of thinking. So-called left-brain and right-brain thinking.

Left-brain thinkers typically process thoughts in more textual and abstract terms, while right-brain thinkers are usually more graphic and visually imaginative.

At one table the researcher placed four left-brain thinkers. At another there were four right-brainers. The third table there were two of each, left- and right-brain dominant.

He gave each table group the same problem to solve and an hour to do it. At the end of the hour the left-brain group had a correct solution. So did the right-brain group, but, while correct, theirs was a totally different and unexpected approach. The mixed group argued and fought the whole time and was never able to arrive at any common understanding or agreement on the problem, much less on a solution.

Surely this was a small group and can only be used to illustrate the idea, but my personal experience shows it is a very real and common situation.

When creating a team it is often useful to make sure they can work well together and give them a small problem to solve before they take on 'the big one.'

The Blackboard Swap

Because everyone has limits, why would it not be possible that two people of different cognitive modes of thinking might clash simply because one or the other become mentally 'overloaded' trying to discern what the other is talking about.

I had such an experience. A very intelligent person with whom I was working blew up at me one day. We were discussing a complicated technical matter and I was drawing a diagram on his office blackboard when he stood up and screamed, "D**n it, Al! Why do you always have to draw pictures when you talk!?"

This very smart person had a PhD in an abstract area of mathematics called lattice theory, something I was totally clueless about but greatly respected, just as I would respect the sudden appearance of Albert Einstein.

I suddenly realized the nature of our problem and when we talked about our cognitive differences for a few minutes, we jointly agreed that from that point on, I would write *words* on his blackboard (to describe the pictures in my mind) and he would translate his abstract thoughts into *pictures* on my office blackboard! This worked admirably and we never had that problem again!

A Right-Brain Computer Language

This left-brain/right-brain difference may also help explain why the computer language called APL was never widely accepted by the general programming community.[244] Many engineers and technical people still use APL because, for those who are able to understand it, it is more robust and they can write programs much faster. Studies show that most engineers are right-brain oriented thinkers.

80 Percent Were Left-Handed!

A colleague, Dr. Ray Polivka, called me excitedly one day in 1986 with a most amazing story. He had just returned from a meeting of experts in that very abstract computer language called APL. Ray has written books on APL and I was about to host a different meeting on that language.[245]

60 people we in attendance at Ray's meeting. In the course of the meeting it was discovered that 80 percent of them were left-handed. This was a highly unusual occurrence, since the U.S. national average is only nine percent who are left-handed.

All the people in this meeting were expert senior programmers, fluent in both APL and in the more standard computer languages. These attendees were the developers of the computer application that interprets and executes APL code. They were from many companies and several countries.

At that meeting, someone grumbled aloud, wondering why most computer programmers did not accept and use the APL language, since it has been shown that it can be an order of magnitude faster to code in this language than most others. (It should be noted that it takes considerably longer to acquire skill in this language than more common languages, such as C and C++).

Another attendee offered an opinion that, since mastering APL requires a degree of graphic spatial visualization, it is therefore more of a right-brain oriented language. He then mentioned some research that has shown that right-brain oriented people are more likely to be left-handed. He asked for a showing, who was left-handed. Startlingly, 48 of the 60 attendees – 80 percent – were left-handed!

---

[244] APL, originated with the unassuming name "A Programming Language" originally designed by IBM Fellow and mathematician Dr. Kenneth E. Iverson. See, *IBM Systems Journal* (Twenty-fifth Anniversary APL issue), Vol. 30, No. 4, 1991.

[245] Thompson, Norman D. and Raymond P. Polivka, *APL2 In Depth*, Springer, 1995

There has been a decades-long disagreement between APL-favoring programmers and the rest of the coding community – many of whom, although familiar only with the appearance of its unusual notation, seem to be unable to cognitively work with its implied spatial concepts.[246]

Japanese Experience – Language, Thought and Visual Thinking

Several years ago Mitsuru Ohba, a professor at Hiroshima City University and I were talking at dinner, discussing languages in general. My friend and I were comparing English with Japanese and similar languages (e.g., Chinese and Korean.) Ohba-san is fluent in both Japanese and English.

Written Japanese characters – Kanji-kana – are most often *pictures* of things, actions and concepts. But written English words (and most other western languages) are representations of the *sounds* we speak when we refer to things, actions and concepts.[247] I enquired if indeed it might be possible to think certain thoughts in Japanese that are very difficult or even impossible in Western languages.

Ohba-san replied, "Oh yes, that is well known in Japan." He went on to state that there are more left-handed people in Japan than in the western world – a clue to more graphic, right-brain thinking.

(Apparently, thinking about some problems in English (as with other western languages) requires the extra neural step of translating English symbols to sounds and then to concepts, thus an apparent extra step and extra workload on a finite human brain.)

Two people can perceive a problem totally differently, and language can play a strong role. That doesn't make either of them wrong – just different. Can anything be lost by taking a little time to agree on what the problem is and what exactly we're talking about before we go *gung ho* toward a 'solution'?

WHEN THINGS GET TOO COMPLEX

Human Complexity Limits

In 1956, Harvard professor George Miller reviewed thirty-odd previous scientific studies of human perception and made the amazing discovery that humans are limited in what they can think about. He proposed the 'seven, plus or minus two' rule.[248] That is, most people are limited to between five and nine thoughts which they can carry in their heads at any one time. That seemed to be the limit, and is referenced today in many areas, from advertising to the design of aircraft cockpits.

Beyond Seven Plus-or-Minus Two

A few years after George Miller's study, two other cognitive scientists, Averbach and Sperling, discovered that there might be a much higher limit, as long as the person was not required to *articulate* – i.e., to speak, write or communicate – any thoughts. Through a very clever series of experiments they showed that people are capable of holding – for a short time – about 25 simultaneous visual images, under some conditions. But as soon as they were required to 'output' any of these thoughts, the internal 'stack' suddenly drops from approximately 25 down to 7 (plus or minus.) 'Output' can be anything that

---

[246] The APL language exists today; in June, 2016 it celebrated its 50th anniversary. For the curious person, go to *TryAPL.org*

[247] Further complicating the matter, studies of English show that fully 30% of the written characters in English words are not phonetic, thereby requiring even more internal "lookup" activity. Learning to read is overwhelming for some children. "Phonics" methods have helped many children make the transition to reading text, and eventually to handwritten script.

[248] Miller, George A., "The Magical Number Plus or Minus Two: Some Limits on Our Capacity for Processing Information", *The Psychological Review*, 1956, vol. 63, pp.81-97.

requires external communication and can include writing down a thought or telling someone, or even verbalizing it. [249] Deeper study of this phenomenon is a fascinating pursuit.

Averbach and Sperling's work hasn't received as much publicity as Miller's, possibly because of the technical journal in which it was originally published in 1961.

Other Evidence of Greater Mental Capacity

"Flow" – Averbach and Sperling's finding are suggestive of what happens to practitioners of deep meditation, or what the best-selling author Csikszentmihalyi calls 'flow'. [250] The idea of insulating deep thinkers from distractions seems to be partly related to the seminal work by architects who designed the IBM Research Laboratory in Santa Theresa, California. [251] They determined that highly productive and creative computer programmers needed to have quiet, peaceful and spacious places to work, without interruptions. They subsequently designed the entire building and the work spaces and communication facilities to meet these requirements.

The Still, Small Voice – Biblical Scripture suggests a similar result. Paraphrasing the prophet Elijah, "I looked for the Lord in the windstorm, the earthquake and the fire and did not find him, but in the sound of a gentle whisper." [252] Some translations refer to the gentle whisper as the "still, small voice." Clearly, deep thinking and revelation are not to be found in loud noise and cacophony.

A Need to Repress – Some have speculated that the loud music that is popular with hormonally nascent young people helps them suppress deeper thoughts that may be uncomfortable especially to the emotionally and spiritually unprepared.

Chemical-Induced Calmness – Some drugs can suppress. But others can sedate and calm. Wine and spirits have been a part of most earthly cultures since the beginning of time. [253] Some individuals say they find greater ability to create, think and find peace and union with the Universe when they are sedated with natural or artificial chemicals, such as mescaline, certain mushrooms, LSD and other so-called hallucinogens. But there is a strong moral and societal resistance to these methods because they can lead to out of control behavior and addiction among our weakest.

And in our millisecond-conscious western culture, anyone who sits calmly meditating in public for more than a few minutes may be regarded as ill or mentally incapacitated. People in white coats may soon appear to save them.

PERSONALITY TYPES

Predicting Inter-Personal Barriers

Further separating us from effective dialogue may be our disparate personality types. In an attempt to understand differences in personality, the Myers-Briggs Type Indicator (MBTI) method has become popular in some areas of psychology. [254]

---

[249] Averbach, E, and G. Sperling, "Short-term Storage of Information in Vision", *Symposium on Information Theory*, C. Cherry (Ed.) London, Butterworth, 1961, pp. 196-211.

[250] Csikszentmihalyi, Mihaly, *Flow: The Psychology of Optimal Experience*, HarperCollins, 2008, 285.pp.

[251] McCue, Gerald M., "IBM's Santa Teresa Laboratory—Architectural design for program development", *IBM Systems Journal*, Vol 17, No. 1, 1978, pp.4-25

[252] *1 Kings 19:11-12, (NIV)*

[253] Interesting exceptions – Some Christian sects and all Islamic sects.

[254] Myers, Isabel Briggs with Peter B. Myers (1995) [1980]. *Gifts Differing: Understanding Personality Type*. Mountain View, CA: Davies-Black Publishing

The MBTI method proposes four different measures/types of a personality. Each of these four can have two opposite values, so there are sixteen different combinations or types.

- **E/I** – Extraversion vs. Introversion
- **S/N** – Sensing vs. iNtuition
- **T/F** – Thinking vs. Feeling
- **J/P** – Judgment vs. Perception

When combined, 16 different personality types emerge. Of course, few people are all one extreme type or another. For example someone may possess both a measure of extraversion *and* introversion – somewhere in the middle between 'E' and 'I'.

The resultant 16 type combinations can be characterized as in this table:

INTJ	Scientist or Architect	**INFJ**	Protector or Advocate
INTP	Thinker or Logician	**INFP**	Idealist or Mediator
ENTJ	Executive or Commander	**ENFJ**	Giver or Protagonist
ENTP	Visionary or Debater	**ENFP**	Inspirer or Campaigner
ISTJ	Duty Fulfiller or Logistician	**ISTP**	Mechanic or Virtuoso
ISFJ	Nurturer or Defender	**ISFP**	Artist or Adventurer
ESTJ	Guardian or Executive	**ESTP**	Doer or Entrepreneur
ESFJ	Caregiver or Consul	**ESFP**	Performer or Entertainer

This is one way of illustrating the great difference in our cognitive styles and personalities – the way we think and act.

But most interesting is when one considers the different kinds of interaction between two individuals. Each person can have one of these 16 different types and there are 16 times 16, or 256 different interaction combinations. Actually there are only 136 *unique* combinations of types.[255] A unique combination might be an ISTF person interacting with an ESTP, or an ENTP interacting with another ENTP) That's still quite a lot of diverse combinations!

We need to be aware of and respect our differences when we are attempting dialogue, especially in difficult moments. Imagine a situation where, for example, an ENTJ (Executive/Commander) is trying to communicate with an ISFP (Artist/Adventurer) about an important matter with which neither is very familiar. This is another illustration of how difficult it can be to understand one another and our need to back off a bit when discussions get heated. Are we being disagreed with on substance? Or are we seeing things differently?

(Note: the Myers-Briggs measurement is still regarded as controversial among some cognitive psychologists and in addition to a faithful set of followers, it has its many detractors who disagree with the extent of its accuracy and applicability.)

---

[255] Since there are 16 different four-letter types, there are 16 x 16, or 256 different combinations. But there are only 256 - 16 = 240 combinations of *different* types. Of those 240 only 120 are unique combinations (e.g., ENTP ⇔ ISTJ is the same as ISTJ ⇔ ENTP). Now, by adding in the 16 pairs of like types (e.g., INTJ ⇔ INTJ, INFJ ⇔ INFJ, INTP ⇔ INTP, etc.), we see that there are 120 + 16 = 136 *unique* combinations.

AUTISM, SAVANTS AND OTHER LIKE-MINDED PEOPLE

So far, we have assumed that human differences are explainable in commonly understandable terms. But what about people who have brains that are provably 'wired' differently?

Autism Spectrum Disorder – ASD – affects an increasingly large number of children.[256] It is characterized by persistent social communication and interaction impairments and restricted, repetitive patterns of behavior, interests or activities. There is a test for it, the Autism-Spectrum Quotient (or AQ) test but that is only an indicator and not a proof of the disorder.

People with ASD are often very different in their manner of communicating and the things that interest them. And many on the ASD spectrum – from the milder end, called Asperger's Syndrome to the other extreme – severe autism – can be very sensitive to noises and unusual sounds.

Autistic people are often weak in verbal skills but perform well or very well in tasks requiring visual of mental imagery skills.

Many on the ASD spectrum hold responsible jobs and can function in society. But their behavior may cause us to misjudge them.

Albert Einstein was slightly autistic. And supposedly so were a number of other geniuses, including Susan Boyle the singer, likewise Dan Aykroyd the actor, Isaac Newton and Thomas Jefferson.

So called 'savants' – people who can perform amazing mental tasks are usually autistic. One such person, Stephen Wiltshire requires only one helicopter tour of a city, such as London or Rome, in order to draw the entire landscape in all its detail, down to the last window ledge. Another savant, Leslie Lemke only needs to hear a musical work played once before she can play it on a piano. That includes any musical style, including complex classical pieces. These are gifted autistic people.

Autistic author Temple Grandin has written extensively about autism and how it affects people both positively and negatively and current research into its suspected causes.[257] According to Grandin, only about ten percent of autistics are savants but most savants are autistic.[258]

ANCIENT AWARENESS

St. Paul acknowledged in Chapter 12 of his letter to the early Christians in the city of Corinth that we are each created with different gifts:

> *To each individual the manifestation of the Spirit is given for some benefit. To one is given through the Spirit the expression of wisdom; to another the expression of knowledge according to the same Spirit; to another faith by the same Spirit; to another gifts of healing by the one Spirit; to another mighty deeds; to another prophecy; to another discernment of spirits; to another varieties of tongues; to another interpretation of tongues. ... Some people God has designated in the church to be, first, apostles; second, prophets; third, teachers; then, mighty deeds; then gifts of healing, assistance, administration, and varieties of tongues. ... Strive eagerly for the greatest spiritual gifts.*
>
> *1 Cor. 12:7-10, 28, 31, (NAB)*

---

[256] Recent government statistics show that between 1 in 60 to 1 in 40 new births are children with ASD, with a greater percentage appearing in male births.

[257] Grandin, Temple, *The Autistic Brain: Helping Different Kinds of Minds Succeed*, Houghton Mifflin Harcourt, New York, 2014 (Chapter 3, "Sequencing the Autistic Brain" presents an excellent overview of current research into the hereditary and so-called *de novo* (after conception) causes of Autism and other brain disorders.)

[258] *Ibid.*, Chapter 6

CONCLUSION

The Social Media Paradox

We are closer today and farther apart than ever. People are no more different than they ever were but something has changed in the way we interact.

Our innate created human differences and our acquired and adopted ways make it difficult to understand and talk with some people. We have begun to divide into cliques and subgroups, each of which thinks alike but can no longer understand or communicate with others who think differently. Even worse, as we *isolate* from those other groups we allow progressively less opportunity to get to know and understand them. *This is our garden where hostility grows.*

Our electronic technology and the Internet have greatly weakened traditional methods that once helped us get to know, adapt to and work with different and unusual people. Our great technological 'revolution' has brought us into closer contact but our human weaknesses, cognitive differences and fears have driven our understanding and empathy farther apart. People who think differently, for whatever reason, are more likely to be pushed away rather than included. Rejected, they join cliques that increasingly dislike others.

After a few unpleasant encounters between these groups, any hostility causes even more clustering and group division. It is so much easier to surround ourselves with people who agree with us, who don't make us feel uncomfortable and if need be, who can defend us. We retreat to our safe spaces – our 'tribes' and close friends to the exclusion of others.

> **NO WiFi Available. Talk to each other.**
>
> *Sign in Store Window*

Exhausted and Distracted

Our weaknesses are made worse by lack of relaxed time together. One study showed that the average American father spends about five minutes a day in conversation with his children. Americans work longer hours than almost any other people in the developed world. We are the Exhausted Nation. We have little relaxed time to share with our families, neighbors or communities.

We are burying ourselves in electronic entertainment and social media. Children don't play outside with other children – they sit indoors and communicate through their screen devices. Roughhousing and informal sports are a thing of the past in many communities. Less real interaction leads to more estrangement and hostility.

The Work before Us

Part of the cure is to *make time* to be with other people and their communities and defer judgement until we can dialogue together and begin to peacefully work toward common interests and goals. Families should do the same. Get off Facebook and Twitter. Go out and actually talk face to face with real people. It may be almost as difficult as learning a new language. *Think about it.*

More work lies ahead.

APPENDIX D. PRAYER FOR THE PROTECTION OF RELIGIOUS LIBERTY [259]

O God our Creator, from your provident hand we have received our right to life, liberty, and the pursuit of happiness. You have called us as your people and given us the right and the duty to worship you, the only true God, and your Son, Jesus Christ. Through the power and working of your Holy Spirit, you call us to live out our faith in the midst of the world, bringing the light and the saving truth of the Gospel to every corner of society.

We ask you to bless us in our vigilance for the gift of religious liberty. Give us the strength of mind and heart to readily defend our freedoms when they are threatened; give us courage in making our voices heard on behalf of the rights of your Church and the freedom of conscience of all people of faith.

Grant, we pray, O heavenly Father, a clear and united voice to all your sons and daughters gathered in your Church in this decisive hour in the history of our nation, so that, with every trial withstood and every danger overcome — for the sake of our children, our grandchildren, and all who come after us — this great land will always be "one nation, under God, indivisible, with liberty and justice for all."

We ask this through Christ our Lord.

Amen.

---

[259] Copied from the website of the United States Conference of Catholic Bishops – *www.usccb.org/*

APPENDIX E. SAMPLE CIVILITY PLEDGE – 2001

A Call for Increased Public Civility and Dignity

Pledge to the Citizens of the Town of Beekman

The Town of Beekman has been under a cloud for several years; Local papers have had a string of editorials decrying town officials' repetitive failure to conduct themselves with dignity and civility. Under several previous administrations, town meetings have had to be brought to order by law enforcement officials. Elected officials have refused to cooperate or work with other elected officials.

Many citizens have expressed discomfort in the manner in which they personally have been treated and how the town's business has been conducted. Sadly, in past years our town has become something of a laughingstock in the county.

Therefore, I the undersigned candidate for election pledge that if elected I will work toward a greater degree of civility in the conduct of Town and/or County business, both by personal example and by requiring the same of those town employees whom I appoint or help to appoint, specifically:

Main objective

- The citizens of this town who elect me come from many different backgrounds and ways of thinking. Those who express their concerns deserve my full attention. I will attempt to treat every citizen and official with the patience, respect and dignity due a respected member of my own family.

- As a leader, it is my responsibility to bring people together on issues. I will help the town find common ground. I will avoid trading in rumors that injure the good name or reputation of others.

Promotion of harmony

- I will listen to issues and complaints from citizens and my fellow officials in a fair and balanced manner, recognizing that some may test my patience. Nonetheless, I will endeavor to give everyone a fair hearing and try to explain my disagreements in a polite and civil manner.

- I may disagree with and debate issues but I will not attack persons, nor will I trade in rumor or innuendo at the expense of the dignity of another person or group.

- I will be proactive, and will encourage others to work proactively, in following these precepts as they conduct the town's business fairly and in the full light of day.

Resolution of disputes

- If another person misrepresents or offends me, I will first try to resolve the problem with that person directly and privately, one-on-one.

- Then, if that person refuses, I will try to peacefully arbitrate and resolve the problem with the help of one or two other people.

- Only if these first two steps fail will I discuss the matter publicly.

Finally

- If I find that I become unable or unwilling to support or fulfill the above, I will voluntarily resign my office and make way for those who can.

I the undersigned agree that the above is in the best interests of my town and I will adhere to these principles to the best of my ability. I further acknowledge that this agreement may be publicly communicated with my fellow townspeople.

(Name) _____ (Date) _____

(Please return early. Signed returns will not be acknowledged after Friday, October 26, 2001)

APPENDIX F. HOW ALL 50 STATE CONSTITUTIONS REFER TO 'GOD'

Alabama 1901, Preamble.
We the people of the State of Alabama, invoking the favor and guidance of Almighty God, do ordain and establish the following Constitution ...

Alaska 1956, Preamble.
We, the people of Alaska, grateful to God and to those who founded our nation and pioneered this great land ...

Arizona 1911, Preamble.
We, the people of the State of Arizona, grateful to Almighty God for our liberties, do ordain this Constitution ...

Arkansas 1874, Preamble.
We, the people of the State of Arkansas, grateful to Almighty God for the privilege of choosing our own form of government ...

California 1879, Preamble.
We, the People of the State of California, grateful to Almighty God for our freedom ...

Colorado 1876, Preamble.
We, the people of Colorado, with profound reverence for the Supreme Ruler of Universe ...

Connecticut 1818, Preamble.
The People of Connecticut, acknowledging with gratitude the good Providence of God in permitting them to enjoy ...

Delaware 1897, Preamble.
Through Divine Goodness all men have, by nature, the rights of worshipping and serving their Creator according to the dictates of their consciences ...

Florida 1885, Preamble.
We, the people of the State of Florida, grateful to Almighty God for our constitutional liberty, establish this Constitution ...

Georgia 1777, Preamble.
We, the people of Georgia, relying upon protection and guidance of Almighty God, do ordain and establish this Constitution ...

Hawaii 1959, Preamble.
We, the people of Hawaii, Grateful for Divine Guidance ... establish this Constitution ...

Idaho 1889, Preamble.
We, the people of the State of Idaho, grateful to Almighty God for our freedom, to secure its blessings ...

Illinois 1870, Preamble.
We, the people of the State of Illinois, grateful to Almighty God for the civil, political and religious liberty which He hath so long permitted us to enjoy and looking to Him for a blessing on our endeavors ...

Indiana 1851, Preamble.
We, the People of the State of Indiana, grateful to Almighty God for the free exercise of the right to choose our form of government ...

Iowa 1857, Preamble.
We, the People of the State of Iowa, grateful to the Supreme Being for the blessings hitherto enjoyed, and feeling our dependence on Him for a continuation of these blessings, establish this Constitution ...

Kansas 1859, Preamble.
We, the people of Kansas, grateful to Almighty God for our civil and religious privileges. establish this Constitution ...

Kentucky 1891, Preamble.
We, the people of the Commonwealth of grateful to Almighty God for the civil, political and religious liberties ...

Louisiana 1921, Preamble.
We, the people of the State of Louisiana, grateful to Almighty God for the civil, political and religious liberties we enjoy ...

Maine 1820, Preamble.
We the People of Maine ... acknowledging with grateful hearts the goodness of the Sovereign Ruler of the Universe in affording us an opportunity ... and imploring His aid and direction ...

Maryland 1776, Preamble.
We, the people of the state of Maryland, grateful to Almighty God for our civil and religious liberty ...

Massachusetts 1780, Preamble.
We ...the people of Massachusetts, acknowledging with grateful hearts, the goodness of the Great Legislator of the Universe ... in the course of His Providence, an opportunity ...and devoutly imploring His direction ...

Michigan 1908, Preamble.
We, the people of the State of Michigan, grateful to Almighty God for the blessings of freedom ... establish this Constitution ...

Minnesota 1857, Preamble.
We, the people of the State of Minnesota, grateful to God for our civil and religious liberty, and desiring to perpetuate its blessings ...

Mississippi 1890, Preamble.
We, the people of Mississippi in convention assembled, grateful to Almighty God, and invoking His blessing on our work ...

Missouri 1845, Preamble.
We, the people of Missouri, with profound reverence for the Supreme Ruler of the Universe, and grateful for His goodness ... establish this Constitution ...

Montana 1889, Preamble.
We, the people of Montana, grateful to Almighty God for the blessings of liberty. establish this Constitution ...

Nebraska 1875, Preamble.
We, the people, grateful to Almighty God for our freedom ... establish this Constitution ...

Nevada 1864, Preamble.
We the people of the State of Nevada, grateful to Almighty God for our freedom establish this Constitution ...

New Hampshire 1792, Part I. Art. I. Sec. V.
Every individual has a natural and unalienable right to worship God according to the dictates of his own conscience ...

New Jersey 1844, Preamble.
We, the people of the State of New Jersey, grateful to Almighty God for civil and religious liberty which He hath so long permitted us to enjoy, and looking to Him for a blessing on our endeavors ...

New Mexico 1911, Preamble.
We, the People of New Mexico, grateful to Almighty God for the blessings of liberty ...

New York 1846, Preamble.
We, the people of the State of New York, grateful to Almighty God for our freedom, in order to secure its blessings ...

North Carolina 1868, Preamble.
We the people of the State of North Carolina, grateful to Almighty God, the Sovereign Ruler of Nations, for our civil, political, and religious liberties, and acknowledging our dependence upon Him for the continuance of those ...

North Dakota 1889, Preamble.
We, the people of North Dakota, grateful to Almighty God for the blessings of civil and religious liberty, do ordain ...

Ohio 1852, Preamble.
We the people of the state of Ohio, grateful to Almighty God for our freedom, to secure its blessings and to promote our common ...

Oklahoma 1907, Preamble.
Invoking the guidance of Almighty God, in order to secure and perpetuate the blessings of liberty ... establish this ...

Oregon 1857, Bill of Rights, Article I. Section 2.
All men shall be secure in the Natural right, to worship Almighty God according to the dictates of their consciences ...

Pennsylvania 1776, Preamble.
We, the people of Pennsylvania, grateful to Almighty God for the blessings of civil and religious liberty, and humbly invoking His guidance ...

Rhode Island 1842, Preamble.
We the People of the State of Rhode Island grateful to Almighty God for the civil and religious liberty which He hath so long permitted us to enjoy, and looking to Him for a blessing ...

South Carolina 1778, Preamble.
We, the people of the State of South Carolina. grateful to God for our liberties, do ordain and establish this Constitution ...

South Dakota 1889, Preamble.
We, the people of South Dakota, grateful to Almighty God for our civil and religious liberties ... establish this ...

Tennessee 1796, Art. XI. III.
That all men have a natural and indefeasible right to worship Almighty God according to the dictates of their own consciences ...

Texas 1845, Preamble.
We the People of the Republic of Texas, acknowledging, with gratitude, the grace and beneficence of God ...

Utah 1896, Preamble.
Grateful to Almighty God for life and liberty, we establish this Constitution ...

Vermont 1777, Preamble.
Whereas all government ought to ... enable the individuals who compose it to enjoy their natural rights, and other blessings which the Author of Existence has bestowed on man ...

Virginia 1776, Bill of Rights, XVI ...
Religion, or the Duty which we owe our Creator ... can be directed only by Reason ... and that it is the mutual duty of all to practice Christian Forbearance, Love and Charity towards each other ...

Washington 1889, Preamble.
We the People of the State of Washington, grateful to the Supreme Ruler of the Universe for our liberties, do ordain this Constitution ...

West Virginia 1872, Preamble.
Since through Divine Providence we enjoy the blessings of civil, political and religious liberty, we, the people of West Virginia, reaffirm our faith in and constant reliance upon God ...

Wisconsin 1848, Preamble.
We, the people of Wisconsin, grateful to Almighty God for our freedom, domestic tranquility ...

Wyoming 1890, Preamble.
We, the people of the State of Wyoming, grateful to God for our civil, political, and religious liberties, establish this Constitution ...

Appendix G. Substance Addiction – Help and Recovery

Why did 70,000 people die of drug overdoses in the U.S in 2017? Why has drug use skyrocketed and why are millions of people becoming addicted to drugs and alcohol? Do we understand the causes and can we do anything about it?

Who is at Risk?

Why hasn't fifty years of "Just say 'NO' " eliminated the drug scourge that continues to destroy our children, one by one? There is hardly an elementary school child today who hasn't come across a drug user. Platitudes and abstractions don't prepare them to confront their own fears, temptations and crises.

According to mental health professionals, the leading cause of addiction is the prior mental state of the addict. Put in simple terms, the person is often overwhelmed to the point of depression and anxiety with the stresses of life. Substance abuse becomes a form of self-medication.

That's the bad news. The better news is that there is hope and treatment where it is wanted and accepted.

Weak, Depressed Children

Why aren't we raising strong children anymore? There seems to be too little peace of mind and too much turmoil in growing up. Turmoil and stress that, sixty years ago, was unimaginable during peacetime.

This new generation is weaker and *less* able to handle life's problems. On college campuses the word, 'snowflake' now refers to more than the weather. It refers to children – who should be on the crest of adulthood – who melt at the slightest inconvenient thought, word or action of another.

Has life ever dealt you 'ups and downs'? How would your children be able to handle *your* past setbacks? Some kids become overwhelmed by events many adults would regard as trivia. For example, being the last one chosen – or rejected – for the baseball team. Failing an exam or a homework assignment. Being ignored or rejected or even bullied by someone who yesterday was a friend. Being 'un-friended' on social media. There are so many hurts to endure and little strength or armor to prevent the wounds.

Childhood insecurity has always been part of life. It is worse when there's no one to talk with about it. In times past we would run to our parents or grandparents. Today, most of them are over their heads with all that's changing so rapidly. Many sincere, loving, well-meaning adults are totally out of touch or unavailable.

And it is harder to endure when our young people have little acquired 'immunity' from a lifetime of being overprotected.

Lives of Quiet Desperation

Today's kids assume the world is totally falling apart. They constantly hear of terrorism, "wars and rumors of war." They may have had friends who died from overdoses or suicide. And, as always there are occasional horrible natural disasters somewhere. The TV and Internet relentlessly, aggressively push it in their faces, day after day. Their world is spinning out of control. There is no respite from the daily bombardment of bad news. And lacking experience or judgement, they cannot cope.

Have you heard about the awful 800 pound gorilla in the corner that no one wants to talk or think about? It's the constant fear of parental divorce. Kids hear mommy and daddy argue and fear strikes deep. Every kid today knows someone whose apparently happy family has suddenly disintegrated.

In 1960 almost every American mother stayed home and raised the family. Times have changed all that. Today the majority of moms are out in the workplace. Many by choice, and many more to keep the family from sinking in a sea of taxes and acquired debt.

Family economics are at a low point. Americans pay more in taxes than for food and clothing combined. More than half of American families are living from paycheck to paycheck. One quarter of Americans have zero money saved for emergencies.

Can your kids talk openly with you – or at least someone – about their deepest fears, without being lectured and admonished? A lot of kids think that the turmoil and fear in their lives is normal and indeed many quietly habituate and adapt to it. But when the ups and downs get overwhelming and someone suggests an exciting distraction – for the unarmed, unprepared kid, the trouble soon begins.

BECOMING AN ADDICT – THE PROCESS

Why Do Kids Turn to Drugs??

Why do people do drugs? Despite all the simplistic propaganda, it's not because someone offers them and then they get 'hooked'. Sure that can happen, and we need to teach them to avoid if that happens. But something else is usually first.

It's state of mind. The happy child, engaged in a caring family and with a decent life and friends isn't a prime candidate. The child who learns to handle disappointment isn't a prime candidate. A loved child is much safer. But sometimes even all that is not enough. There's always the unexpected and we have to be alert.

It's the kid whose life starts to overwhelm them – inexperience and poor emotional defenses. Not necessarily emotional or mental illness, although that is a factor. Just the child's emotional state. No one knows why, but some children are weak and they easily succumb, while others are strong and able to handle emotional upsets. Perhaps a clue is in the statistic that shows adolescent children from fatherless homes are 10 times more likely to wind up in chemical abuse centers.[260]

So, just like starting a fire, first you need the dry wood. Then the tinder. Then the spark. The dry wood of internalized, unexpressed stress, the tinder of a particularly tough event and the spark of distraction & excitement – perhaps in the form of an offer to, "Try this!"

A Few Functional Addicts

Too many adolescents don't believe that addictions are permanent. They believe they could stop when they want to. They know and hear that some people can manage their addictions – even stop using if they want. Optimism and ignorance overwhelm common sense and they believe getting 'hooked' only happens to other kids – '*those losers!*'

Some people – a very few functional addicts –can control their use. I once worked for a very capable person who I later discovered was a regular cocaine user, but could function adequately when he needed to. I have also known a couple of 'social alcoholics' who could function when they had to – and do it well. Only close friends and family members even knew. But these are the very rare exceptions.

Onset of the Disease

It would be nice if we could raise our kids in some faraway place where there is no TV or bad influences. The fantasy of *Little House on the Prairie* comes to mind.[261] But the real-world is that kids can get hooked before we know it. I've personally known people who have burned their brains out and

---

[260] *https://thefatherlessgeneration.wordpress,com/statistics*
[261] A widely read children's series of books (and later a TV series) written by Laura Ingalls Wilder about 80 years ago that remain popular to this day.

been permanently damaged by drugs and alcohol. Naloxone[262] and "just say 'NO' " alone won't save our kids. *We* must do the job.

Before there is any hope of healing, someone has to recognize the problem and possibly intervene. Assuming there are caring parents, relatives, or friends, the first step is *awareness*. It comes in many ways. Sudden school grade crash. Change in attitude, behavior or appearance. Strange pills or packs of powder hidden in secret places. Revelation from a friend. Or, God forbid, a call from the hospital or a uniformed officer at the door. Whatever it takes, the recognition too often comes after the damage has begun.

Drug addiction and alcohol addiction are *diseases*. In the past we often incorrectly blamed the patient or their family for many diseases (e.g., stomach ulcers, depression, and schizophrenia). Blame doesn't cure. Research now shows that, like many diseases, some addictions are acquired and others facilitated by our genetic structure.

Counselling and punishment aren't effective alone, any more than pretending there is no real problem. ("… and we really shouldn't talk about it outside the family!") Not talking about and treating this disease is called *enabling* the afflicted one and results in postponing and ultimately denying them proper treatment.

Condemned by the Enabler

If you or your family are suddenly caught up in this crisis, you need to understand that you are not the first to be there. First, admit there is a problem. Addiction is a treatable disease and there is hope. Denial and delay can make it too late to help. But if help is wanted and summoned it is available.

Deniers can be 'enablers'. An enabler is someone who does all the wrong things for loving reasons thinking they're protecting their addict. Instead, they unknowingly reinforce the self-destructive behavior. They pay his overdue electric bill, because he lost his job. They buy her groceries when her pantry is empty. They let him live in their home and treat him like a baby, feeding, clothing, cleaning up after him.

Out of an intention of love the enabler will do everything to help, except what is really needed: to intervene and arrange treatment for the addiction and its underlying problems.

SUPPORT AND TREATMENT

A new beginning can start with an invitation to the addict to attend a meeting. *Narcotics Anonymous*[263] (NA), *Alcoholics Anonymous*[264] (AA) or one of the several other local or national self-help groups. Non-using family members or friends can start the process and get help from *Nar-Anon*[265] or *Al-Anon*[266], two family support groups.

Alateen[267] is another fellowship support group for young people and teens whose lives have been affected by someone else's drinking. These groups have websites and toll-free phone numbers and anonymity is strictly observed.

---

[262] Naloxone, an overdose-reversing drug, available as an easily administered nasal spray, over the counter without prescription in most states. When there is an opioid overdose, **knowing how to use Naloxone and keeping it within reach can save a life**. The nasal spray can be administered by anyone and has been reported to have little to no side effects if opioids are not present. *But always check first with a doctor or pharmacist before considering this option.*

[263] *Narcotics Anonymous* – Get started online at: *www.na.org/meetingsearch*

[264] *Alcoholics Anonymous* – State by state groups, online at: *www.aa.org/pages/en_US/find-aa-resources*

[265] Family help: *Nar-Anon* – Online at: *www.nar-anon.org/find-a-meeting/*

[266] Family help with alcohol problems – Online at: *al-anon.org/find-a-meeting*

[267] For young people and teens – Online at *www.al-anon.alateen.org* (Click on "Alateen – for teens")

These programs have a proven approach, usually employing a so-called '12-step' method, which eventually involves a sponsor – someone who has been abstinent for some time and is willing to stay in communication and help. There are also some other groups that do not use group meetings, 12-step or sponsors, but they are said to be less effective.

For some, especially those who are sent against their will by the courts, there are rehabilitation and treatment centers for every kind of addiction. They range from free, church-sponsored and government paid, to high-priced private clinics where the wealthy may send their children or themselves. Outcomes vary.

A positive outcome ultimately is more likely when there is a positive desire and attitude on the part of the addict. History shows it is almost impossible for an addict to recover without the help of another understanding and capable person and that is why these support groups have become so important.

RECOVERY AND VIGILANCE

Evidence shows that recovery is faster with support than trying to do it alone. Relapse is always a danger and having a sponsor and a group who understand the struggles can be a valuable asset. Also having a peer group to support and guide the family is invaluable.

Most professionals agree there is no such thing as a cure for addiction. This disease permanently changes the brain physiology. The abstinent addict must remind him- or herself of this and be eternally vigilant, "one day at a time," every day, and forever.

Those who follow this path can recover their lives and go on to be productive and a benefit to themselves and a blessing to those around them.

———————

N.B. – Any Internet addresses, QR codes and telephone numbers in this book are offered as a resource. They are not intended in any way to be or to imply an endorsement, nor does the author vouch for the content of these sites, numbers or references.

APPENDIX H. PERSISTENT CHALLENGES FOR FAMILIES AND CHILDREN

The purpose of this appendix is to underline some of the more pressing problems faced by our next generations and what we might be able to do now to guide them. Many of us are deeply concerned about what is happening to the so-called Millennial generation and their emotional and intellectual unpreparedness for adult life in a dangerous and unpredictable world.

But we are even more concerned about the newest, post-Millennial generation who are measurably delayed in emotional and social maturity and are, in the words of one researcher, "at the forefront of the worst mental health crisis in generations."

The toys our children's children are playing with are destroying their minds and their souls and a great battle lies ahead to understand and confront this new percolating evil.

Finally it is time to call out those fringe feminists and their sick agenda which continues to promote destruction of the basis of family stability.

WEAK FAMILIES AND MISGUIDED YOUTH

Families have evolved over time from the earliest days when a clan was ruled by an authoritarian male head in a so-called 'trustee family' to the 'domestic family' of the 20th Century and now more and more we continue the decline toward today's powerless 'atomistic' family in which sexual preferences and individual autonomy begin to rule over traditions of family obligation. The atomistic family is right at the bottom and sociologists say it is leading to the destruction of our civilizations. [268]

Our crumbling families are doing a wretched job of guiding our youth. The inevitable result is a new generation of children whose social habits and perceived needs are unrecognizable to the older generations. Many of these children are unprepared for the challenges of the real world and they are truly suffering, as evidenced by their social behavior, medications, counsellors and their suicide rates.

There was a time when young people turned to older adults for lessons in living and learned some wisdom without having to make their own mistakes. Many kids today are sailing alone and unguided in dangerous and uncharted waters.

PARENTS WHO LOSE CONTROL

Most parents are too busy – assuming that they are living together with their children. If they are separated or divorced, they are even busier and more stressed.

Many of these parents are desperate to regain control over their children's lives but are unable, as they themselves struggle, just to survive.

Today's kids are saturated with movies, videos, pornography of all kinds, and addictive video games – some of them quite horrible by grandparent standards. All while going through the usual problems of growing up, with the hopeful goal of becoming members of a civilized society.

Meanwhile their parents are working like crazy to pay for all the things they have bought on credit and will have to pay off over time. Including hundreds of dollars for game boxes, smartphones, tablets and computers. And if parents are separated or divorced, as one happy salesman recently commented, "Then we will sell *twice* as many of what (an intact family) needs."

---

[268] Jarvis, Douglas E., *The Family and the Western Political Order*, PhD. Thesis, Carleton University, Ottawa, Ontario, 2014.

Parents give in to children's demands at a remarkable rate. It's almost like they feel that denying their child an electronic toy is akin to child abuse. But real abuse is what happens to the child when the parents are too distracted to notice what kids are learning from these monster 'toys'.

If you try to conduct a conversation with a child playing one of those addictive smartphone games, it is totally impossible.

CHILDREN'S VENOMOUS VIDEO GAMES

Destroying Children's Souls

We are constantly fed mixed messages about graphic video and video game violence. The folks who create and sell these games claim they do nothing to harm developing plastic minds.

That is a blatant lie.

Not only do they harm average minds but they trigger incredible evil in the minds of mentally disturbed people who can go on to do horrible deeds. Columbine murderers Dylan Klebold and Eric Harris enjoyed playing the shooting game called "Doom". This is a program that contains satanic imagery and lets users participate in graphic violence. The player 'lives' through the eyes of the shooter. One analyst estimates that there are more than 20 million players of this game alone around the world. (Yes, we are exporting this kind of trash – WMDs – "weapons of mental destruction" to innocent minds around the world.) [269, 270]

Three years ago I received in the mail an unsolicited six-month subscription to a 'gaming' magazine. This was a real eye-opener. The blood and guts and gore and horror depicted is beyond telling.[271] The moral lessons 'taught' by these games are chilling to say the least: They teach that murder for profit is OK; prostitution is normal; stealing is good; every form of evil is portrayed as noble, because it is exciting and therefore 'fun'.

So-called 'experts' tell us that these are just games and have no lasting impact on children. Dozens of studies later they are still debating this. A recent article in *USA Today* quotes a new study that finally shows that these game players actually become more physically aggressive. The article mentions 24 earlier studies that confirm these players are more violent and aggressive.[272]

There will undoubtedly be another 24 such studies which will also be actively discounted, ignored or suppressed by those Big Money interests which they threaten.

Video Games – A 100 Billion Dollar Industry

In 2017 the video game market accounted for more than 100 billion dollars in sales and is *growing steadily at more than ten percent per year* – faster than our population is growing and faster than our national economy.

There is a lot of advertising and promotional money out there to 'buy' favorable studies and continue to keep parents in the dark about how incredibly evil these games are. And only the most naïve and ignorant among us would believe that the owners of these game-producing companies don't want to bias our thinking.

We are being deceived, our children's minds are being damaged and it is time to wake up and act!

---

[269] See note on 'Hollywood exports' earlier in this book.

[270] I get weary listening to all the political bobble-heads castigating our past leaders who spoke of exporting "nation building"; I wonder at their ignorance of our ongoing exporting of nation-erosion through our mind-poisoning electronic 'entertainment'.

[271] Pay a visit to your local book chain store and browse through some of these 'gaming' magazines for a good look at what our children's after-school education looks like.

[272] Snider, Mike, "Study confirms link between violent video games and physical aggression", *USA Today*, October 2, 2018

Is it possible that a video or game can alter an adult mind but will have no lasting effect on that of a child? Is there any evidence or counter-evidence?

Corporations spend large sums of money for training videos, games and simulators to change how their employees think and work – to promote and change habits, skills, ideas and behaviors.

Making and selling corporate and industrial training videos, simulators, games and other electronic aids is a multi-billion dollar business – by one estimate, also over 100 billion dollars yearly. If these things are specifically made to change the thinking and habits of adult minds, then how much more susceptible are the minds of young children to the same media?

Irrefutable medical studies show that a young person's brain is still developing well past the age of 24. To assert that kids are somehow not affected is blatant nonsense and yet these greedy purveyors of corruption and filth continue to hide behind the First Amendment. Meanwhile our legislators do nothing and parents are overwhelmed by life's other complexities.

If by law, drugs, alcohol and tobacco are restricted from children, why have we not done the same for these more toxic *mental* poisons? Children's minds are being severely damaged, especially those on the margins who have preexisting psychological or developmental problems.

It is well past time to take control and stop the lies by those who are selling death and disaster to our children. It's time to let our children advance and grow and learn the joy of a normal childhood.

What Can We Do?

Barring a national fight to restrict the worst of these videos and video games from young children, the fight must be fought in our own homes and communities. [273] Without a national ban, our bests hope is to be very careful about giving smartphones, game boxes and computers to our children. Then we must take steps to prevent them from downloading objectionable applications ('apps'.)

It gets harder to do if children already have these devices and apps. You might want to have your child take you through some of these games so you can see what's on his/her phone or tablet or computer. Then, be very gentle. Setting boundaries needs to start with caution. Today's kids have a way of doing what *they* think best, regardless of parental wisdom and choice. It's part of their growing up process – called 'rebellion'.

Do it with love and caring and where possible, get your immediate community behind you – whether it's the church, the PTA, or the Rotary Club. And most of all, it will not be effective if one parent, grandparent or guardian is against it and tries to undermine the other's efforts.

Where Are All the Neighborhood Children?

A few days ago my wife and I took a pleasant Sunday afternoon ride through the local countryside. We drove through many different neighborhoods and upper middle-class housing developments and passed hundreds of houses with flower gardens and neatly mowed lawns. Weekday mornings these neighborhoods are crowded with school busses.

I estimate we passed 400 houses. Seeing few signs of life, we started looking to see if any children were outside playing. In about an hour and a half we saw a total of three children and one of them was just going into his house. I can only guess that some were playing their games, watching TV or deep into social media. [274]

---

[273] By law, we forbid under-age children to buy tobacco or alcohol products. Is it unreasonable to propose jail to those who would sell these damnable computer products to our children – with or without parental approval? Just as forbidding tobacco and alcohol are for the public good, so also is forbidding these games and videos in our best national interest.

[274] This is a conservative estimate based on actual housing density and 40 mph travel. Assuming (conservatively) one child per household, one can assume there were approximately 397 children inside their houses – that's fewer than one percent playing outside.

TEENS AND SMARTPHONES – A MENTAL HEALTH CRISIS

Post-millennials – teens – are on the brink of a national mental-health crisis. Depression, anxiety and suicide rates are suddenly soaring and are provably exacerbated by too much screen time. These kids are lonelier and less likely to spend time together. When they do, they have more unease when they need to interact.

So says researcher Jean M. Twenge who has been researching generational differences and trends for 25 years.[275]

Teens today – she calls them the *iGen* generation – differ from millennials in how they spend their time. A 2018 survey by Common Sense Media discovered that 89 percent of American teens owned a smartphone (iPhone, Android, etc.). That is up from 41 percent only six years earlier in 2012.[276]

Isolated and Feeling Left Out

Twenge says kids are typically isolating themselves in their bedrooms, hanging out on social media – Facebook, Snapchat and Instagram – and are more inclined to feel isolated and left out.

She quotes one 13-year old who described the situation, "I think we like our phones more than we like actual people."

Bullying – aggressive 'cyberbullying' – has increased rapidly among middle- and high school boys and girls. As they spend less face time together these kids often become more troubled.

Mood Disorders and Suicides

Teens are spending an average of two and a half hours a day on their smartphones and many of them are sleeping with them or near them, checking them before bed, during the night and first thing in the morning.

Teens that need an average of nine hours of sleep are getting about seven. According to Twenge, in the four years from 2012 to 2015, 22 percent more teens failed to get seven hours of sleep. Sleep deprivation is linked to a multitude of problems, including compromised thinking and reasoning, more illness and weight gain, high blood pressure and mood and mental health problems.

Suicide rates have risen dramatically for 12 to 14-year-olds. In the eight-year period from 2007 to 2015, two times as many boys and three times as many girls killed themselves. *Suicide is a permanent solution to a temporary problem.* But these 'temporary' problems seem overwhelming to young, unprepared minds.

Twenge suggests that, "Some mild boundary-setting could keep kids from falling into harmful habits." She also admits that, "Prying the phone out of our kids' hands will be difficult." [277]

Clearly, we are poorly prepared for this new smartphone age and parents are going to need help.[278]

Outlaw Some Smartphone Apps for Teens?

We made changes in our laws regarding children's access to alcoholic beverages and tobacco products. Why should we not consider doing the same for other potentially harmful things?

Before this new generation faces a national disaster – and we seem to be on the cusp of one now – perhaps it is time to get serious about regulating access to smartphone devices for young, still-forming, plastic minds.

---

[275]Twenge, Jean M., "Have Smartphones Destroyed a Generation?", *The Atlantic Monthly*, September, 2017 (Adapted from Twenge's book, *iGen: Why Today's Super-Connected Kids Are Growing Up Less Rebellious, More Tolerant, Less Happy – and Completely Unprepared for Adulthood – and What That Means for the Rest of Us*, Simon and Schuster, 2017

[276] *www.commonsensemedia.org/research/social-media-social-life-2018*

[277]Twenge, Jean M., *op. cit.*

[278] See earlier notes in Chapter 2 regarding Thomas Kersting's "Smartphone Contract" for kids.

But be prepared for a strong push-back from the special interests – the manufacturers and distributors of these devices *and* the social media companies such as Facebook, Alphabet (Google, YouTube), Instagram, Snapchat and Twitter and their ilk.

Concerned citizens are going to need to be very creative and careful in how we approach any possible regulation. Remember, these mega-corporations already give a great deal of money to politicians. (Did someone mention superannuated politicians? Oh yes, see "Term Limits" on page 85.)

MILLENNIALS – PRACTICING FOR FAILURE

Millennials – those young folks who were born near the turn of the 21st Century are in line to become the leaders of tomorrow. They are very different from the people who grew up in the Great Depression and then went on to win a terrible war against enemies determined to conquer us – the Germans and the Japanese. That earlier group, called 'The Greatest Generation,' grew up in hardship and poverty, rescued America, and made this the greatest and strongest country on earth. Many older Americans fear what would become of our nation should we have another all-out war in which these young people would be called upon to defend us.

Effeminate Men

A recent study has found that Millennial women prefer much older men – in some cases, twice their age. The theory is that Millennial men are undependable and lacking in masculine traits, such as a protective, supportive nature.[279]

Fleeing From Reality

Young college adults increasingly demand campus 'safe spaces' where they can avoid 'unbearably uncomfortable conversation and ideas'. Many of them violently protest campus speakers with whom they disagree, forcing them to cancel or not to speak at all.

Tenured, left wing professors teach (coach) them but fail to convey American history and the origins of this great country and the Constitution which was distilled from the successes and mistakes of the past. On many campuses socialist government is presented as a sensible future choice.

Recently a group of Millennials, when asked their opinion about a list of policy proposals, agreed with 80 percent of the topics, but when they were told the items were from President Trump's agenda, their agreement fell to 30 percent. Emotion rules the day and critical analysis turns up missing.

Too many colleges and universities indoctrinate and fail to educate.

Inconceivable Surrender?

We have no idea how these Millennials will react to real stress – such as another Pearl Harbor or 9/11 attack. Renowned author, economist and syndicated columnist Dr. Thomas Sowell remarked a few years ago that he was absolutely frightened that if Iran should use a nuclear device and destroy one or two U.S. cities and then demand our surrender, he believed President Obama, who spent eight years talking about how bad America is, might just capitulate and *surrender*![280]

Unimaginable!? Yes, but very possible. And people like Barack Obama are the heroes of this new generation that may soon be leading our country.

This is scary. Very, very scary.

---

[279] Jacobs, Jessica, "Why Millennial Women Want to Date Older Men", *acculturated.com/millennial-women/*, August 18, 2015

[280] Dec. 10, 2014 interview by Rush Limbaugh.
www.rushlimbaugh.com/daily/2014/12/10/dr_thomas_sowell_s_greatest_fear/

Snowflakes

There was a time, before all the flat screens and computer games when kids actually grew up talking and playing with one another. And if they disagreed, they would talk about it – even exchange a few insults and sometimes a few blows. Then they would quickly resolve the problem and continue to play. The word 'impulsive' was synonymous with childhood. And kids were expected to be hyperactive from time to time. Parental guidance – sometimes strong, Ritalin-free guidance – usually fixed most cases of hyperactivity.

Once upon a time childhood insults were a normal form of communication.

Now we have arrived at a time when – as incredible as it may seem – children ages 2-5 spend an average of 22 hours a week – one quarter of their waking hours – watching television! [281] Older kids spend almost twice that much watching TV or playing computer games and eating junk food. These children are living in and acclimating to all this fantasy and linear, one-track thinking instead of practicing the skills of real human interaction.

Meanwhile, parents, when they're not reading *Psychology Today* or other self-help aids, hover over them, making sure they don't get hurt or emotionally upset. If they are a bit impulsive or hyperactive they are diagnosed with ADHD, and medicated with Ritalin or Adderall.[282]

Childhood insults are now seen as a form of menacing, bullying and danger.

All Grown Up?

Fast forward – The flat-screen kids are now in college, being taught by professors who 'survived' the '60's and according to several surveys, prefer socialistic and left-leaning responses to political issues. Even thinking about free markets, capitalism, and conservative ideas is abhorrent to many. Necessary discussion is limited to Orwellian *Newspeak* lists of what *not* to talk about.[283] Education is too often without historical context and costly lessons of the past are lost. No open conservative discussion is permitted. These topics are discounted, as 'non-subjects,' and students are left to believe that the great drooling masses are unaware that these issues have already been 'decided' by highly intelligent, mostly-white, elite, tenured professors.

Protection for Fragile Customers

College costs have risen so much faster than inflation for the past two decades that students have come to believe they are 'consumers' and college just another 'commodity'. [284] And since the "customer is always right," and they are the customers, therefore they and their demands must be right.

It would then seem reasonable that paying-customers could demand 'safe spaces' where they can retreat to avoid contrary ideas. Equally reasonable that their instructors provide them with 'trigger warnings' if the day's lesson might be unsettling. Upsetting topics might touch on sensitive issues such

---

[281] Perlmutter, David, MD., "Brain Development: How much TV Should Children Watch?", *Huffington Post, The Blog*, May. 25, 2011

[282] (This footnote is added as an aside which may be useful to some readers.) New research shows that **ADHD in some cases is caused or exacerbated by certain foods in the diet**. The British medical journal, *Lancet*, published what has been called the first peer-reviewed study that confirms this fact that some allergists have been suggesting for years. The study concludes, "A strictly restricted elimination diet is a valuable instrument to assess whether ADHD is induced by food. The prescription of diets on the basis of IgG [the antibody immunoglobulin G] blood tests should be discouraged." Pellser, Lidy M, et. al., "Effects of a restricted elimination diet on the behavior of children with attention-deficit hyperactivity disorder (INCA study): a randomized controlled trial", *Lancet*, 2011; 377:494-503.

[283] Orwell, George, op.cit.

[284] College costs have been growing at roughly twice the rate of the cost of living, even outpacing the rapid rise in medical costs, according to a 2013 *US News & World Report* study. Another 2015 study by *CNBC* says that college tuitions have been outpacing the annual inflation rate by about six percent over the long term.

as 'pro-life,' or 'Islamic terrorism,' or the American Flag or the Pledge of Allegiance, or God forbid, the meaning of 'State's Rights' or the history of the Confederate Flag.

It's nice to be all grown up and in college. But what are we preparing them for?

Great Pain on the Path to Maturity

Some of these post-adolescents will be forced to change when they get into the real world and have to meet deadlines, work with people they don't like and take orders from impatient bosses. Some of them will survive. But it will be considerably more difficult for them than it was for us of the older generations who learned how to interact – and deal with physical and emotional discomfort – as kids.

A recent study, posted online, found that a very large percent of Millennials prefer socialism – *until they get a job.*[285]

DESTRUCTIVE MILITANT FEMINISM

> *What is pro-woman about denying that the hard work of raising healthy, stable and loving children is important?*
>
> Erica Komisar [286]

Sadly, militant feminism continues to severely denigrate the role of fathers and men in general. One has only to look at how men are portrayed in current TV shows and popular media as bumbling, clueless, semiconscious imbeciles. Many recent box office winners show children who possess super-hero powers. One has to wonder if their popularity results from a subconscious longing for a real, but missing masculine role model – a real man who can solve real home problems.

The Other Side of Feminism

Feminist, author, professor and artist Camille Paglia is well known for condemning a feminism that demeans men and their accomplishments and fails to prepare women and men for the dangerous world we live in. Paglia thinks deeply, is well informed and worth listening to.

Camille Paglia

In a 2016 talk on "The Battle of Ideas" she takes on modern destructive feminism head-on. A 15 minute excerpt of her talk, subtitled "Why Feminism is the Collapse of Western Civilization" can be viewed on YouTube, either by clicking on the QR code on the right or visiting the website directly at *youtu.be/mb2JEX8DYYE* .

CONCLUSION

Many of the problems of our misguided youth and the generations to follow and their failing families will not be solved soon. Much of this has come about at an astonishing pace. But now is the time we must begin to chip away at the worst of the problems as we continue the main effort to strengthen our families, our faith institutions and our educational processes.

Try to stay informed and especially aware of what is happening in the lives of our children. Support those groups and political leaders who understand the problems and are not afraid to oppose Big Money interests that are destroying our children's futures.

---

[285] Ekins, Emily, "Millennials like socialism – until they get jobs", *The Washington Post*, March 24, 2016
[286] Komisar, Erica, "The Human Cost of Sweden's Welfare State" *Wall Street Journal*, July 11, 2018

N.B. – Any Internet addresses, QR codes and telephone numbers in this book are offered as a resource. They are not intended in any way to be or to imply an endorsement, nor does the author vouch for the content of these sites, numbers or references.

APPENDIX I. PERSISTENT CHALLENGES TO A CIVILIZED SOCIETY

In this appendix we enlarge on some of the topics covered in earlier chapters. These are issues that will likely be with us for many years and decades and with which we must cope as we work to face them.

More than anything, our country needs an attitude of unity of purpose if we are to set our differences aside, come together and work to re-awaken the slumbering spirit of this great nation.

Many Challenges

We have become a nation more divided than any of us have ever before seen. The root causes are many. Everyone who examines the folds of our social fabric professes to know part or all of the reason. But there is great concern and debate on what to do about it. Even some of the Post-Modernists among us are very concerned and seeking a spiritual and unifying solution.[287]

Our long-term challenges are many: Our increasingly dysfunctional political establishment, our failing public educational system and our news media that are so biased they don't show any evidence of self-awareness of how biased they are.

The evil impulses of mankind are nothing new but our technology aids and magnifies the resulting tremendous suffering, mass migration and death we hear of almost daily. And then there is our inexplicable (to many of us), nonchalant approach to the mass killing of our unborn babies.

No dystopic summary is complete without mentioning the persistent threats to peace from China, Russia, Iranian-backed terrorism and militant Islam. The coming threats of cyberwarfare and space weapons are relatively new and unfamiliar to many of us.

Lastly we salute those heroes who are always beside us and facing these challenges, but seldom noticed in the shadows of our busy and hectic lives.

DYSFUNCTION IN THE PUBLIC ARENA

Diversity, Illusion, Freebies and Irrelevance

The political Left promotes a kind of 'diversity' that divides us into opposing 'identity groups'. Diversity helps them win votes. Clever, creative, computerized milking of the many goats of diversity helped Barack Obama win two elections by identifying groups and subgroups of so-called victims and targeting them with an excellently planned and executed system. (His opponent, Mitt Romney didn't have a chance with his totally out-of-date system.) [288, 289] Politicians on the left promise instant accommodations to the requirements and requests of these subgroups which wins them many additional votes.

The political Right speaks of 'unity' while they disagree and argue among themselves. Witness the 2017 failed effort to repeal and replace The Affordable Care Act by a supposedly Congressional Republican majority. At this writing, the current 115th U.S. Congress can't seem to agree on anything as they continue to divide over dogmatic differences, refusing to compromise their perfect illusions. All

---

[287] Patten, Terry, *A New Republic of the Heart: An Ethos for Revolutionaries*, North Atlantic Books, Berkeley, CA, 2018, See especially Chapters 10 & 11.

[288] Issenberg, Sasha, "How Obama's Team Used Big Data to Rally Voters", *MIT Technology Review*, *www.technologyreview.com/s/509026/how-obamas-team-used-big-data-to-rally-voters/*, December 19, 2012

[289] Wolffe, Richard, *The Message – The Reselling of President Obama*, Hatchett Book Group, New York, 2013. (See especially, Chapter 6)

"sound and fury, signifying nothing." [290]   Someone recently described the Congressional Republicans as "Two hundred Paul Reveres, all yelling and screaming and riding furiously in different directions."

Meanwhile, poor communicators that these Republicans are and almost always have been – these uncompromising, supposed believers in the free market mechanisms of Hayek[291] and Friedman[292] are left stunned when they lose election after election to the votes of the beneficiaries of all the socialistic quick-fixes and 'freebies' handed out by the jubilant political Left.

The Republican Party has been dominated by inarticulate people who, although they espouse many practical and effective ideas, are totally inept and incompetent at explaining them to the average voter. In the words of Dr. Thomas Sowell, "…when they come on the air, they sound as if this is the first time they have ever thought about what they are going to say…." [293]

Two Immediate Priorities

It is time to put some of our ruling elites on the unemployment lines. While we have a bit of relative peace and quiet time to breathe and think and while America is between major crises – political and economic madness, wars and riots – we need to get our act together. Two urgent things must be done:

First, we will become a stronger country with *legislatures that better represent the needs of the country* and when political office is no longer looked upon as a lifetime career. We need more turnover in our politically elected offices. Interestingly, there is a scriptural precedent for this.

In the Bible we learn that Adam and Eve, originally destined to live forever in the Garden of Eden, messed up and were kicked out. No longer eligible for permanent 'employment', God showed us the first example of '*human term limits*'.

Some of our eternal political leaders continue to 'mess up' – breaking pre-election promises, buying votes with taxpayer money, accepting forbidden fruit and lavish emoluments from others with evil intent, etc. The precedent has been set; now let's cancel *their* employment. It's called *political term limits*.

Second, we have to *regain control of our educational systems*. The teachers' unions – NEA and AFT, and their subsidiary unions – must be placed on a short leash – and soon. Our educational system is an absolute failure at teaching students how this country and our Constitution and rule of law works. This is no recent concern. Allan Bloom wrote about it more than 30 years ago and little has changed.

> *Students now arrive at the university ignorant and cynical*
> *about our political heritage, lacking the wherewithal to*
> *be either inspired by it or seriously critical of it.*
> *Allan Bloom, 1987* [294]

Our entire public education system is so incredibly ineffective and boring that most students – who eventually become potential voters – cannot wait to get out of school and stop 'learning'. It is ludicrous

---

[290] Bill S., Circa 1606

[291] Hayek, Friedrich, *The Road to* Serfdom, University of Chicago Press, 1944, [1994 reprint edition]

[292] Friedman, Milton and Rose Friedman, *Free to Choose, The Classic Inquiry Into the Relationship Between Freedom and Economics*, Harcourt, Inc., 1980

[293] Sowell, Thomas, "Republicans' forte not communication", *Poughkeepsie Journal*, March 21, 2000, p. 4A (This eighteen year old commentary was recently echoed 16 years later in *The Wall Street Journal*, by William McGurn, who commented that the Republicans have an economic message for middle America, but they make it very boring." ("Grow, Baby, Grow", *WSJ*, Feb. 16, 2016, p. A 15)

[294] Bloom, Allan, *The Closing of the American Mind – How Higher Education has Failed Democracy and Impoverished the Souls of Today's Students*, Simon and Schuster, New York, 1987

that teachers get permanent employment guarantees after as little as one to three years on the job. This tenure idea serves no one and is at the heart of all that is bad about our public schools.

Unions hold immense power over our state and federal legislators and contribute billions of dollars to help re-elect their favorite politicians who in turn continue to keep our educational systems in a state of perpetual failure.

It is no exaggeration to say that our teachers' unions have in effect been managing and controlling our public education system. In a normal business corporation, when a manager does a terrible job – the owners will fire that manager and find a new one. The reason it hasn't happened so far is that these 'managers' – the big teachers' unions – behave like they are the owners, and they are in bed with the people who make the rules.

It's time to reassert <u>our</u> ownership. Our children's future depends on it.

Just those two actions alone – term limits and un-tenure – will begin the long process of repairing a great many of our problems and help to turn the country back over to the people. But only if we the people unite to take a more active part in the running of this country.

For that to happen, one priority must be addressed first:

The Rest of the Story – Please!

Our news media – cable, broadcast and streaming – must be called to task and made to understand their responsibility to cover ALL the news. Not just the salacious, the stupid, the one-sided and the inane. Too much of the voting public has little idea of the really important news because they are continually being fed a mixture of baloney and apple pie.[295]

Many opinion and talk shows seem to regard Americans as a bunch of stupid morons who couldn't possibly understand the whole truth. (Remember Hillary Clinton's "deplorables?"). Over the past few decades most news broadcasts contain less actual news and more and more sound bites and entertainment. And many studies have determined that most of what the media calls "news" is very biased and potentially one-sided.

For example, the recent Russia/Trump brouhaha during one news week occupied more than 90% of one network's program time, as they continued to ignore many other important national and worldwide developments of far greater significance. All this, apparently, because there are a great many people in and out of the media who are trying to undermine the President.

But in the process they are strangling our whole country.

MAN'S CONTINUING INHUMANITY TO MAN

Tyranny, Suffering and Death

Nobel Prize winner Elie Wiesel's gripping story of the Holocaust in his book *Night*, tells the true and horrible story of one of mankind's worst periods.[296] It was a time when a democratic-government-turned-socialist mutated into a violent tyranny which decided that all their problems were caused by

---

[295] The First Amendment does not protect news media from being shamed or rejected by a free market. But we may need to legislate new controls over mergers and acquisitions to keep news organizations more balanced between local, national and global news, and to prevent them from further merging into uncontrollable behemoths that no longer respond to the needs or will of the people. We may already be past that point, as we now have six giant corporations which control almost all of our U.S. news.

[296] Elie Wiesel, *Night*, Hill and Wang, publisher, 2006 (Translated from the French edition, 1958)

minorities in their midst and strong leadership could fix them. They became determined to exterminate millions of people who were 'not like them' – Jews, Catholics, homosexuals, gypsies, and many others – to 'purify' their country so that a superior Aryan race could repair their brokenness.

And the rest of the world did little to stop it.

Wiesel wrote this account of his family's capture and extermination at the hands of the Nazis, imploring us to study so we would never again repeat what had happened there and then.

Our current social dysfunction cannot compare with what happened then, but one only has to look at more recent history – the genocides of the Hutus in Rwanda, the Khmer Rouge killing fields in Cambodia, The Cultural Revolution in China, and the recent mass killings of Syrian citizens by their own government – and see that we humans have learned very little.

In our lifetime, democracy has transformed into socialism and then to tyranny, violence and incredible suffering in neighboring Venezuela.[297]

Don't say, "It could never happen here." Pray that *it won't happen here*, because mankind has not lost its capacity for laziness, forgetfulness and incredible evil.

Speaking of Evil...

Modern medicine has evolved in amazing ways. Doctors often operate on unborn children to repair heart defects and other anomalies before they are born. The baby is given an anesthetic before the operation and treated post-op with the same care as any other person. The anesthetic is necessary to prevent trauma because medical science says that unborn babies can feel pain after their tenth week *in utero*.

Unfortunately, there is something called '*women's health care*' where babies are 'operated' on after the tenth week *without* anesthesia. This operation is performed with surgical instruments and suction devices which rip the unborn baby apart and expel it piece by piece from their mother's womb.

Having lived through and witnessed a number of ugly trauma myself, I have a very strong stomach, but it was not strong enough to help me when I witnessed my first video of an actual abortion.

For more than forty years I have studied what my file folder label calls "MITM" – *Man's Inhumanity to Man*. The single, strong conclusion: The more we are able to regard another human as a ***thing*** and less as a ***living person***, the easier it is to ignore, torture, kill or discard that person with indifference and without awakening or disturbing our conscience. Jesus implored us to get to know strangers and treat them as brothers and sisters because it is not always natural and we find some people harder to approach.

Just as the Nazis killed people with indifference, we are doing the same to the unborn. We have reduced to zero the difference between our abortionist culture and those Nazi killers.

Mother Teresa said it clearly, while accepting her Nobel Peace Prize in 1979:

> *The greatest destroyer of peace today is the cry of the innocent,*
> *unborn child. For if a mother can murder her own child in her*
> *womb, what is left for you and me is to kill each other.*

The Us Versus Them Problem

We are all prejudiced one way or another. 'Prejudice' means to pre-judge and we do it as a natural protection. It's a built-in primitive reflex that helped our distant ancestors protect their tribe or family

---

[297] There is much evidence that unwatched democracy can lead to tyranny. Plato, in his *Republic* first described the process of descent 25 centuries ago, as democracy leads to too much casual freedom, then to laziness and to dependence and ultimately to tyranny (*Plato, Book VIII*). Friedrich Hayek and Milton Friedman describe a similar progression as Democracy leads to Socialism and thence to rule by a very strong person which leads to totalitarianism and tyranny. The current rapid descent to tyranny in Venezuela is not the exception but rather the rule.

group from strangers. Deep prejudice is not something we think about – it seems to be an automatic reaction of our nervous system.

Every country on earth has its sins where it has wrongly judged another nation and caused harm. Whether it was the Romans and the Celts, or the American settlers and the Native Americans, (from whom I am distantly descended,) or the USA and the North Vietnamese. The list is almost endless. Sometimes the attack was intelligently planned and at others it was driven by ignorance. Vietnam was driven by a goal to stop the expansion of Communism, but the way the war started – the 'Gulf of Tonkin Incident' – was stupid and in retrospect forced upon an ignorant Congress and American people. Vietnam was a tipping point. America's culture took a downward turn and there was no going back.

Peaceniks, Slogans and Noble Wars

Flowers and anti-war songs can get some of the people stirred up. They can also exacerbate an existing divide. So it was during the Vietnam era. Two different views of the war effort were emerging and the people were becoming polarized. But government slogans and anti-war songs did not bring us together. Our leaders said they were intent on containing the spread of Communism. But thanks to technology, for the first time in history we witnessed the bloody horror of war on our TV sets. War would never again be far away and noble.

In retrospect we had little idea of the history or intentions of the people we were fighting. Wouldn't it be nice if we could understand other people before we have to go and kill them to get to know them and their needs and culture?

Some cynical wit once remarked, *"War is how Americans learn geography."* It's also how we learn foreign cultures and languages, such as Arabic.

Not all Wars are Inevitable

World War I, in retrospect was inevitable. WW-II was not, according to some historians who contend that if the rest of the world had understood the desperate post-WW-I economic situation in Germany imposed by the victors we might have prevented the great German monetary crisis that led to the rise of Nazi Socialism and the European – and world-wide – tragedy that followed.[298]

DOES EVERYONE WANT TO KILL US?

Things are not too good in the world out there. And our young people, devoid of any serious study of world history, think this is all new and their world has gone out of control (they may have been distracted by gender studies and other meaningless trivia). News Flash, tender snowflakes! It always has been chaotic! People haven't changed, they just have bigger swords.

Iran is headed by apocalyptic Islamists whose religious doctrine declares the most holy thing they can do is destroy the entire world so their missing Mahdi – the new Caliph – can reappear and rule a rebuilt world in a perfect version of subservient Islam.[299] ISIS (a.k.a., ISIL) wants to conquer, convert and enslave the entire world to establish a draconian Seventh-Century form of Islam.

North Korea is led by a 'most unusual' human being who apparently is either way ahead of the rest of the world in his thinking, or just suicidal. He has considered blowing up everyone else with his new atomic and rocket toys and until recently has said he especially wants to annihilate the United States.

---

[298] The proper name of the Nazi Party is the National Socialist German Workers' Party
[299] See *Appendix B. Peaceful/Militant Islam and American Culture.*

The Russians lost the Cold War and now want to reassert their 'superiority'. They seem to feel their lot will be much better if they can decide elections in foreign countries. They also want to steal every trade and government secret they can get their hands on. Marxist conflict theory still rules the hearts of the Kremlin.

Let's not forget our trading partners the Chinese. China seems to be competing with the Russians to see who can cyber-hack the most foreign governments and businesses and steal the most trade secrets.

Communist Party Chairman Xi Jinping is literally now in charge of nearly every facet of Chinese life and government. Chairman Xi has taken on himself more power than any other leader since Chairman Mao Tse-Tung and has brought the leadership of the growing armed forces closer under his wing. Historically, the Communist Chinese have had not one, but two governments. There is a civil government and there is the powerful military that owns and runs many of the largest business enterprises and wields enormous economic and political power.

The U.S. has begun to challenge the Chinese incursion and island building in the South China Sea which has heretofore been acknowledged as open international waters. Chairman Xi recently instructed his military advisers overseeing the South China Sea to "prepare for fighting a war." As the U.S. continues to apply other pressure – trade tariffs and sanctions – on the Chinese and the Russians, the two powers are becoming more aligned and as of this writing are currently planning large scale joint military exercises.

Students of history see some similarities between this and the events that led up to the Japanese war in the Pacific three quarters of a century ago.

The old *Mad Magazine* character, Alfred E. Newman used to say, "What, me worry?" *Maybe.*

Is the Giant Sleeping Again?

Any war upon us by an external enemy will be devastating. In 1941 the Japanese took us by surprise and almost defeated us. Before the war, the people were divided. There were the hawks and pacifists, the interventionists and isolationists, the militants and the statesmen. When Pearl Harbor was bombed and most of our Pacific Fleet destroyed or damaged and then when three of our merchant cargo ships were sunk in the Atlantic by the Germans we finally woke up and came together. The pacifists and isolationists – who had spent years working to reduce our military strength – suddenly became very silent.

Who cannot forget those famous words of Japanese General Yamamoto, in the movie, *Tora, Tora, Tora,* "I fear all we have done is to awaken a sleeping giant and fill him with a terrible resolve." Indeed, once awake, America came together quickly with a unified mind and single resolve and purpose and with a massive unified nation-wide effort, we rebuilt and deployed our military strength and with much sacrifice and shed blood, we finally defeated our enemies.

Things are different now, but I have no doubt we could and would awaken and do it again. There's nothing like a common enemy to make people forget their squabbles and differences and focus on the need to survive.

But we might have to melt a few of our precious 'snowflakes' first.

Wake Up Call No. 1 – Cyberwarfare

America is in an undeclared war with external enemies. Despite many warnings, America's power distribution systems have been infected with foreign-implanted software 'changes' that could cause our total power grid to collapse. This has been described as a national emergency.

Foreign enemies don't have to attack us with bombs and missiles. All they need do to bring us to our knees is shut down our power grid. Our entire banking systems run on this electricity. Our entire commerce system which takes our food from farm to processors to market depends on electricity. Our telephones and cell phones and TVs and Internet all depend on electricity. Cities' water and sewage systems would cease to function. A foreign enemy could catastrophically cripple our entire country in a matter of hours if they dared do so.

In December, 2015 in the country of Ukraine, 225,000 people lost electric power for many hours. The electrical generation and distribution system was not at fault. The problem was Russian government hackers who remotely took control of Ukraine's power grid.[300]

It is almost a national habit that we wait until a problem occurs and then the legislature creates sudden, urgent new laws. And then we lawyer-up an investigation to see whom to blame. This *ex post facto*, after the fact approach is our traditional way. Anyone who suggests a thorough *potential problem analysis* to see what *might* go wrong is at risk of being accused of wasting time on "what if" games.

We successfully placed the first humans on the moon because NASA used potential problem analysis (PPA) extensively to prepare for almost every imaginable "what if" deviation from plan. PPA, known for some time but largely unapplied, goes way beyond typical management planning and has developed into a science.[301]

Wake Up Call No. 2 – Space War

Hostile enemies and potential adversaries know they could cripple us by destroying a few of our earth satellites. More than 2,000 man-made satellites are currently circling the earth of which almost 700 are U.S. satellites. (Russia has more than twice that many.)

Our most vulnerable military satellites analyze military communications, facilities and operations in China, Russia, Iran and North Korea. Priority weather and communications satellites have become an essential part of our businesses and our national defense.

The Global Positioning System (GPS) is absolutely essential to our military and our national defense and has become essential to private commerce as well. Truckers use GPS to find their way to deliveries; private individuals no longer use paper maps, but rely instead on GPS. It is hard to imagine a modern America without GPS.

In order to destroy a satellite no rocket-launched space weapon is necessary. A few accurate blasts of a powerful, earth-bound laser could take out almost any one of these satellites. Because of the way these ground based lasers work and the manner in which they can be deployed, they would be incredibly hard to locate and destroy if there were a military conflict. For example a single, well-concealed laser weapon (or a battery of them) could take out our entire GPS system in a few days.

HEROES ALL AROUND US

Every day, in every American city, we have thousands of citizens who put their life on the line to help other people. These men and women are called firemen, policemen, emergency medical technicians (EMTs), ambulance drivers – and there is a host of others who keep our electricity and water flowing and our transportation systems running – these folks are mostly invisible to us until we need them.

And consider the people who staff our 911 dispatch centers? There are many stories of these people braving blizzards and hurricanes to get to their job to help those in need. This is a grueling, emotionally difficult job and it continues to be hard to find reliable people who can handle the constant stress.

---

[300] Fairley, Peter, "Cybersecurity at U.S. Utilities Due For an Upgrade", *IEEE* Spectrum, May, 2016

[301] Kepner, Charles H. and Benjamin B. Tregoe, *The Rational Manager – A Systematic Approach to Problem Solving and Decision Making*, McGraw-Hill, New York, 1965. (This early book gives a good overview of PPA. Additional research has followed, but sadly much of it is seldom applied on large, expensive government projects.)

Our great republic would have ceased to exist many years ago without the brave soldiers, sailors marines, airmen and others who defend us. A disproportionate number of these men and women are from small towns in "fly-over country." [302] Their heroism is regularly ignored by news reporters, few of whom have ever served in any military capacity.

You won't read about these heroes or see much on TV until one of them falters or a mission goes wrong. Then the warped media will salivate all over it. Don't misunderstand, there's nothing wrong with reporting serious problems – indeed an informed citizenry is essential to a functioning democracy. But it's also nice to have a little balance.

The non-stop blather and perpetuation of misinformation from most of the mainstream news and entertainment media encourages protesters, some of them violent. Media distortion does little to promote factual understanding or civic peace. The *Black Lives Matter* movement is an example. Its beginning was *exacerbated by misleading press reports* which touched a nerve and the movement has grown all over the nation. And that set of lies and the movement it fostered continues to endanger many of our police and first responders.

The next time you see a soldier or veteran thank him or her for their service.[303] And do likewise when you see a policeman, fireman, first responder or other public servant. A sincere 'thank you' won't cost you anything and won't make up for their typically lower wages,[304] but it may give them some more hope for the goodness of the common man. They are there for you and a civil society cannot function or exist without these dedicated heroes.

═══════════════════════

N.B. – Any Internet addresses, QR codes and telephone numbers in this book are offered as a resource. They are not intended in any way to be or to imply an endorsement, nor does the author vouch for the content of these sites, numbers or references.

---

[302] Phillips, Michael M., "Brothers in Arms: The Tragedy in Small-Town America", *The Wall Street Journal*, September 22, 2017

[303] More than 40 years after the Vietnam War, I met a man about my own age who was wearing a "Vietnam Vet" cap. I thanked him for his service. He paused, looked at me with puzzlement and remarked that this was only the third time anyone had ever done so.

[304] I continue to be amazed at the professional athletes who will not stand and respect the National Anthem which honors the nation that has allowed them to become millionaires. But maybe in my ignorance I'm missing something?

APPENDIX J. USING QR CODES IN THIS BOOK

A QR (Quick Response) Code is a machine-readable symbol consisting of an array of black and white squares, typically used for storing an encoded URL (Universal Resource Locator – Internet address).

A smartphone or tablet with the appropriate application (app) can read this with its camera and can take you directly to an Internet site without your needing to type its address.

(The QR Code can also contain other information, such as short textual phrases which can be displayed, but that feature is not used in this book.)

There are several types of QR Code. Those used in this document are specifically designed to take you to web sites, including video presentations.

OBTAINING THE QR CODE-READING APP:

If you have an Android phone or tablet, use the *Google Play Store* app and search for 'QR Code reader'. If you have an Apple iPhone, open the *Apple Store* app and search for 'QR Code reader'.

There are several free versions of this reader and each will usually display an advertisement first.

TO USE THE QR CODE APP:

Point your device's camera at the QR Code and press the indicated button and the app should take you directly to the indicated website. (It may ask for your permission first.)

MORE INFORMATION

More QR Code Information

This form of two-dimensional bar code was developed for industrial uses, first in Japan in 1994. QR Codes are used for many purposes besides Internet access. For more information on QR Codes in general, visit: *en.wikipedia.org/wiki/QR_code* . Or if you already have a QR scanner, click on this QR Code ➔

N.B. – Any Internet addresses, QR codes and telephone numbers in this book are offered as a resource. They are not intended in any way to be or to imply an endorsement, nor does the author vouch for the content of these sites, numbers or references.

Bibliography

A little learning is a dangerous thing
Drink deep or taste not the Pierian Spring.
There shallow draughts do intoxicate the brain
Whilst drinking largely sobers it again.
                                    Alexander Pope

Alley, Cornelia, *An American Odyssey 1535 – 1615*, CreateSpace Independent Publishing Platform, North Charleston, SC, 2017

al-Misri, Ahmad ibn Naqib (Translated by Nuh Ha Mim Keller), *Reliance of the Traveler – A Classic Manual of Islamic Sacred Law*, Amana Publications., Beltsville, MD, 1994

Bachman, Mark, *Winning Muslims to Christ*, Answer Publications, Roanoak, Il, 2005

Bennett, William J., *The Moral Compass – Stories for a Life's Journey*, Simon and Schuster, New York, 1995

Bloom, Allan, *The Closing of the American Mind – How Higher Education has Failed Democracy and Impoverished the Souls of Today's Students*, Simon and Schuster, New York, 1987

Butler, Samuel, *The Way of All Flesh*, Grant Richards, 1903

Carnegie, Dale, *How to Win Friends and Influence People*, Simon and Schuster, 2009

Carson, Ben, M.D., and Candy Carson, *America the Beautiful – Rediscovering What Made This Nation Great*, Zondervan Press, 2012

Carson, Ben, M.D., and Cecil Murphey, *Gifted Hands, The Ben Carson Story*, Zondervan Press, 1996

Catechism of the Catholic Church, 2nd ed., (Publication No. 5-110), United States Catholic Conference, Washington, DC, 1997

Chandler, Paul-Gordon, *Pilgrims of Christ on the Muslim Road – Exploring a New Path Between Two Faiths*, Rowman & Littlefield Publishers, Inc., 2007

Christian America? – Perspectives on our Religious Heritage, (Edited by Daryl C. Cornett), B&H Publishing Group, Nashville, TN, 2011

Clinton, Hillary, *It Takes a Village: And Other Lessons Children Teach Us*, Simon & Schuster, New York, 1996

Cogan, John F., *The High Cost of Good Intentions – A History of U.S. Federal Entitlement Programs*, Stanford University Press, 2017

Confucius, *Confucius – The Analects (Lun yü) (Translated by D.C. Lau)* Penguin Books, London, 1979

Cramer, Kathryn, *Roads Home: Seven Pathways to Midlife Wisdom*, William Morrow and Co., New York, 1995

Csikszentmihalyi, Mihaly, *Flow – The Psychology of Optimal Experience*, Harper & Row, New York, 1990

DeTemple Jill, and John Sarrouf, "Disruption, dialogue, and swerve: Reflective structured dialogue in religious studies classrooms", *Teaching Theology & Religion - Wiley Online Library*, 2017, pp. 283–292 (doi.org/10.1111/teth.12398) de Toqueville, Alexis, *Democracy in America*, (In two volumes, Vol. 1 and 2), (Translation by Arthur Goldhammer), The Library of America, New York, NY, 2004

Esolen, Anthony, *Out of the Ashes – Rebuilding American Culture*, Regnery Publishing Co., Washington, DC, 2017

Farrell, Warren, and John Gray, *The Boy Crisis, Why Our Boys Are Struggling and What We Can Do About It*, BenBella Books, Inc, Dallas, TX, 2018

Feynman, Richard P., *The Pleasure of Finding Things Out*, Perseus Publishing, Cambridge, MA, 2000

Fisher, Roger and William Ury, with Bruce Patton, Editor 2011, *Getting to Yes, Negotiating Agreement Without Giving In*, Penguin Books, Original Edition, 1981

Frankl, Viktor E., *Man's Search for Meaning*, Beacon Press, Boston, 1992

Frey, Carl Benedikt and Michael A. Osborne, *The Future of Employment*, Oxford Martin School, University of Oxford, September 17, 2013

Friedman, Milton and Rose Friedman, *Free to Choose, The Classic Inquiry Into the Relationship Between Freedom and Economics*, Harcourt, Inc., 1980

Gardner, Howard, *Frames of Mind: The Theory of Multiple Intelligences*, 3rd Edition, Basic Books, 2011

Goldberg, Bernard, *Bias, A CBS Insider Exposes How the Media Distort the News*, Regnery Publishing, Inc., Washington, DC, 2002

Grandin, Temple, *The Autistic Brain: Helping Different Kinds of Minds Succeed*, Houghton Mifflin Harcourt, New York, 2014

Grandin, Temple, *Thinking in Pictures: My Life With Autism*, Random House, New York, 2006

Haber, Ralph Norman, Editor, *Contemporary Theory and Research in Visual Perception*, Holt, Rinehart and Winston, Inc., New York, 1968

Hahn, Scott, *The Lamb's Supper: The Mass as Heaven on Earth*, Doubleday, New York, 1999

Hahn, Scott, *Understanding "Our Father": Biblical Reflections on the Lord's Prayer*, St. Paul Center for Biblical Theology, 2002

Hamilton, Alexander, James Madison and John Jay, *The Federalist Papers*, New American Library, New York, 1961

Hamilton, Alexander, *The Basic Ideas of Alexander Hamilton*, (Ed. by Richard B. Morris)Pocket Books, Inc., 1957

Hartman, Andrew, *A War for the Soul of America –A History of the Culture Wars*, University of Chicago Press, 2016

Haugeberg, Karissa, *Women Against Abortion, Inside the Largest Moral Reform Movement of the Twentieth Century*, University of Illinois Press, 2017

Hayek, Friedrich, *The Road to Serfdom*, University of Chicago Press, 1944, [1994 reprint edition]

Herdan, Gustav, *Language as Choice and Chance* (Note, there is a later version, *The Advanced Theory of Language as Choice and Chance*), P. Noordroof, N.V., Groningen, Holland, 1956

Hirsch, E.D., Jr., *Cultural Literacy – What Every American Needs to Know*, Houghton Mifflin Co., 1987

Hirschman, Albert O., *Exit Voice and Loyalty, Responses to Decline in Firms, Organizations and States*, Harvard University Press, Cambridge, MA, 1970

Horowitz, David and Richard Poe, *The Shadow Party: How George Soros, Hillary Clinton and Sixties Radicals Seized Control of the Democratic Party*, Nelson Current, publisher, 2006

Jarvis, Douglas E., *The Family and the Western Political Order*, PhD. Thesis, Carleton University, Ottawa, Ontario, 2014

Jefferson, Thomas, *The Life and Selected Writings of Thomas Jefferson*, (Ed. by Adrienne Koch & William Peden), Random House, New York, 1944

John Paul II, Pope, *The Role of the Christian Family in the Modern World (Familiaris Consortio)*, Pauline Books & Media, Boston, Anniversary Edition, 2015

Jomier, Jacques, O.P. (Translated from the French by Edward P. Arbez), *The Bible and the Qur'an*, Ignatius Press, San Francisco, 2002

Kepner, Charles H. and Benjamin B. Tregoe, *The Rational Manager – A Systematic Approach to Problem Solving and Decision Making*, McGraw-Hill, New York, 1965

Kersting, Thomas, *Disconnected, How to Reconnect our Digitally Distracted Kids*, CreateSpace Independent Publishing Platform, 2016

Komisar, Erica, *Being There: Why Prioritizing Motherhood in the First Three Years Matters*, Penguin Random House, New York, 2017

Kuralt, Charles, *American Moments*, Simon and Schuster, New York, 1998

Lafontaine, Raymond & Béatrice Lessoil-Lafontaine, *êtes-vous auditif ou visuel? un concept de communication*, Les Nouvelles Editions Marabout, Verviers, Belgique, 1984

Laforet, Fr. Nicholas J., *Unbelief, Its Causes and Cures*, (Originally published in 1869. Translated from the French. Later, revised, enlarged and edited by James Cardinal Gibbons), Sophia Institute Press, Manchester, NH, 2016

Lamott, Anne, *Travelling Mercies – Some Thoughts on Faith*, Random House, New York, 1999

Lapointe, Joseph, *The Last Real People – Meet Adirondackers who match their mountains ... the tough, caring, outlandish folk of the North Country*, Pinto Press, Mt. Kisco, NY, 2000

Lewis, C.S., *Mere Christianity*, Macmillan Publishing Co., New York, 1960

Lewis, C.S., *The Four Loves*, Harcourt Brace Jovanovich, 1960

Liebman, Joshua Loth, *Peace of Mind*, American Book – Stratford Press, Inc., New York, 1948

Loewen, James W., *Lies my Teacher Told Me: Everything Your American History Textbook Got Wrong*, The New Press, 2018

Lost Rondout, A Story of Urban Removal, A video by Stephen Blauweiss and Lynn Woods, 2016

Lucado, Max, *Cure for the Common Life – Living in Your Sweet Spot*, Thomas Nelson, Inc., 2005

Mallouhi, Christine A., *Waging Peace on Islam*, InterVarsity Press, Downers Grove, Illinois, 2000

Martin, Judith, *Miss Manners' Guide for the Turn-of-the-Millennium*, Pharos Books, New York, 1989

Masud, Enver, *The War on Islam*, Madrasah Books, Arlington, VA, 2002

MacNutt, Francis, *Deliverance from Evil Spirits – A Practical Manual*, Baker Publishing Group, Grand Rapids, MI, 2009

McDowell, Josh, *More Than a Carpenter*, Tyndale House Publishers, Wheaton, IL, 1977

Mead, Margaret, *Male and Female; A Study of the Sexes in a Changing World*, Harper Collins, 2001

Morley, Patrick, *The Man In The Mirror: Solving the 24 Problems Men Face*, Zondervan Publishing House, 1997

Myers, Isabel Briggs with Peter B. Myers [1980]. *Gifts Differing: Understanding Personality Type*. Mountain View, CA: Davies-Black Publishing, 1995

Negroponte, Nicholas, *Being Digital*, Alfred A. Knopf, 1995

Oppong-Baah, Rev. Msgr. Dr. John, *A Father's Voice to Children*, ProBranding Consult, Accra, Ghana, 2007

Oppong-Baah, Rev. Fr. Dr. John, *Facing the Reality of Mid-Life Crisis*, Rijnbeek Printing Press, Ghana, West Africa, 2004

Orwell, George, *Nineteen Eighty-Four*, The New American Library, 1949

Prayers Against the Powers of Darkness, United States Conference of Catholic Bishops, (Available online at: *store.usccb.org/prayers-against-the-powers-of-darkness-p/7-567.htm*)

Packard, Vance, *The Hidden Persuaders*, David McKay Company, NY, 1957

Parker, Star, *Uncle Sam's Plantation – How Big Government Enslaves America's Poor* and *What We Can Do About It*, WND Books, Nashville, TN, 2003

Patten, Terry, *A New Republic of the Heart: An Ethos for Revolutionaries*, North Atlantic Books, Berkeley, CA, 2018

Plato, *Republic,* (Trans. By G.M.A. Grube, 2nd Ed.; Revised by C.D.C. Reeve), Hackett Publ. Co., Inc., Indianapolis, IN, 1992

Popenoe, David, *Families Without Fathers: Fathers, Marriage and Children in American Society*, Routledge, 2017

Qureshi, Nabeel, *Seeking Allah, Finding Jesus: A Devout Muslim Encounters Christianity*, Zondervan, 2018

Roberts, Gen. Henry M., *Robert's Rules of Order*, (Revised and updated edition, Ed. by John Sherman), Barnes & Noble Books, 1993

Rodgers, Nigel, *Roman Empire – A complete history of the rise and fall of the Roman Empire…*, Anness Publishing, Ltd., New York, 2011

Saint-Jure, Fr. Jean Baptiste, S.J., and St. Claude de la Colombière, S.J. (Translated by Prof. Paul Garvin), *Trustful Surrender to Divine Providence – The Secret of Peace and Happiness*, Tan Books and Publishers, Inc. Rockford, IL, 1983

Sarah, Robert Cardinal, *God or Nothing*, Ignatius Press, 2015

Spencer, Robert, *Stealth Jihad – How Radical Islam is Subverting America without Guns or Bombs*, Regnery Publishing, Washhington, DC, 2008

Spencer, Robert, *The Politically Incorrect Guide to Islam (And the Crusades)*, Regnery Publishing, 2005

Spencer, Robert, *The Truth About Muhammad, Founder of the World's Most Intolerant Religion*, Regnery Publishing, 2006

Stark, Rodney, *The Triumph of Christianity, How the Jesus Movement Became the World's Largest Religion*, HarperCollins, 2011

Starnes, Todd, *The Deplorables Guide to Making America Great Again*, FrontLine, Lake Mary, FL, 2017

Taplin, Jonathan, *Move Fast and Break Things, How Facebook, Google and Amazon Cornered Culture and Undermined Democracy*, Little, Brown & Company, 2017

Tegmark, Max, *Life 3.0: Being Human in the Age of Artificial Intelligence*, Alfred A. Knopf, New York, 2017

"The Growth of Incarceration in the United States – Exploring Causes and Consequences", *National Research Council*, Jeremy Travis, et. al, Editors, The National Academies Press, Washington, D.C., 2014

The Book of Hadith – Sayings of the Prophet Muhammad, (Selected by Charles le Gai Eaton from Robson's translation of *Mishkat al-Masabih*, Re-translated by Mahmoud Mostafa; Arabic text with English translation), The Book Foundation, Watsonville, CA, 2008

The Holy Qur'an: Text, Translation and Commentary, (Translation by Abdullah Yusuf Ali, Arabic text and translation on opposite pages; extensive notes and commentary), Tahrike Tarsile Qur'an, Inc., Elmhurst, NY, 2012

The New American Bible. St. Joseph Edition, Catholic Book Publishing Co., New York, 1992

Toffler, Alvin, *Future Shock*, Bantam Books, Inc., New York, 1974

Trifkovic, Serge, *The Sword of the Prophet – Islam, history, theology, impact on the world*, Regina Orthodox Press, Inc., 2002

Treadgold, Warren, *The University We Need, Reforming American Higher Education*, Encounter Press, 2018

Trump, Donald J., *Crippled America: How to Make America Great Again*, Simon and Schuster, New York, 2015

Twenge, Jean M., *iGen: Why Today's Super-Connected Kids Are Growing Up Less Rebellious, More Tolerant, Less Happy – and Completely Unprepared for Adulthood – and What That Means for the Rest of Us*, Simon and Schuster, 2017

Vadanya (Chris Pauling), *Introducing Buddhism*, Barnes & Noble Books, New York, 2001

What Works: William J. Bennett's Research About Teaching and Learning", Edited and Updated by Dana B. Ciccone, PhD, Published by The Wooster Book Co., Wooster, OH, 1996

Whorf , Benjamin Lee (Selected Writings, Ed. by John B. Carroll), *Language, Thought and Reality*, The M.I.T. Press, Cambridge, MA, 1982

Wiesel, Elie, *Night*, (Translated from the French by Marion Wiesel), Hill and Wang, New York, 2006

Williams, Armstrong, *Reawakening Virtues: Restoring What Makes America Great*, New Chapter Publisher, Sarasota, FL, 2011

Wolffe, Richard, *The Message – The Reselling of President Obama*, Hachette Book Group, New York, 2013

Zimmerman, Carle C., *Family and Civilization*, Intercollegiate Studies Institute, 1947

Index

About the Author

During World War II, Al O'Hara grew up on his grandmother's farm in upstate New York while his father was off fighting in the war. On that farm his great uncle taught him that anything was possible if you used whatever brains God gave you and worked hard enough. Always curious, he started building tree houses and rafts and bridges as a child. Later his interests progressed to electronics and physics.

Prior to the end of his high school education (he attended five high schools) he had been written off by teachers as slow and mediocre. Finally, outstanding teachers in a private school helped him discover talents and abilities in math and literature that restored his self-confidence and fired up a lasting interest in learning.

In college he converted the attic of his fraternity house into a laboratory where he invented and developed new miniature electronic circuits. From these he then designed and partially constructed a digital computer. Newly graduated as an electrical engineer he was hired by IBM's Federal Systems Division and put to work with some of the best and brightest mathematicians and engineers on several state-of-the-art projects. IBM then sent him to Cape Canaveral to design some of the equipment that put the first American astronauts in space. Later, he worked on the earliest developments in computer graphics hardware and software. He holds several fundamental patents in data communications, computer graphics and computer design.

After a long engineering, programming and management career with IBM he retired and with a business partner, started a management consulting business. He then retired again after 11 years of that adventure.

Today he is a licensed Professional Engineer, a licensed Amateur Radio Operator and a certified scuba diver. An amateur musician and amateur carpenter, he also enjoys hiking, canoeing and fishing.

In the past he has dabbled in politics and has helped organize and lead political and community groups which have been successful in 'overthrowing' two imperious local governments.

A past founder, director and officer of a private school, grades seven through twelve, he has also taught numerous adult education courses and served as an adjunct instructor at a local college. He has worked as a volunteer in a local mental health hospital and served as member and officer on several public and professional boards.

After studying and searching many of the world's religions he and his wife converted late in life to the Roman Catholic faith. Active in his church, he helps run an annual Christian retreat for men. He busies himself with extensive reading, writing, prison ministry, training dogs and mowing the lawn, not necessarily in that order.

His personal military service was limited to service in the National Guard and by osmosis, the first 16 years of his life under the tutelage of his army officer father. Before World War II as an 'army brat' he moved many times. Later his family moved again for military and business objectives. Now having moved a life-total of 35 times he is settled, married to a wonderful wife and living in a rural area of mid-upstate New York. He has four grown children and two mixed-heritage dogs.

O'Hara has lived all over the east, west and south of the United States and talked about life with thousands of people of all cultures, races and skills. This book is the result of eight decades of asking questions and listening to the pain, fortunes and aspirations of so many of them.

Copyrights and Permissions

The following permissions of owners or copyright holders of published material are hereby acknowledged.

Mahoney, Jeffrey, Letter to the Editor, *Poughkeepsie Journal* (New York), June 23, 2017.

Excerpts from "Overcoming the Spirit of the Age", by Billy Graham, © 2017 Billy Graham, used by permission, all rights reserved.

Annie Lane column. June 28, 2017. Copyright, © 2017, Annie Lane. Reproduced by permission of Annie Lane and Creators Syndicate, Inc.

Photo, Courtesy Northwest Florida Daily News: 7/10/2017 news article, declared public domain.

All other references, by permission and/or fair use.

Scripture References:

NIV – Scripture quotations are taken from the New International Version (NIV): Scripture taken from The Holy Bible, New International Version ®. Copyright© 1973, 1978, 1984, 2011 by Biblica, Inc.™. Used by permission of Zondervan.

KJV – Holy Bible, King James Version. Scripture quotation from The Authorized (King James) Version. Rights in the Authorized Version in the United Kingdom are vested in the Crown. Reproduced by permission of the Crown's patentee, Cambridge University Press.

NAB – Holy Bible, New American Bible – Scripture texts in this work are taken from the New American Bible, revised edition © 2010, 1991, 1986, 1970 Confraternity of Christian Doctrine, Washington, D.C. and are used by permission of the copyright owner. All Rights Reserved.

NASB – New American Standard Bible – Scripture quotations taken from the New American Standard Bible® (NASB), Copyright © 1960, 1962, 1963, 1968, 1971, 1972, 1973, 1975, 1977, 1995 by The Lockman Foundation. Used by permission. www.Lockman.org.

ESV – Holy Bible, English Standard Version – Scripture quotation is from The ESV® Bible (The Holy Bible, English Standard Version®), copyright © 2001 by Crossway, a publishing ministry of Good News Publishers. Used by permission. All rights reserved.

45690491R00126

Made in the USA
Middletown, DE
19 May 2019